"Written from the real-life trenches (hope. The book combines meaty bit and rich theology to provide a comft... ....g .... valicy of darkness. In addition to the pastoral tone of the book, White takes a unique and intriguing journey through parts of the genealogy of Jesus."

—**Cameron Cole**, author of *Therefore I Have Hope: 12 Truths That Comfort, Sustain, and Redeem*

"Andy White expresses a powerful truth about the Christian faith. He gleans from examples in Matthew's genealogy of Jesus and from his own 'spiritual genealogy' that faith is not just a set of beliefs and practices. Faith is the way to live a certain kind of story, journey, and pilgrimage toward a future not known with certainty but, nonetheless, constructed by God and one traveled by Christ himself. Consequently, regardless of the setbacks, losses, and shocks that occur, our faith-story is never over."

—**Dennis L. Sansom**, chair, Department of Philosophy, Samford University

"*Seeds of Redemption* is a gentle and serious reminder of how our life path may go through a valley of death and darkness, yet God never seems to give up on us. Though we sometimes look to be struggling alone, God is near and brings the victory to us for his glory. Andy White opens our eyes to see that Jesus's followers seem to go through persistent trials and hardships, but that these situations can build character and bring out a new creation with new passion and zeal for faith in God, thus radiating his glory and beauty."

—**Samuel M. Mugisha**, bishop, Anglican Diocese of Shyira, Musanze, Rwanda

"With references to literary classics, movies, and diverse spiritual writers, Andy White uses examples from the genealogy of Jesus to meet us in the midst of life's heartache and pain and to remind us that grace not only redeems our brokenness, but it equips us to be agents of that grace to others in a world desperately in need of redemption. A must-read for both the hurting and the hopeful!"

—**Kristy Dempsey**, award-winning children's book author

"Andy White's book is not just another treatise about broken humanity and suffering. Linking specific biblical characters and their narratives with current, commonly experienced human conditions, Andy explains how setbacks, loss, betrayal, failures, and plain old sin are part of Jesus' redemptive story—his story—in our lives today. Poignant human anecdotes, insightful quotes, fascinating film analogies, and scholarly textual perspectives help the reader better understand the meaning-making process of Jesus's love during our toughest times. In the end, our pain is always about Jesus, and Andy faithfully honors that reality."

— **Geoff Paetzhold**, International Counseling & Consulting, Inc.,
Smyrna, Georgia

"*Seeds of Redemption* is an honest and compelling exploration of how the life God gives can germinate and grow out of the dark soil of pain, sorrow, failure, and loss. By looking at various figures from Matthew's genealogy of Jesus, Andy White helps us see that God enacts his drama of redemption through stories of struggle that nevertheless bear a beautiful weight of glory."

—**Wes Vander Lugt**, Gordon-Conwell Theological Seminary

Seeds of Redemption

Seeds of Redemption

Buried Treasure in the Sacred Ground of Struggle

Andy White

RESOURCE *Publications* · Eugene, Oregon

SEEDS OF REDEMPTION
Buried Treasure in the Sacred Ground of Struggle

Resource Publications
An Imprint of Wipf and Stock Publishers
199 W. 8th Ave., Suite 3
Eugene, OR 97401

www.wipfandstock.com

PAPERBACK ISBN: 978-1-7252-9496-7
HARDCOVER ISBN: 978-1-7252-9497-4
EBOOK ISBN: 978-1-7252-9498-1

05/20/21

To my children,
Caroline, Drew, and Mari-Helen,
whose beautiful lives remind me every day
of the goodness of God!
With much love . . .

This is the genealogy of Jesus the Messiah the son of David, the son of Abraham: Abraham was the father of Isaac, Isaac the father of Jacob, Jacob the father of Judah and his brothers, Judah the father of Perez and Zerah, whose mother was Tamar, Perez the father of Hezron, Hezron the father of Ram, Ram the father of Amminadab, Amminadab the father of Nahshon, Nahshon the father of Salmon, Salmon the father of Boaz, whose mother was Rahab, Boaz the father of Obed, whose mother was Ruth, Obed the father of Jesse, and Jesse the father of King David. David was the father of Solomon, whose mother had been Uriah's wife, Solomon the father of Rehoboam, Rehoboam the father of Abijah, Abijah the father of Asa, Asa the father of Jehoshaphat, Jehoshaphat the father of Jehoram, Jehoram the father of Uzziah, Uzziah the father of Jotham, Jotham the father of Ahaz, Ahaz the father of Hezekiah, Hezekiah the father of Manasseh, Manasseh the father of Amon, Amon the father of Josiah, and Josiah the father of Jeconiah and his brothers at the time of the exile to Babylon. After the exile to Babylon: Jeconiah was the father of Shealtiel, Shealtiel the father of Zerubbabel, Zerubbabel the father of Abihud, Abihud the father of Eliakim, Eliakim the father of Azor, Azor the father of Zadok, Zadok the father of Akim, Akim the father of Elihud, Elihud the father of Eleazar, Eleazar the father of Matthan, Matthan the father of Jacob, and Jacob the father of Joseph, the husband of Mary, and Mary was the mother of Jesus who is called the Messiah. Thus there were fourteen generations in all from Abraham to David, fourteen from David to the exile to Babylon, and fourteen from the exile to the Messiah (Matt 1:1–17).

Contents

Acknowledgments | ix

Introduction | 1

Chapter 1: Invitation for the Marginalized—Matthew | 11

Chapter 2: Good News When It's Bad—Abraham | 22

Chapter 3: Faith in the Face of Uncertain or Unwanted Outcomes
—Isaac | 32

Chapter 4: Liberation from Hidden Bondage—Jacob | 43

Chapter 5: Grace of Exposure—Judah | 54

Chapter 6: Power of the Vulnerable—Tamar | 65

Chapter 7: Present Helper When Afraid—Rahab | 76

Chapter 8: Healing When Grieving Loss—Ruth | 88

Chapter 9: Significance When Feeling Small—Jesse | 98

Chapter 10: Forgiveness for the Guilty—David, Bathsheba,
and Uriah | 108

Chapter 11: Meaning in the Struggle to Survive and Succeed
—Solomon | 119

Chapter 12: Justice in the Face of Evil—Manasseh and Amon | 131

Chapter 13: Future Hope While Longing for Home
—Hezekiah and Josiah | 144

Chapter 14: Beauty Arising and Growing Out of the Ashes
—Babylon | 157

Bibliography | 167

Acknowledgments

S o many people over the years have loved me and contributed to my life, as well as to my family—family members, friends, former pastors and youth pastors, mentors, coaches, teachers, professors, supporters, people from my years in college ministry, and work associates. While I would love to thank many of them by name, for the purpose of bringing the dream of this book to life, I'd like to extend my warmest gratitude to a few.

My parents, Charles and Sandra White—for having provided me with a loving and nurturing home and for their commitment and sacrifices to make sure I had opportunities to grow and thrive. Sadly, my mother died a few weeks after I had submitted the final manuscript for publishing. I feel I could add a whole new dimension to the chapters on grief and future hope having experienced this painful season of mourning. Seeds of redemption, I trust somehow, lie as buried treasure in this too. I would also like to acknowledge and thank my grandparents, the late Charles and Helen White; the late Alphus Yoe, Jr.; and my 100 year old grandmother, Marion Nash Yoe.

Wipf and Stock Publishers—for their willingness and desire to take on this project. I am grateful for their detailed and structured guidance each step of the way and for bringing this book to fruition.

Wes Vander Lugt, my friend and former pastor at Warehouse 242, provided me with the encouragement I needed to get it published, read the manuscript, and offered meaningful suggestions to enhance its message.

Julie Cramer's editing revisions and coaching suggestions significantly improved the book overall. She helped pull everything together and encouraged me through the finish line.

Those who kindly took time to write thoughtful endorsements for the book.

During the time I've invested completing this book, a weekly small group has served as a safe haven for personal sharing, laughter, healthy discussions, and prayer. Thank you Scott, Jeff, Larry, Jack, Matt, Stevan, Owen, Harold, Simon, and others who participated at some point. Thanks to our facilitator and friend, Kurt Graves, for his care, stimulating questions, and thoughtful insights.

My seminary professors, among other things, imparted a love for God's unfolding story of redemption, helped sharpen my writing skills, and equipped me with very useful study tools and resources.

Jorja White, my ex-wife and good friend, journeyed with me through everything personal I share in the book. Uncommon insight, fierce advocacy for the vulnerable, and passionate love for people flow like a fountain from her huge heart. Her influence permeates several pages in the book. Also, her father, the late Dean Hollowell, and mother, Jeanette Hollowell, along with her entire family, have always cared for me as one of their own.

Caroline, Drew, and Mari-Helen are treasures beyond description. I am extremely grateful for their precious lives, huge hearts, unique personalities and gifts, the love we share, the adventures we've experienced as a family, and the ones yet to come!

Introduction

"'I don't like anything here at all,' said Frodo, . . . 'But so our path is laid.' 'Yes, that's so,' said Sam. 'And we shouldn't be here at all, if we'd known more about it before we started. But I suppose it's often that way. The brave things in the old tales and songs, Mr. Frodo: adventures, as I used to call them. I used to think that they were things the wonderful folk of the stories went out and looked for, because they wanted them, because they were exciting and life was a bit dull, a kind of a sport, as you might say. But that's not the way of it with the tales that really mattered, or the ones that stay in the mind. Folk seem to have been just landed in them, usually—their paths were laid that way, as you put it. But I expect they had lots of chances, like us, of turning back, only they didn't. And if they had, we shouldn't know, because they'd have been forgotten. We hear about those as just went on—and not all to a good end, mind you; at least not to what folk inside a story and not outside it call a good end. You know, coming home, and finding things all right, though not quite the same—like old Mr. Bilbo. But those aren't always the best tales to hear, though they may be the best tales to get landed in! I wonder what sort of a tale we've fallen into?"[1] —J.R.R. Tolkien

I n the movie *Cast Away*, Chuck Noland, a time-management fanatic and systems analyst at FedEx, specialized in solving productivity problems. His hectic schedule regularly took priority over his long-term relationship with Kelly and he kept delaying marriage. An urgent complication occurred in Malaysia during one Christmas season, disrupting Chuck's plans to propose to her. While flying over the Pacific Ocean, his flight encountered a violent storm resulting in a tragic crash in the boundless

1. Tolkien, *The Two Towers*, 696.

1

expanse of waters below. Miraculously, Chuck somehow broke free from the submerging wreckage and pulled himself into an inflatable life-raft. During the traumatic event, however, Chuck lost consciousness and the raft's emergency locator transmitter was lost. He floated all night before washing ashore on an uninhabited island where he would have to adapt and learn to survive with no means of escape.[2]

In the similarly themed classic, *Robinson Crusoe,* written by Daniel Defoe, Crusoe recounted his initial reaction of helplessness upon being shipwrecked on a deserted island: "After I got to shore and escaped drowning, instead of being thankful to God for my deliverance, having first vomited with the great quantity of salt water which was gotten into my stomach, and recovering myself a little, I ran about the shore, wringing my hands and beating my head and face, exclaiming at my misery, and crying out I was undone, undone."[3]

Each of us faces unforeseen shipwrecks of some sort. Not the kind that leaves us deserted on some isolated, uninhabited island, but the kind that leaves us, nonetheless, with this same desperate sense of feeling undone. I began writing this book in August 2008 during an unfolding financial crisis in the United States. I was enduring an unusually stressful season of transition and vocational and financial uncertainty. Prior to that time, our family already had experienced some life-altering events—and little did we anticipate the hardships that would come later. But we are not special or unique. Life is difficult. Each of us has—or at some point will have—faced struggles that wreak havoc in our lives, threaten to weaken our faith, strip us of hope, rob us of joy, extinguish our vitality, and diminish our capacity to love. Perhaps you have experienced or currently are experiencing one or more of the following: being fired from a job, underemployed, or unemployed; keeping your head above water in a debt crisis, foreclosure, and/or bankruptcy; coping with depression; wondering aimlessly with no sense of meaning, or purpose; regretting poor choices or lost opportunities; feeling guilt from something you've done or left undone; feeling trapped, isolated, and emotionally detached in a dying or dead marriage; weathering the storm of divorce; struggling to break free from an addiction; grappling with loneliness and isolation; adjusting to an empty nest; surviving emotional, psychological, and/or physical abuse; facing the disappointment of unmet expectations or longings never realized; fearing the possibility of losing someone or something of great value; confronting injustice and suffering backlash because of it; stomaching a betrayal; working through the

---

2. *Cast Away.*
3. Defoe, *Robinson Crusoe,* 49.

heartache of a breakup or end of a once important relationship; fighting a losing battle with cancer or coping with some health issue; contending with a stressful work environment; grieving the death of a loved one; fighting self-doubt and insecurity; repeating old negative patterns and habits; taking care of a special-needs child or an elderly parent; suffering from a traumatic experience or accident; or bearing one or more of these burdens of a close friend or family member.

Don't be fooled. People amid success can experience shipwrecks no one else notices. Consider, for example, the breakdown of trust, communication, and relationships that can happen within some wealthy families over financial issues. Many professionals and business executives under enormous pressure can struggle with sleeplessness and rely on anxiety medication to help them cope with the unrelenting stress associated with their huge responsibilities. Many live under fear of a triggering event that could cause it all to collapse.

We face struggles not only as individuals, but also as communities. Think about the devastation that wars, mass shootings, hurricanes, tornadoes, and forest fires cause. In 2004, an earthquake in the Indian Ocean triggered tsunamis that killed an estimated 225,000 people in 14 countries, making it one of the deadliest natural disasters in recorded history. A magnitude 7.0 earthquake hit Haiti in January of 2010. A magnitude 9.0 earthquake struck in the Pacific Ocean off the coast of Japan in March 2011, triggering a tsunami that flooded more than 200 square miles of coastal land. In the past several years we've witnessed other nations experience revolutions, internal warfare, and toppling of regimes which had been in place for decades. The pandemic in 2020 certainly disrupted and, in many cases, upended the lives of millions of people worldwide. According to John Hopkins University's Coronavirus Resource Center, there were more than 13 million cases of COVID-19 and around 265,000 consequential deaths identified in the United States by the end of November 2020. Millions of people who were laid off from work because of the pandemic lived in a constant state of anxiety. Due to shelter-in-place orders across the country, millions suffered loneliness and boredom because of the isolation.

Perhaps you can relate to what Frederick Buechner once wrote: "I have seen sorrow and pain enough to turn the heart to stone. Who hasn't? Many times, I have chosen the wrong road, or the right road for the wrong reason . . . I have followed too much the devices and desires of my own heart . . . yet often when my heart called out to me to be brave, to be kind, to be honest, I have not followed at all."[4]

4. Buechner, *A Crazy, Holy Grace*, 62.

Confronting hardships and profound emotions can threaten to consume us like a forest fire. We can feel fear, stress, mental disorientation, chronic exhaustion, lack of motivation, and cycles of negativity. We can experience genuine doubts about God, or unexpected emotional outbursts. Shame, a painful feeling of unworthiness, can intensify when we are unable to fix or rise above the problem. Wanting to appear okay, we might hide behind a mask in secrecy and silence. Doing so can make matters worse. To survive, some of us try as best we can to ignore our problems by burying our heads in the sand and acting like nothing is wrong. Others attempt to escape by working more, sleeping more, bingeing in front of a television or computer screen, or eating, drinking, or medicating on some other drug of choice. Others who tend to be more controlling experience intensified stress as they seek to fix a problem they cannot solve or control. At times, depending on the situation, nothing seems to help. Well-intentioned friends can offer harmful and/or ill-timed advice when they minimize the problem by saying things such as: *It will be okay; It will all work out; It's all happening for a good reason; God never gives us more than we can handle; Keep thinking about the many blessings you still enjoy*; or, *Someone's always got it worse than you do.* For many people, they simply cannot see a light at the end of the proverbial tunnel. If they see any light, they are more likely to interpret it as that of an oncoming train. If this describes your situation, then why not be honest and experience the freedom of expressing your emotions and honestly exclaim like Robinson Crusoe that you are "undone, undone"?

A few years ago, I crossed paths with an acquaintance in a parking lot. Shortly into our conversation, we began lamenting a particular life tragedy of a mutual friend. At one point in the interaction, however, he stated something quite simple, yet richly profound. "His story isn't over." It reminded me of a professor in seminary who often stated that exact same thing about the Israelites. Whether they were enslaved in Egypt, wondering in the wilderness, rebelling against God, being defeated in battle, or experiencing exile far away from home, he would exclaim, "But the story ain't over!"

Many of the stories we read, hear about, or watch in the movies have a good ending. The rescuers save the kids trapped in the cave; the alcoholic becomes sober; the servant maid marries the prince; the losing team makes a miraculous comeback. Yet so many real-life stories spiral downward and don't end well. As you face your own hardships, you may be asking—as Sam in the opening quote—what sort of a tale you've fallen into.

While seeking a resolution or wishing for help in a cultural context where individualism is valued, you may feel isolated. Many people function in an environment of pretense, putting on an act that all is well while hiding their problems. We are too ashamed to risk vulnerability. We don't want to be judged or perceived as needy or weak. Therefore, we remain silent and independent, which results in feeling uncared for, detached, disconnected, and misunderstood by those closest to us. Frederick Buechner explains how humans tend to erect walls to hide behind:

> "The inner state you end up with is a castle-like affair of keep, inner wall, outer wall, moat, which you erect originally to be a fortress to keep the enemy out but which turns into a prison where you become the jailer and thus your own enemy. It is a wretched and lonely place. You can't be what you want to be there or do what you want to do. People can't see through all that masonry to who you truly are, and half the time you're not sure you can see who you truly are yourself, you've been walled up so long. Fortunately there are two words that offer a way out, and they're simply these: 'Help me.' It's not always easy to say them—you have your pride after all, and you're not sure there's anybody you trust enough to say them to—but they're always worth saying."[5]

Perhaps currently you don't feel the need for help yourself. But you most likely know someone who *is* experiencing some sort of shipwreck. How we respond to others in need can reveal much about our own character or unperceived internal shipwrecks. Picture in your mind a recent global calamitous event such as the pandemic as well as one in someone's life you know personally. Do you find yourself feeling a genuine sense of compassion, or rather a sense of judgment or apathy? Have you grasped and felt the gravity of the situation or attempted to minimize or ignore it? Have you attempted to reach out to the one you know personally? Have you sought to be present with them, or avoid them altogether? Maybe you're so caught up in your own agenda, you've forgotten about them. Clearly, we do not have the capacity to feel compassion, show concern, or get involved in every single problem out there. In many cases, there is nothing we could do even if we wanted to. In some cases, we could do something, but perhaps it's best we do nothing. Why? Because sometimes helping can cause more harm in the long run. Consider the parent who does everything for his or her child, inevitably preventing the child from ever assuming personal responsibility and growing up. My point is to ask yourself: when others are in crisis, what is revealed to be true of your heart? If through some reflection, you realize your own heart is calloused, self-righteous, or judgmental then perhaps your life is shipwrecked as well—and perhaps even more so than the shipwrecked person about whom you were thinking. By the way, if you think

---

5. Buechner, *Whistling in the Dark*, 60.

you've got it all together, there's a word for your condition—denial. But take heart, your story is not over either!

Why? Because ironically, within these struggles are seeds of redemption. I do not pretend to know much about seeds. I do know that they must be buried in dirt (and therefore, in the dark) to grow. Without seeds, the earth would be a barren place unable to support the many forms of life which exist. From seeds grow roots unseen, and then out of the darkness and soil emerge life-giving plants. Certain seeds become trees and eventually forests. The ground of struggle in which we find ourselves buried is sacred ground. Don't dismiss grief, anger, despair, or other negative emotions, as we many times refer to them, as signs of a lack of faith. Rather, "embrace those dark angels as the best, most demanding spiritual teachers"[6] you may ever know. It's critically important, Barbara Brown Taylor testified, to let "emotions flow—even the loud and messy ones— because if they are kept from making their noise and maybe even tossing the furniture, they can harden like plaque in a coronary artery, blocking anything else that tries to come through. Eruptions are good news, the signal that darkness will not stay buried."[7]

One evening back in August of 2008, while overwhelmed with anxiety, I engaged in one of my main stress-relieving activities—jogging. During that hour or so of cardio workout, prayer, and quiet thought, a passage of Scripture randomly surfaced to the forefront of my mind. It was not a passage one would consider immediately relevant to the struggles I was facing such as Psalm 23 or the exhortation from 1 Peter 5:7 to cast all our anxieties upon God because he cares for us. No, the passage that came to my mind is one that perhaps has put many a reader to sleep. It was the genealogy of Jesus as recorded in Matthew chapter 1. Here were normal human beings, both men and women from all walks of life, each having faults, facing hardships, making bad decisions, engaging in harmful behavior, and experiencing failures relevant to our own. And unlike so many families and institutions which seek to minimize, justify, deny, or conceal any problems or failures among their members, the Bible does not do so. The genealogy is not simply a list. The stories represented in the genealogy are quite wild and fascinating, perhaps like yours and mine.

The genealogy scrolls through around forty names. That is too many to cover in one book. Besides, the Bible does not provide much information, if any at all, for several of them. In each chapter I focus on a particular person from the genealogy, starting with Matthew, the author of the gospel

---

6. Taylor, *Learning to Walk in the Dark*, 78.

7. Taylor, *Learning to Walk in the Dark*, 84.

who documented the list. It is not my goal to provide an exhaustive study on each person, but, instead, to focus on a particular struggle that he or she faced relative to our own as well as the seeds of redemption buried in the ground of that struggle. Redemption is multi-dimensional, and I am just scratching the surface. In essence, to redeem is to "'buy free,' literally to 'buy back.' A free person has been seized and is being held for ransom. Someone else pays the ransom on behalf of the captive and thus 'buys back' his or her original freedom. The point of redemption is to free the prisoner from bondage, to give back the freedom he or she once enjoyed."[8] What we consistently see throughout the genealogy is God redeeming where it is not sought, deserved, or appreciated. Central to all these stories is the redeemer himself, Jesus. After all, the genealogy is ultimately about him.

Allow me to provide a brief example from one of the chapters that can also help tie this together. Take Solomon, for instance. He wrestled to find meaning in life. Victor Frankl was a preeminent psychotherapist during the twentieth century and a Holocaust survivor. Frankl, when trying to convey the meaning of one's life, invoked the analogy of a movie: "It consists of thousands upon thousands of individual pictures, and each of them makes sense and carries a meaning, yet the meaning of the whole film cannot be seen before its sequence is shown. On the other hand, we cannot understand the whole film without having first understood each of its components, each of the individual pictures. Isn't it the same with life?"[9] This analogy is most helpful in conveying the whole of the genealogy in Matthew 1. One cannot understand the whole meaning of Solomon's life or any of the others in the genealogy without understanding the entire story being ultimately about Jesus and his purpose in coming. And one cannot comprehend the meaning of the story of Jesus without also knowing and understanding those stories imbedded in the names of those in the genealogy. So, get ready. I will be diving into stories of struggle and redemption in the lives of Matthew, Abraham, Isaac, Jacob, Judah, Tamar, Rahab, Ruth, Jesse, David, Solomon, Manasseh, Amon, Hezekiah, and Josiah as well as the only place mentioned in the genealogy—Babylon.

Seeds take time to grow. From Abraham, the first person listed in Matthew's genealogy, to Jesus was perhaps around two thousand years. God promised Abraham a son when he was seventy-five years old. Isaac was not born until twenty-five years later. The Israelites remained slaves in Egypt for more than four hundred years. Moses spent forty years in voluntary exile before God called him back to Egypt to deliver his people out of bondage.

8. Wolters, *Creation Regained*, 57.

9. Frankl, *Man's Search for Ultimate Meaning*, 143.

The Israelites wandered in the wilderness for forty years before entering the promised land. Judah's captivity in Babylon lasted a long time. But we don't typically like to wait. We can be so intensely focused on where we think we should be or want to be that we experience tremendous difficulty patiently waiting in the present moment. Henri Nouwen—a Catholic priest, professor, writer, and theologian—once exhorted his readers "to be present fully to the moment, in the conviction that something is happening where you are."[10] It's tempting to suppose God will work at some other time and in some other place. But *this present moment is pregnant with possibility because God is always working.* The reason I am referring to struggles as sacred ground is because God is with us in the struggle. Guard yourself, therefore, against the temptation to believe this moment is void of any meaning or significance even though it may be painful, sad, stressful, boring, or confusing. We should be willing "to stay where we are and live the situation out to the fullest in the belief that something hidden there will manifest itself to us."[11] Do not interpret waiting as passively sitting around doing nothing. We are to proactively *live* out whatever situation we are in to the fullest. Patiently persevering through present challenges means some degree of suffering. Such waiting involves breathing an expectant hope and faith in a God who loves us, moves in mysterious ways and in his own time, and is working out all things for good. Such waiting does not require one to have answers or certainty, but rather a hopeful willingness to explore through unknown mystery. Such waiting results in a renewed, engaged, energized walk through the journey uncertain of the outcome, but maintaining confident assurance in a good God. Such waiting understands the significance of small things. Seeds, once buried in dirt and darkness, in time become trees, and eventually forests. Such waiting produces the joy of knowing that God's story of redemption is not over. Keep in mind our view and understanding of what good is could be different from God's view. C.S. Lewis wisely said, "Our good is to love him . . . and to love him we must know him: and if we know him, we shall in fact fall on our faces."[12] Our good is to love our neighbor as we love ourselves. We will love him, our neighbor, and ourselves as our assurance grows of his love for us. Though it sounds strange, "hope born of faith becomes matured and purified through difficulty."[13]

Nouwen warned against wishing for things to go in a specific direction. We might wish for relief: for the pain to stop, the problem to be

---

10. Durback, *Seeds of Hope*, 158.

11. Durback, *Seeds of Hope*, 158.

12. Lewis, *The Problem of Pain*, 46.

13. Nouwen, *Turn My Mourning into Dancing*, 53.

resolved, the relationship to heal, the career opportunity to work out, the debt to go away, the cancer to disappear, or simply for the sun to shine. At times, what we wish for happens. But the reality is, despite all our efforts, so much of life is out of our control and things are not the way they are supposed to be in this broken world. Regarding some of our struggles, our wishes are at times aligned with things we treasure perhaps more than God himself or with the values of our surrounding culture and not with the ways of Jesus. And we are blind to it. Suffering has a way of opening our eyes, awakening us to truth, and freeing us from a bondage of which we were unaware. Theologian Martin Marty once concluded, "Brokenness and wounding do not occur in order to break human dignity but to open the heart so God can act."[14] Many of you can probably relate to something Barbara Brown Taylor gained from her own experiences. "I have learned things in the dark that I could never have learned in the light."[15] Franciscan priest, Richard Rohr, made this wise observation: "It is often when the ego is most deconstructed that we can hear things anew."[16] For what God is doing could be completely different from what we are wishing for. Then there are those struggles which simply are realities in life for all of us. For example, someone we love has cancer or some other disease and is dying. We would all wish and pray for that person to heal and live. Yet death may result despite our desperate prayers and wishes. We must therefore hope rather than wish as Nouwen advised: "I have found it very important in my own life, to let go of my wishes and start hoping. Hope is willing to leave unanswered questions unanswered and unknown futures unknown. Hope makes you see God's guiding hand not only in the gentle and pleasant moments but also in the shadows of disappointment and darkness."[17]

This book reflects on God being ever at work in and through the struggles of various persons listed in Jesus's genealogy. Like them, we bear the image of God and face similar struggles. Og Mandino once wrote, "Search for the seed of good in every adversity. Master that principle and you will own a precious shield that will guard you well through all the darkest valleys you must traverse. Stars may be seen from the bottom of a deep well when they cannot be discerned from the mountaintop. So will you learn things in adversity that you would never have discovered without trouble. There is always a seed of good. Find it and prosper."[18]

14. Marty, *A Cry of Absence*, 123.

15. Taylor, *Learning to Walk in the Dark*, 5.

16. Rohr, *Falling Upward*, xxxiv.

17. Nouwen, *Turn My Mourning into Dancing*, 60.

18. Mandino, *A Better Way to Live*, 118.

Seeds buried in the ground need water. Amid our struggles, we need God's mercy. Rohr also wrote, "Water always falls and pools up in the very lowest and darkest places, just like mercy. And mercy is just grace in action."[19] As you read through this book, I pray you would know and experience the redeeming mercy of God falling and pooling up in the places of your struggles. May deeper roots of faith and hope germinate from seeds of redemption. May a growing soul, wisdom, and a widened capacity to love arise and grow. May a beautiful and unexpected story of glory flourish out of and beyond the soil of your hardships.

To begin this reading journey in *Seeds of Redemption—Buried Treasure in the Sacred Ground of Struggle*, why don't you take a minute, find a quiet place to kneel, and pray the prayer below to him whom Jesus said to address simply as, "Father." I recognize some of your struggles are so painful that you would rather not pray. Perhaps you are struggling to believe God is even real at all. If this is the case, I simply invite you to keep reading. This is the opening prayer from a book entitled *The Valley of Vision*.

> Lord, high and holy, meek and lowly, thou hast brought me to the valley of vision where I live in the depths but see thee in the heights. Let me learn by paradox that the way down is the way up, that to be low is to be high, that the broken heart is the healed heart, that the contrite spirit is the rejoicing spirit, that the repenting soul is the victorious soul, that to have nothing is to possess all, that to bear the cross is to wear the crown, that to give is to receive, that the valley is the place of vision. Lord, in the daytime stars can be seen from deepest wells, and the deeper the wells the brighter thy stars shine. Let me find thy light in my darkness, thy life in my death, thy joy in my sorrow, thy grace in my sin, thy riches in my poverty, thy glory in my valley.[20]

19. Rohr, "A Santa Claus God," lines 28–29.
20. Bennett, *Valley of Vision*, 1.

CHAPTER 1

Invitation for the Marginalized

Matthew

"Jesus had no trouble with the exceptions, . . . He ate with outsiders regularly, to the chagrin of church stalwarts, who always love their version of order over any compassion toward the exceptions."[1]
—Richard Rohr

*L*es Misérables is one of my favorite books. Victor Hugo's French histori-cal fiction was published in 1862 and is considered one of the great-est novels of the nineteenth century. The protagonist, Jean Valjean, steals bread during an economic depression to feed his family, and is subsequently caught and imprisoned where his very name is erased. No longer Jean Valjean, he becomes identified as number 24601. With each escape he at-tempts, he tacks time onto his sentence, which balloons to nineteen years. During this period, Valjean endures severe mistreatment. He has no bed on which to sleep, and prison means chains, a cell, exhausting labor, and whip-pings. Beatings are the only means by which he ever receives physical touch. No one speaks a friendly word to him or performs a kind act on his behalf. "From year to year this soul had withered more and more, slowly but fatally. With this withered heart, he had a dry eye. When he left the galleys, he had not shed a tear for nineteen years."[2] Upon release, Valjean is forced to carry a yellow passport, identifying him to the public as a former convict. Any ray of hope regarding the idea of freedom quickly fades. For wherever he goes after his release, Valjean endures rejection as an outcast, and alienation worse than if he had leprosy. His encounter with the unforgiving world il-

---

1. Rohr, *Falling Upward*, 56.
2. Hugo, *Les Misérables*, 100.

lustrates that, "Liberation is not deliverance. A convict may leave the galleys behind, but not his condemnation."[3]

Condition of being marginalized

To be marginalized is to be excluded, rejected, alienated, or pushed out of a community. It is a place of powerlessness and insignificance. Perhaps the most alienated group in America today is the prison population. "Very few prisoners have access to education, substance abuse programs, counseling, training, therapy, drug therapy and treatment for mental illness, and just simple human-to-human contact."[4] This is not new. Back in the 1800s, French researchers Alexis de Tocqueville and Gustave de Beaumont determined that "in America, (a criminal) is an enemy of the human race and every human being is against him."[5] Michelle Alexander wrote, "Criminals, it turns out, are the one social group in America we have permission to hate. In 'colorblind' America, criminals are the new whipping boys. They are entitled to no respect and little moral concern."[6] On an extraordinarily hot day in July 2020 I learned that North Carolina's largest women's prison does not have air-conditioning. To put that in perspective, consider that leaders of an animal shelter—who run a program for the inmates on how to train dogs—remove their animals every summer because they consider the prison conditions unsafe. Animal rescue facilities are climate-controlled, and prisons are not.

Matthew 9:9–13 records the time when Jesus entered Matthew's life. Matthew chose not to reveal anything about his past, family, education, achievements, community involvement, or political association. He was content to identify himself as a tax collector. Mention of a tax collector would have aroused anger among Jews who were under the forced rule of the Roman Empire, which annually appointed officials to collect taxes from every household based upon property and income. Taxation financially weakened the Jews, while it empowered the empire they despised. Tax collectors gathered as much as they could from the public while only paying a fixed amount to the imperial treasury. Understandably, Jews equally detested tax collectors as much as their employer. Tax collectors "were notoriously unscrupulous, growing wealthy at the expense of others of their

---

3. Hugo, *Les Misérables*, 103.
4. Gilliard, *Rethinking Incarceration*, 120.
5. Graber, *The Furnace of Affliction*, 120.
6. Alexander, *The New Jim Crow*, 141.

own people."[7] According to rabbinical literature, Jews were to extend their hatred even to the family of the tax collector because they were "universally regarded as no better than robbers or thieves."[8] The Gospel of Matthew, with its special Jewish interests, "contains the most frequent derogatory references to tax collectors,"[9] and the most strict Levites "viewed tax collectors not only as traitors, but as immoral and rapacious."[10] Matthew was sitting in a tax collector's booth when Jesus approached him.

Compassion of Jesus contrasted with the compliance of Javert

Though brief, the story of Jesus's initial encounter with Matthew captures the beautiful heart of his mission: inviting the alienated outsider to belong as one of his close followers. Matthew 9:9–13 (MSG) says:

> "Passing along, Jesus saw a man at his work collecting taxes. His name was Matthew. Jesus said, 'Come along with me.' Matthew stood up and followed him. Later when Jesus was eating supper at Matthew's house with his close followers, a lot of disreputable characters came and joined them. When the Pharisees saw him keeping this kind of company, they had a fit, and lit into Jesus's followers. 'What kind of example is this from your Teacher, acting cozy with crooks and riffraff?' Jesus, overhearing, shot back, 'Who needs a doctor: the healthy or the sick? Go figure out what this Scripture means: 'I'm after mercy, not religion.' I'm here to invite outsiders, not coddle insiders.'"

While most Jews would have avoided the perceived traitor, Jesus saw Matthew, and approached him. Later in the same chapter, Matthew records another situation where Jesus sees a crowd of people described as harassed and helpless like sheep without a shepherd. Seeing them in this state triggers within him compassion. *Splagxnizomai* is the Greek word used in Matthew 9:36, which scholars sometimes translate as, "moved with pity," or "moved with compassion." This same Greek word is also used to describe Jesus's response in Mark 1:41 when a leper with rotted skin, covered face, emaciated body, and torn clothes approached him. To say Jesus was moved with compassion, or a deep feeling of affection, sympathy, and mercy would certainly

---

7. Bromily, *The International Standard Bible Encyclopedia*, 4:742.
8. Bromily, *The International Standard Bible Encyclopedia*, 4:742.
9. Bromily, *The International Standard Bible Encyclopedia*, 4:742.
10. Carson and Moo, *An Introduction to the New Testament*, 147.

convey the meaning in part. But it still would not capture the full extent. There really is not an English word equivalent. *Splagxnizomai* means his guts were tied up in knots with a combination of passion, pity, anger, frustration, and love. Imagine for a second how a parent would feel if one of his or her children had been beaten up at school by an older bully and needed to go to the hospital. One pastor described *splagxnizomai* as horrified love.[11] A feeling of horror that something is not right and love which compels someone to action. Atticus Finch, the central attorney in Harper Lee's *To Kill A Mockingbird,* tried to teach his daughter, Scout, a huge life lesson one day when he said, "You never really understand a person until you consider things from his point of view . . . until you climb into his skin and walk around in it."[12] Compassion, though, does not stop at merely understanding; it compels one to action. Matthew would learn early on about Jesus's compassion. Upon seeing Matthew, Jesus approached him and extended an invitation: "Follow me." The invitation included a close association with and opportunity to learn from Jesus in an ongoing, committed relationship.[13]

From there, they went to Matthew's house to enjoy a meal together with others. In the Ancient Near East, to share a meal with someone was a guarantee of peace, trust, fraternity, and forgiveness. It symbolized a shared life. For an orthodox Jew to say, "I would like to have dinner with you," implied a deeper request for friendship.[14] Jesus was having dinner not only with Matthew, but also with other tax collectors, sinners, crooks, and riffraff.

This enraged the Pharisees. They could not fathom why Jesus engaged in intimate table fellowship with those they viewed as immoral and corrupt. How could a teacher, knowledgeable about God's law, possibly associate so closely with those of such ill repute? To them it was inconceivable. So, they asked the disciples, "Why does your teacher eat with tax collectors and sinners?" Brennan Manning offered this explanation:

> In the year 1925, if a wealthy plantation owner in Atlanta extended a formal invitation to four colored cotton pickers to come to his mansion for Sunday dinner, preceded by cocktails and followed by several hours of brandy and conversation, the Georgia aristocracy would have been outraged, neighboring Alabama infuriated, and the Ku Klux Klan apoplectic. Sixty or seventy years ago in the deep South, the caste system was inviolable, social and racial discrimination inflexible, and indiscretion made

---

11. Cassidy, "Scandalous Savior."
12. Lee, *To Kill A Mockingbird,* 39.
13. Brown, *Dictionary of New Testament Theology,* 1:481–82.
14. Manning, *The Ragamuffin Gospel,* 57.

the loss of reputation inevitable. . . . In first century Palestinian Judaism the class system was enforced rigorously. It was legally forbidden to mingle with sinners who were outside the law: table fellowship with beggars, tax collectors . . . and prostitutes was a religious, social, and cultural taboo.[15]

The antagonist in *Les Misérables* is Javert. First introduced in the book as a prison guard at Toulon where Valjean served out his prison sentence, Javert later becomes a police inspector. Throughout the story, Javert is preoccupied with pursuing Valjean to make sure he is justly punished. Central to Javert's purpose for existence is law and order. It is his passion, code, and religion. He believes life is to be lived in perfect compliance with the straight line of the law. The most important values, ideals, and beliefs flow out of the government's and courts' decrees. Therefore, one's chief end in life must be perfect adherence to the law. To fall short of this standard means punishment. Punishment is embedded deeply in the decrees as part of that law and order. Therefore, punishment is always the right course of action to take regarding any lawbreaker. Compassion, kindness, and mercy are not written into the code of law. So, neither does Javert manifest any of these attributes. Why would he? If he demonstrates any benevolence, kindness, or compassion, he would be betraying his most deeply held religious convictions. Javert seeks to perfect his duties as a chief enforcer of those laws and decrees. For Javert, justice means inflicting punishment to maintain order. To Javert whose duty is to the law alone, lawbreakers deserve no redemption. And so, he ruthlessly holds people accountable to that law.

The Pharisees, like Javert, were absorbed with holding people ruthlessly accountable to the Law. Like Javert, their goal was to be irreproachable or faultless. As a powerful police inspector, Javert embodied a system that wielded power not to correct and restore those who had violated the law, but rather to punish and destroy them. The Pharisees in Jesus's day, obsessive about morality, "barred from the community those who did not or could not conform"[16] to their standards. To put it simply, they did not like or accept anyone who was not like them. C.S. Lewis once asserted, "The essential vice, the utmost evil, is Pride. Unchastity, anger, greed, drunkenness, and all that, are mere fleabites in comparison: it was through Pride that the devil became the devil: Pride leads to every other vice: it is the complete anti-God state of mind."[17] But they were utterly blind to the immorality of their obsession with morality; of their guilt in pursuing guiltlessness; and

---

15. Manning, *The Ragamuffin Gospel*, 56–57.

16. Blue, *Healing Spiritual Abuse*, 25.

17. Lewis, *Mere Christianity*, 121–22.

how this corruption vandalized human dignity. "The proud person offends against God by self-exaltation, against other people by self-pre-occupation, and against self by self-deception. The delusion increases until one fancies oneself so high as to be invulnerable."[18] Psychiatrist and bestselling author, Dr. M. Scott Peck asserted that today's Pharisees who perpetrate evil are "the self-righteous who think they are without sin because they are unwilling to suffer the discomfort of significant self-examination."[19] Lewis warned, "Prostitutes are in no danger of finding their present life so satisfactory that they cannot turn to God: the proud, the avaricious, the self-righteous, are in that danger."[20]

Each of us is responsible for our own decisions and actions. To whatever degree some person or group may have cut us off, we should reflect humbly on whatever part we may have played in contributing to the alienation. It may be true that our own contribution was one percent, and theirs was ninety-nine. Or, maybe our own alienation is due mostly or completely to our own actions that hurt others. In the case of Matthew, the tax collector, perhaps he was corrupt. Perhaps he did abuse the system, collecting more taxes from people than was required and pocketing the excess. You might recall the story of another tax collector, Zacchaeus, whom Jesus called down from the sycamore tree saying, "Zacchaeus, hurry and come down, for today I must stay at your house." In response, Zacchaeus said to Jesus, "Behold, Lord, half of my possessions I will give to the poor, and if I have defrauded anyone of anything, I will give back four times as much" (Luke 19:5–9). He accepted responsibility for his wrongdoing and was ready to go back to every single person he had wronged to make it right. And Jesus celebrated Zacchaeus's contrition by saying, "Today salvation has come to this house." Jesus was not blind to Zacchaeus's abuses as a tax collector. True compassion does not enable harmful behavior.

But it is also critical for our own health and wholeness to understand when our alienation is the result of someone else's problems. Of all the issues Jesus could have exposed and opposed, he zeroed in on the abusive self-righteousness of the Pharisees. I will elaborate more on this when we get to the chapter on Tamar. Some of us may blindly be participating in a culture of Javerts or modern-day Pharisees, which can thwart ministry and harm people.

18. Bromily, *The International Standard Bible Encyclopedia*, 3:960.

19. Peck, *People of the Lie*, 72.

20. Lewis, *The Problem of Pain*, 96.

Closed groups

A common biblical metaphor to describe the church is the "body of Christ." Acts 2:42–47 describes the early church functioning and growing in a beautiful and healthy way, "having favor with all the people" (v. 47). But what can happen when this body has lost its head and is not acting as the body *of Christ*? Years ago, I learned a lot about closed organizational families from a book entitled, *The Incestuous Workplace,* a scandalous title, I know. Many of its insights help explain why many churches and parachurch organizations today hinder Christ's teachings and ministry. What author William L. White refers to in this book as "closed systems" can include for-profit companies, community-service entities, nonprofit entities, and religious groups. White analyzes the propensity of members within closed organizations to be isolated from the outside world and increasingly have their personal, professional, and social needs met inside the organization. Such dynamics can end up causing much disruption and even the collapse of the organization. Such dynamics characterized the Pharisees's community. Closed systems tend to have an inflexible definition of values, beliefs, acceptable behaviors, and a high degree of intimacy among members. Bad problems arise in the stories of closed systems when their passion for these things gets perverted. How does this happen? Controlling leaders act as strict gatekeepers regarding the "flow of ideas and people into the organization" as well as "the ability of members to develop and sustain professional and social relationships and activities outside of the organization."[21] They resist change and "tend to expel that which is different."[22] In the most extreme cases, a tyrannical or authoritarian management style operates under the belief "that workers must be controlled by fear, force or charismatic persuasion."[23] Members deviating from norms can expect a harsh response. Those within such organizations tend to view the outside world as a threat. Therefore, outsiders are to be feared and mistrusted. Members learn the belief system cannot be challenged. Those courageous enough to challenge those beliefs may be "extruded from the organizational family."[24] Leaving a closed organizational family can be extremely difficult. Commitment, devotion, and loyalty are so strongly valued that "leaving is viewed as a betrayal."[25] I have only scratched the surface of White's brilliant work.

---

21. White, *The Incestuous Workplace,* 40.
22. White, *The Incestuous Workplace,* 40.
23. White, *The Incestuous Workplace,* 41.
24. White, *The Incestuous Workplace,* 53.
25. White, *The Incestuous Workplace,* 66.

Perhaps these insights will stimulate you to constructively evaluate whatever organization or church body of which you are a part. For those interested, the book also provides critique of *open* organizational systems as well as direction on how organizations can promote health.

Jesus rebelled against the Pharisees's closed organizational system. For example, take the Samaritans, whom the Jews viewed as repugnant and repellant religiously and socially, while "Christ's disposition toward the Samaritans was always one of blessing."[26] In fact, how did Jesus respond to the Pharisees's question about why he was hanging out with the crooks and riffraff? *Healthy persons need not visit a doctor.* The Pharisees could not recognize their own sickness or need for a physician. In their self-deception, they were shocked about Jesus associating with outcasts; therefore, something had to be wrong with Jesus instead of themselves. They were convinced that they were the good guys on the "right side of the law," and Jesus deserved punishment just as Javert believed about Valjean. Their behavior was based on this delusion. Jesus, perceiving their delusional state, exhorted them to relearn the heart of God as revealed in the words of the Old Testament prophet, Hosea: "I desire mercy, not sacrifice" (6:6). As leaders, the Pharisees should have understood that God had not dealt with them according to their rule-keeping compliance. They should have recognized that Jesus, by associating with the marginalized, was being consistent with God's compassionate nature.

Before Hosea had spoken those words, Israel had experienced peace and prosperity. But instead of engaging in thankful adoration of God and generous love toward others, they acted immorally and worshipped idols. Eventually, their corrupt hearts and behavior brought about their destruction and downfall at the hands of the Assyrians in 722 BC. To provide Hosea with an experience which would enable him to understand God's position toward Israel, God told Hosea to marry Gomer, a prostitute who would be unfaithful to him. "The LORD said to me, 'Go, show your love to your wife again, though she is loved by another man and is an adulteress. Love her as the Lord loves the Israelites, though they turn to other gods'" (Hos 3:1). Israel had acted as an adulteress; yet even still, God loved the children of Israel. In quoting Hosea 6:6 to the Pharisees, Jesus likened them to the unfaithful Israelites. It was Jesus's way of pointing out their adultery and calling them to repentance.

26. Hunter, *To Change the World*, 192.

Jesus joins us

"Sacrifice" to the Hebrew ear referred to external ceremonial worship of God involving blood, ritual, and offerings. These outward forms of sacrifice, however, were meaningless to God without true devotion from the heart, authentic compassion, mercy, and love for one's neighbor. But Israel had missed it. The Pharisees had missed it. Mercy in the Old Testament was used to communicate "the deep, tender feeling of compassion that was awakened by the trouble, weakness, suffering, or vulnerability of another in need of help."[27] As Brennan Manning pointed out, Jesus "spent a disproportionate amount of time with people" who were alienated.[28] These were those described in the gospels as: "the poor, the blind, the lame, the lepers, the hungry, sinners, prostitutes, tax collectors, the persecuted, the downtrodden, the captives, those possessed by unclean spirits, . . . the least, the last, and the lost sheep of the house of Israel?"[29]

We, the marginalized, do not remain alone in the ground of struggle. Jesus joins us there. His own story began in exclusion. In the insignificant little town of Bethlehem, where no inn had room for his mother, Jesus was born in the most unfit place for the Lord of Lords. He entered our world in a stable, or cave as some have interpreted, spending his first night on earth in a feeding trough. His first visitors were shepherds, a marginalized, unnoticed, non-influential lower social class of nomads who dwelled in fields apart from society. Considered a threat at birth by King Herod, Jesus was taken by Mary and Joseph out of their home country to Egypt at the angel of the Lord's instruction. Herod sought to kill the child. His boyhood home was Nazareth, an unimportant small village. Upon being told, "'We have found the one Moses wrote about in the Law and about whom the prophets also wrote—Jesus of Nazareth, the son of Joseph,' Nathanael responded, 'Nazareth! Can any good thing come from there?'" (John 1:46). Most of Jesus's life was spent working an ordinary, mundane job as a carpenter. To inaugurate his ministry, Jesus, after being baptized, was led *outside* of society into the wilderness for forty days and nights. Isaiah prophesied about the future Messiah:

> "He was despised and rejected by mankind, a man of suffering, and familiar with pain. Like one from whom people hide their faces he was despised, and we held him in low esteem. For he was cut off from the land of the living; for the transgression of

27. Bromiley, *The International Standard Bible Encyclopedia,* 3:322.

28. Manning, *The Ragamuffin Gospel,* 49.

29. Manning, *The Ragamuffin Gospel,* 49.

my people he was punished. He was assigned a grave with the wicked, and with the rich in his death, though he had done no violence, nor was any deceit in his mouth" (Isa 53:3, 8–9).

Jesus was marginalized throughout his life, forsaken, denied, and betrayed by even his closest followers in the end, forsaken by his Father in his dying, and alienated in the tomb upon his death. Jesus was a "falsely convicted criminal who was falsely charged, punitively convicted, mercilessly tortured, and unjustly sentenced to death."[30] The very Son of God endured the worst possible form of alienation—death on a cross.

In *Les Misérables*, Valjean is ill-treated and alienated until he comes to the doorstep of a bishop. The bishop is described as one who spreads kindness, affection, and light everywhere he goes. Such is his reputation that whoever has a need is directed to his home. Instead of alienating the ex-convict like everyone else had done, the bishop gladly welcomes him, treats him with dignity, serves him dinner, and provides him a comfortable bed. Having endured years of torment under a cruel system of injustice and now facing permanent rejection within a law-driven society void of a soul, Valjean is shocked to encounter such extravagant love. Even so, Valjean, hardened by so many years of cruelty, is fixated on surviving. While in the bishop's home that evening, he observes six silver plates belonging to the bishop that he knows he can sell. Concluding this as his only means of survival, Valjean quietly steals these items and sneaks away during the night.

The next day, aware Valjean has taken off with stolen goods, the bishop hears a knock at his door. Three police officers had arrested Valjean. The bishop immediately displays a heart of compassion saying, "I am glad to see you. But! I gave you the candlesticks also, which are silver like the rest, and would bring two hundred francs. Why did you not take them along with your plates?"[31] Can you imagine Valjean's reaction after fully expecting another prison sentence? He walks in downcast and filled with shame. Now, suddenly he looks up at the bishop "with an expression which no human tongue could describe."[32] The police officers seem bewildered and seek to explain their reasons for arresting Valjean. The bishop testifies he had given these silver plates to Valjean the night before, and it is all a mistake. So, the police release him. Valjean is overcome with disbelief. The bishop proceeds to remove the two candlesticks from the mantelpiece, and hand them over to Valjean. With passion and conviction, the bishop looks deeply into Valjean's stunned eyes and encourages him that he no longer belongs to evil,

30. Gilliard, *Rethinking Incarceration*, 148.

31. Hugo, *Les Misérables*, 111.

32. Hugo, *Les Misérables*, 111.

but rather to good. "It is your soul that I am buying for you. I withdraw it from dark thoughts and from the spirit of perdition, and I give it to God."[33] For nineteen years under the code of Javert, Valjean's soul had withered, slowly but fatally. Yet he did not remain alone in that ground of struggle because the bishop joins him there. The bishop's love floods the hard soil of Valjean's alienated and dying soul and resurrects him to new life. Those seeds of redemption flourish as Valjean's life overflows with compassion towards those around him for the rest of his life.

A major obstacle keeping many marginalized persons from viewing themselves from God's eyes of compassion is being so accustomed to viewing themselves from the eyes of modern-day Javerts. Jesus went from the heights of glory to the depths of shame on the cross for those who are broken, needy, vulnerable, struggling, and wounded. No matter who we are, where we have been, or what we have done, God sees us with eyes of compassion. He knows all about us. To him, we are not a number. We have a name and an identity. He extends us mercy and grace. He invites us to belong! Read Luke 14:16–24 about the parable of the great banquet to see how passionate Jesus is about inviting the outcasts of society. He came not to condemn, but to forgive; not to oppress, but to set free; not to lay heavy burdens, but to give rest; not to treat us as an agenda, but as the people we are; not to wound us, but to heal us; not to cause us grief, but to give us joy; not to manipulate us through lies, fear, and intimidation, but to transform us through his love; not to scapegoat blame, guilt, and shame on us because he became the scapegoat of all our blame, guilt, and shame. Why? So that for eternity, *we might belong* in his kingdom. And he invites *us—you*—saying, "Come, follow me."

---

33. Hugo, *Les Misérables*, 112.

CHAPTER 2

Good News When It's Bad

Abraham

"New life starts in the dark. Whether it is a seed in the ground, a baby in the womb, or Jesus in the tomb, it starts in the dark."[1]
—Barbara Brown Taylor

J.K. Rowling, author of the *Harry Potter* series, gave the spring 2008 commencement speech at Harvard. Her parents, having been poor and lacking a college education, wanted her to obtain a degree they believed would pay the bills and secure a retirement. She did not take their advice, studying Classics instead. What she feared more than poverty was failure. A few years after her graduation, she failed on an epic scale. Her short-lived marriage had collapsed, and she was left as an unemployed, poor, single parent. She described this period like being in a dark tunnel, and that "any light at the end of it was a hope rather than a reality." But as she reflected on it all, she began to see the benefits of failure. "I stopped pretending to myself that I was anything other than what I was. . . . Had I really succeeded at anything else, I might never have found the determination to succeed in the one arena I believed I truly belonged. I was set free, because my greatest fear had been realized . . . and I had an old typewriter and a big idea. And so rock bottom became the solid foundation on which I rebuilt my life."[2]

Every one of us could tell a story or stories about when it was bad. I invite you to pause and think of one. Secondly, think of a time, perhaps related to that story, when you received or experienced good news. What effect did it have on you?

---

1. Taylor, *Learning to Walk in the Dark*, 129.

2. Rowling, "The Fringe Benefits of Failure, and the Importance of Imagination," lines 33–34, 57, 75–93.

The impact of good news when it's bad—my story

Around March 2008, after having completed seminary just the year before and having worked several years in full-time vocational ministry, I decided it was time to leave and do something else. Although some issues and themes I address in this book flow out of other painful situations that contributed to that tough decision, I am not going to share those specific stories here. I had no idea what I was going to do next. Even so, I had confidence this was best for my family long-term. Admittedly, I didn't understand the significance that our country was falling into the worst recession since the Great Depression. It became a dreadful season of uncertainty and unrelenting stress. I would not wish the hardships that go along with unemployment and a job search on anyone, especially during a recession. After months of networking, searching, and working transition jobs, I began working in financial services in a commission-based role. That job yielded very little income over the next few years. Therefore, on top of that, I worked a second job making an hourly wage teaching several days a month, which required a lot of travel.

Now, don't get me wrong. I was grateful to be working. I met and worked with some good people along the way. Though we were reluctantly borrowing money to make ends meet, we had a home, food on the table, and good health. Our children were blessed with friendships and a good school system. Close to a billion people around the world who live in extreme poverty and millions more cannot say that. Good Samaritans extended help at critical moments of need and friends were present to encourage us. But the constant financial stress, isolation, and failure to succeed took a tremendous toll on me. I felt ashamed. I felt like a loser. It was bad. On many days and nights, I fought internal battles against this relentless, abusive shame-slinging voice in my head. I interacted regularly with people in a community and at a church who had nice homes and successful careers. Though happy for them, I suffered many humiliations in silence. For instance, at one point I was part of a running group training for a marathon. I could not pay the travel costs involved. One morning during an extended run, the guys asked if I was going. It was the first time I admitted I could not pull it off financially. But I stopped short of telling them that on that particular day, I didn't even have enough money to put gas in my car.

After more than eight years of grinding through this prolonged winter season, I received some good news: an encouraging job offer. It meant moving, but that didn't matter. A salary with benefits and a promising career path gave reason for much celebration! The good news did not eliminate the challenges or drive out all the stress that had preceded it. But after years of scraping to get by, huge burdens lifted, renewed hope stirred within my soul, and I began to feel human again. I felt liberated and glad for the first time in a very long time. That is what good news does.

From good to bad

The genealogy in Matthew 1 starts with Abraham. For a long time, he went by the name Abram. We encounter him at the end of Genesis 11 and at the beginning of chapter 12 when God called him. Before we begin, let's recap what happened before that encounter.

Long before Abraham, God created everything. In Genesis 1, God uses this word *good* to describe Creation: "And God said, 'Let there be light,' and there was light. God saw that the light was good'" (vv. 3–4). What do we consider good? Perhaps the birth of a child, aspects of nature, a particular album, achievement, or event? The Hebrew word for *good* is used six times in this chapter, with its last use underscored in verse 31: "God saw all that he had made, and it was *very good*" (emphasis added). C.F. Keil explains that "God's seeing is not a mere expression of the delight of the eye or of pleasure in His work, but is of the deepest significance to every created thing, being the seal of the perfection which God has impressed upon it."[3] Every single created thing—everything!—carries the seal of God's perfection. Keil went on to say, "By the application of the term 'good' to everything that God made, and the repetition of the word with the emphasis 'very' at the close of the whole creation, the existence of anything evil in the creation of God is absolutely denied."[4] "Evil," therefore, "cannot be blamed on the good creation. . . . Evil is not inherent in the human condition: there once was a completely good creation and there will be again. . . . Nothing in the world ought to be despaired of."[5] So, the first two chapters of Genesis speak of God's good Creation and place the man and the woman in positions of honor as his image bearers.

But then we read chapter 3. Faced with a decision between right and wrong, Adam and Eve chose what was wrong. In chapter 4, their son Cain follows suit by murdering his brother, Abel. Throughout subsequent generations, rebellious and destructive patterns and consequences proliferated into the violence and evil summarized in Genesis 6:5: "The Lord saw how great the wickedness of the human race had become on the earth, and

3. Keil and Delitzsch, *Commentary on the Old Testament* 1:31.
4. Keil and Delitzsch, *Commentary on the Old Testament,* 1:42.
5. Wolters, *Creation Regained,* 51.

that every inclination of the thoughts of the human heart was only evil all the time."

A quick inventory of recent historical events could validate such an assessment of humanity. Philip Hallie, the late professor emeritus of philosophy and the humanities at Wesleyan University in Middletown, Connecticut, and a veteran of World War II, focused his research on Nazi cruelty, particularly on the doctors who conducted experiments on Jewish children in the death camps. In his book, *The Call,* Os Guinness recorded Hallie's thoughts: "'Across all these studies, the pattern of the strong crushing the weak kept repeating itself and repeating itself, so that when I was not bitterly angry, I was bored at the repetitions of the patterns of persecution. My study of evil incarnate had become a prison whose bars were my bitterness toward the violent, and whose walls were my horrified indifference to slow murder. Between the bars and the walls I revolved like a madman. [O]ver the years I had dug myself into Hell."[6]

Genesis 6:5 depicts such a living hell. Even after the story of Noah and the flood, humanity's rebellion proliferated again, reaching its climactic peak in Babel. "Then they said, 'Come, let us build ourselves a city, with a tower that reaches to the heavens, so that we may make a name for ourselves; otherwise we will be scattered over the face of the whole earth" (Gen 11:4). The apex of humanity's rebellion was demonstrated through their arrogant efforts to bring glory to themselves instead of acting as God's image bearers in the world. Noted scholar, author, theologian, and Anglican bishop, N.T. Wright, said, "The story of the Tower of Babel is an account of a world given to injustice, spurious types of spirituality, . . . failed relationships, and the creation of buildings whose urban ugliness speaks of human pride rather than the nurturing of beauty."[7] Ironically, their relentless drive for selfish gain and self-glory through self-effort resulted in self-destruction. "At the end of that story, we find the effects of sin have reached a 'global scale,' with humanity scattered in division and confusion across the face of the earth."[8]

The turning point

So, what was God to do about it? Destroy the earth by some other means than a flood? Genesis 12 is, as N.T. Wright states, "the great turning point."[9] It marks a substantially momentous change indeed for the world. For into

6. Guiness, *The Call,* 91.

7. Wright, *Simply Christian,* 73.

8. Wright, *Knowing Jesus Through the Old Testament,* 9.

9. Wright, *Simply Christian,* 73.

this shattered state of affairs of human rebellion, failure, injustice and con-fusion, God embarks on a rescue mission. He begins his mission of mercy by delivering a message of good news for the entire world to a man named Abraham. Now it wasn't like Abraham was anyone special or deserving. In fact, his "father, Terah, and his ancestors worshiped a whole pantheon of gods, of which the sun was probably the chief god."[10]

With that background in mind, here is what God said to Abraham in Genesis 12:1–3: "The Lord had said to Abram, "Go from your country, your people and your father's household to the land I will show you. I will make you into a great nation, and I will bless you; I will make your name great, and you will be a blessing. I will bless those who bless you, and whoever curses you I will curse; and all peoples on earth will be blessed through you." Imagine hearing such words. What emotions might they stir? What basic logistical hurdles would need to happen? God's initial communication delivered some extraordinarily difficult news that Abraham had to stomach. For God had told him that he would have to leave everything he treasured. This included renouncing and severing all ties with family and thus giving up any ownership rights to property and a future inheritance. Everything Abraham associated with home—family, friends, traditions, work, and familiar places—he would have to leave it all completely behind, never to return to it again. No more dinners and laughter around the evening fire. No more talks with his mother, father, and friends. *Let that sink in.* Consider all that you treasure as it is now—your home, family, favorite places, traditions, friends, place of work, and all else that is familiar and comfortable. Imagine that this has been all you have ever known for seventy-five years. While the biblical account gives no information about Abraham's life prior to God's call, it does tell us that Abraham was seventy-five years old when this hap-pened. On top of this, he had no idea where God was leading. This was the end of Abraham's life as he had always known it.

Yet an ending can also be a beginning, can it not? Growth, and moving on to something new always require ending something and leaving it be-hind. As Barbara Brown Taylor wrote, "New life starts in the dark. Whether it is a seed in the ground, a baby in the womb, or Jesus in the tomb, it starts in the dark."[11] Remember what J.K. Rowling said? Rock bottom became the solid foundation on which she rebuilt her life.

---

10. Williams, *Far As The Curse Is Found*, 106.
11. Taylor, *Learning to Walk in the Dark*, 129.

Good news from a good God

In the Scriptures, people referred to God using different names, which were important in ancient times. The Hebrew word, *Elohim,* is the general name for God found in Genesis 1, "'And the Bible says that 'God' brings the whole creation into existence out of nothing."[12] Another Hebrew name for God is *Yahweh* shown as LORD in small capital letters, such as in Genesis 12:1: "The LORD said to Abram." We see this name used again in Exodus 3 and Exodus 6:1–12 when God calls Moses to lead the people of Israel out of slavery in Egypt. "The name Yahweh is the title God chooses to identify himself as the divine Redeemer, the God who rescues his people from slavery."[13] Yahweh expresses the kind of intimacy a parent shares with his or her child. God is not approaching Abraham as an angry tyrannical master would an unruly, rebellious slave. Rather, God approaches Abraham, as he did Moses, as divine Redeemer who rescues people out of slavery. "The Israelites first come to know God (through Moses) as their Redeemer; only afterward do they learn of his role as the Creator."[14]

This personal redeeming God initiated promises of blessing to not only Abraham, but also through him to *all* peoples on earth. There is, as commentator C.F. Keil explained, "an ascending climax" [15] regarding these promises. God's redemptive purpose "is going to be as wide as all creation."[16] God would purpose to make Abraham and his descendants "the means of God putting things to rights, the spearhead of God's rescue operation" for a world which was badly broken.[17]

God planted his redemptive seed in Abraham's story by promising to build his family into an enduring nation. Through this seed of redemption, all peoples on earth would be blessed. When people hear the phrase, "good news" as it pertains to the Bible, they usually think of only the New Testament. The Apostle Paul, however, connects God's promise to Abraham with its fulfillment in Jesus Christ in Galatians 3:8: "Scripture . . . announced the gospel in advance to Abraham." Galatians 3:16 says, "The promises were spoken to Abraham and to his seed." Scripture does not say, "and to seeds," meaning many people, but "to your seed," meaning one person, who is Christ." Then Paul connects the promise to us! "If you

---

12. Bartholomew and Goheen, *The Drama of Scripture,* 26.

13. Bartholomew and Goheen, *The Drama of Scripture,* 26.

14. Bartholomew and Goheen, *The Drama of Scripture,* 26.

15. Keil and Delitzsch, *Commentary on the Old Testament,* 1:123.

16. Williams, *Far As The Curse Is Found,* 103.

17. Wright, *Simply Christian,* 74.

belong to Christ, then you are Abraham's seed, and heirs according to the promise." (Gal 3:29). N.T. Wright beautifully summarizes the big picture: "Through Abraham and his family, God will bless the whole world. Shimmering like a mirage in the deserts through which Abraham wandered was the vision of a new world, a rescued world, a world blessed by the Creator once more, a world of justice, where God and his people would live in harmony, where human relationships would flourish, where beauty would triumph over ugliness."[18] God would not again destroy the world as he did during the time of Noah; he would redeem it.

The word *gospel* derives from the Greek noun, *angelos,* meaning *messenger,* or the verb *angello,* meaning to announce. The *euangelos* was one who brought "a message of victory or other political or personal *news that causes joy.*"[19] Similarly the Greek verb, *euangelizomai* means "to speak as a messenger of gladness, to proclaim good news."[20] So good was such news that "the immediate reaction on receiving the news was the offering of sacrifice to the gods as a token of gratitude."[21]

Outside the Bible, an example of such celebratory news pertained to the birthday of Caesar Augustus on September 23 in 9 BC. A decree went out saying:

> "It is a day which we may justly count as equivalent to the beginning of everything . . . inasmuch as it has restored the shape of everything that was failing and turning into misfortune, and has given a new look to the Universe at a time when it would gladly have welcomed destruction if Caesar had not been born to be the common blessing of all men . . . Whereas the Providence which has ordered the whole of our life, showing concern and zeal, has ordained the most perfect consummation for human life by giving to it Augustus . . . by sending in him, as it were, a savior for us and those who come after us, to make war to cease, to create order everywhere."[22]

Rome, as the French proverb stated in the late 1100s, was not built in a day. This powerful empire had evolved through hundreds of years of complex political, military, constitutional, social, and cultural conflicts. People suffered through generations of wars and massive bloodshed. After the death of Julius Caesar, his grandnephew, Augustus, or Octavian as he was named,

---

18. Wright, *Simply Christian,* 74.

19. Brown, *New International Dictionary of New Testament Theology,* 2:107.

20. Brown, *New International Dictionary of New Testament Theology,* 2:107.

21. Bromily, *The International Standard Bible Encyclopedia,* 2:29.

22. Brown, *New International Dictionary of New Testament Theology,* 2:108.

was engaged in a prolonged civil strife against Mark Antony. In the Battle of Actium, which was part of the final war of the Roman Republic, Augustus's victory enabled him to consolidate his power over Rome and its dominions. Supreme power, he believed, was the only possible solution for survival. Augustus gathered the reins of government and ruled as an absolute monarch, exercising complete control over the legislature, administration, and armies.[23] So we can understand why then, after such an extended period of exhausting conflict and widespread destruction, this decree effused exuberant joy over an end to war, and a hope that a new day of peace had dawned. Under Caesar Augustus's leadership, the people hoped again now for everything to be reshaped and restored.

The New Testament term for *gospel* or *good news* has roots in the Old Testament. Isaiah 52:7 says: "How lovely on the mountains are the feet of him who brings good news, who announces peace and brings good news of happiness, who announces salvation, and says to Zion, 'Your God reigns!'" God is enthroned as king, and his reign extends over the entire world. The prophet Isaiah believed this proclamation was reason for boundless joy as salvation, redemption, and peace had become reality with God's arrival on the scene.[24]

Paul says the gospel had been preached to Abraham back in Genesis 12. *Euangelion* was central in Paul's beliefs—that "God has acted for the salvation (redemption) of the world in the incarnation, death and resurrection of Jesus."[25] As we see in Matthew 1, Jesus came through the lineage of Abraham. This good news was not just the content of a message, but the execution of that message. It was not just words; real events occurred. God's son actually took on human flesh and lived on this earth at a certain time. Many followed Jesus as he taught, ministered, and performed miracles. Jesus was crucified, then buried in a tomb. But he also bodily arose from the dead! Jesus inaugurated a new peaceable kingdom shaped not by the power of violence and force as was the case with the Roman Empire, but by the power of love. Jesus ushered in a kingdom antithetical to all the culturally prevalent values of the Roman Empire. God's rescue operation which began with good news to Abraham back in Genesis 12 found its fulfillment in Jesus.

Jesus was not simply or only providing a new moral teaching or example to follow. His teachings and example are not what we as human beings need *most*, though they certainly have inspired millions around the world throughout history. For sure, he invites us to follow him. The good

23. Bromily, *The International Standard Bible Encyclopedia*, 4:208.

24. (See also Isa 41:27, 61:1; Ps 40:9–10, 68:11, 96:2).

25. Brown, *New International Dictionary of New Testament Theology*, 2:111.

news that I am referring to is not a message of improvement. As C.S. Lewis said, "We are not merely imperfect creatures who must be improved: we are . . . rebels who must lay down our arms."[26] N.T. Wright says the Good News addresses the fact that:

> "We are lost and need someone to come and find us, stuck in the quicksand waiting to be rescued, dying and in need of new life. . . . With Jesus, God's rescue operation has been put into effect once and for all. A great door has swung open in the cosmos which can never again be shut. It's the door to the prison where we've been kept chained up. We are offered freedom: freedom to experience God's rescue for ourselves, to go through the open door and explore the new world to which we now have access."[27]

Without suffering, failing, or falling in some way, we tend to "stay on the path we are already on, even if it is going nowhere."[28] Experiencing a fall tends to humble us, opening our hardened hearts to receiving the Good News with great joy that we might otherwise miss or dismiss. Henri Nouwen liked to recall "an evening meditation on Dutch television during which the speaker poured water on hard, dried-out soil, saying, 'Look, the soil cannot receive the water and no seed can grow.' Then, after crumbling the soil with his hands and pouring water on it again, he said, 'It is only the broken soil that can receive the water and make the seed grow and bear fruit.'"[29] So, as we live our lives and experience the inevitable breaking that occurs along the journey, we can take comfort and remember that "God whispers to us in our pleasures, speaks in our conscience, but shouts in our pain: it is his mega-phone to rouse a deaf world."[30]

Hope at the end of our rope

I remember a while back reading a post by author and speaker Anne Lamott. She was celebrating an anniversary of sobriety. Many years had passed since she had last woken up sick, hungover, and filled with shame. In addition to her alcohol addiction, she also was broke, suffering from an eating disorder, and could not imagine any way out of all the sickness, lies, and secrets. But she was involved with some sort of recovery group that she said never gave

---

26. Lewis, *The Problem of Pain*, 88.
27. Wright, *Simply Christian*, 91–92.
28. Rohr, *Falling Upward*, xix.
29. Nouwen, *Mornings with Henri J.M. Nouwen*, 53.
30. Lewis, *The Problem of Pain*, 91.

up on anyone. The reason she gave for such hope within the group is what has stayed with me the most: Grace always bats last! We may not struggle with addiction or eating disorders or financial difficulties, but we all drink something, are all disordered, and are all spiritually broke.

When life is bad, what gives you hope? Grace is often the one word used to convey the message of God's good news. Ephesians 2:8 says, "For it is by grace you have been saved, through faith—and this is not from yourselves, it is the gift of God." Albert Wolters points out, "Virtually all of the basic words describing salvation in the Bible imply a return to an originally good state or situation."[31] Consider some of the words throughout this book as describing different aspects or effects of this grace or good news. "To redeem is to buy back, in effect to liberate or return to a lost freedom. To renew is to make new again. Reconciliation is a restoration of a broken relationship and a return to a mended one. Regeneration is a return to life after being dead. Even the word salvation carries the idea of a return to health after a time of sickness."[32] We will continue exploring the depths of this grace throughout the book.

I wrote bits and pieces of this book over those prolonged years of hardship. Do you know why? Because I was constantly in need of good news. God's grace is always available. Yet most of us find it located at the end of our rope. The Good News will make sense only to those who have run out of options. Grace is the primary reason our exhausted souls in the midst of life being bad can be glad; our despairing hearts in the midst of failure can be filled with unspeakable hope; our troubled minds can experience peace; our weakening faith can be strengthened again; and passion to live and love restored. Seeds of redemption are as buried treasure in the ground of our struggles because of the seed of good news planted by God in the soil of Abraham's story. As you consider the bad times in your own life, *rejoice*. The Savior has come. The seed of good news is planted in your story too. Grace bats last.

---

31. Wolters, *Creation Regained*, 57.
32. Williams, *Far As The Curse Is Found*, 287.

CHAPTER 3

Faith When Facing Unwanted
or Uncertain Outcomes

Isaac

"If you tell me Christian commitment is a kind of thing that has happened to you once and for all like some kind of spiritual plastic surgery, I say you're either pulling the wool over your own eyes or trying to pull it over mine. Every morning you should wake up in your bed and ask yourself: 'Can I believe it all again today?' No, better still, don't ask it till after you've read The New York Times, *till after you've studied that daily record of the world's brokenness and corruption, which should always stand side by side with your Bible. Then ask yourself if you can believe in the Gospel of Jesus Christ again for that particular day. If your answer's always Yes, then you probably don't know what believing means. At least five times out of ten the answer should be No because the No is as important as the Yes, maybe more so. The No is what proves you're human in case you should ever doubt it. And then if some morning the answer happens to be really Yes, it should be a Yes that's choked with confession and tears and . . . great laughter."*[1]—Frederick Buechner

Facing unwanted or uncertain outcomes throughout life is simply a part of being human. Consider for a moment how much anxiety over matters we cannot control consumes our mental, emotional, and physical energy. I was not so self-aware about this until I started taking yoga. Guiding us through various exercises, our instructor would tell us to focus on our breathing and release all the tension. And just when we thought we had done so, she would tell us to focus on letting all the tension release in specific areas like the neck, shoulders, arms, stomach, fingers and toes. The

---

1. Buechner, "What Believing Means," lines 2–12.

body does not lie, and I never realized before how much tension I held in my body. (Go ahead and try it yourself).

Facing our own unwanted and uncertain outcomes

My ex-wife, Jorja, and I have three living children and two who died in miscarriages. Caroline is our oldest. Between her and our second-born child, Drew, Jorja had a miscarriage and another between Drew and our third-born child, Mari-Helen. News of each pregnancy caused celebration in our home and among family and friends. But after the first miscarriage, which devastated us, we celebrated each pregnancy thereafter with a lot of caution and underlying anxiety. The second miscarriage went like this: A few weeks into the pregnancy, Jorja had gone in for a routine check-up. When the doctor was unable to identify a heartbeat, we became terrified. Then a few days later, the doctor did another ultrasound. This time he found a beating heart. We were ecstatic yet still guarded and distressed. A couple of days after that, he checked again. This time, there was indeed no heartbeat. The experience kept us on an emotional roller coaster. One minute, all the signs of life, and the next, the outcome any expectant parents dreads most—the death of their child. In chapter eight, I will reflect on the story of Ruth and the theme of grief.

Mari-Helen came into the world on February 1, 2000. During that first year, Jorja felt something was not right with Mari-Helen's development. At the one-year well visit the pediatrician affirmed Jorja's intuition about our daughter—Mari-Helen was very delayed in all her developmental milestones, but the main concern was her communication. She did not babble or coo. She could laugh, but she mustered no meaningful sounds. Initially, the pediatrician thought the issue could be hearing-related but soon ruled it out with a test and referred us to a pediatric neurologist. Waiting for a follow-up appointment after receiving news like this was a form of suffering. An uncertain or unwanted outcome awaited us—and our beloved child—and we could not predict it, stop it, fix it, or control it.

When we don't have facts, isn't it easy to allow our minds to wander all over the place? Within a few minutes into *that* appointment, the neurologist looked at us and said matter-of-factly, "I am unsure if anyone has used the term 'mentally retarded,' but you need to get used to it because that is what we are dealing with here and it is highly likely we will not know the cause." *Several weeks of waiting for that appointment had now turned into probable years of uncertainty.* Questions filled our minds. *What could be wrong? How? Why? What would this mean for her future? To what degree would she be able to function in life?*

Admittedly, this was difficult for me to accept. I lived in a degree of denial: *Maybe the doctor is wrong, or maybe she will improve,* I would say to myself. Although Mari-Helen showed clear signs of developmental delays, the long-term implications were hard to predict with no definitive diagnosis. Problems can fester into larger ones later if we don't accept the truth and take necessary steps to address that reality. Thankfully, Jorja was on top of it. Going forward, a part of our new normal would include genetics testing; doctor visits; physical, speech, and occupational therapy; early childhood intervention; evaluations for school services; applications for respite care; and so on. It would not be until years later that a test would reveal the dysfunctional gene behind her condition—ZNF238.

Then in March 2003, something was going on with Drew, who was five at the time. One day his kindergarten teacher called Jorja to tell her that she had to keep excusing Drew from class so that he could go to the bathroom, and she was concerned. We took Drew to the same pediatrician, and, almost immediately, he knew the problem. Drew had type-one diabetes. The reality of Drew's situation hit me much harder than when we received Mari-Helen's initial assessment. I suppose this was because of the immediacy of the felt impact. Perhaps part of my denial with Mari-Helen was also this false sense as a leader of a ministry organization that I needed to hold it all together. Also, whereas Mari-Helen had no capacity to understand her condition, Drew did. For the next week or so, we remained in children's hospital learning about finger pricks, insulin shots, and carb-monitoring. Can you imagine what Drew was going through as a five-year old? Finger pricks to check blood sugar had to happen before any food intake, at bedtime, or any time his blood sugar felt low or high. For quite some time, we also checked him during the night to make sure his blood sugar levels were good. One type of insulin shot had to be taken at bedtime. The other type of insulin shot had to be taken right after any carb intake or whenever his blood sugar was elevated. That meant a minimum of four to five shots a day. Again, the questions rolled through my mind. *How? Why? Would he have to keep pricking his finger and taking shots like that for the rest of his life? How would it affect his future?* I was anxious and scared for him. I was angry on behalf of him and Mari-Helen. They didn't do anything to deserve this. *Why couldn't they just have a normal life?* These were outcomes we never wanted—or anticipated—for any of our children.

A struggling faith

The struggles of life can weaken our faith, deflate our hope, and diminish our capacity to receive and give love. We can question how God could allow such things. At times, we may feel exhaustion and fall into despair or depression from relentless hardships. On a side note, it is not in the scope of this book to address depression or those who have struggled with suicidal thoughts properly. I have heard sufferers of such sickness describe the condition as having to relive the worst day of their lives over and over. If you or a loved one is experiencing depression or suicidal ideation, please reach out to a professional today.[2] Many of the psalms provide words that express our feelings of doubt and despair. Consider David's words in Psalm 31:9-10 (MSG):"Be kind to me, God—I'm in deep, deep trouble again. I've cried my eyes out; I feel hollow inside. My life leaks away, groan by groan; my years fade out in sighs. My troubles have worn me out, turned my bones to powder." The Bible is filled with stories of people who wrestled with doubt.

In the United States, many people have bought into a false association between the Christian life and the American dream of prosperity. Stories throughout Scripture, however, tell both the beautiful and broken realities that are part of the human journey. Jesus, of course, said, "I am come that they might have life, and that they might have it more abundantly" (John 10:10b). Yet suffering is found throughout Scripture as normal. Jesus suffered temptation, rejection, persecution, betrayal, abandonment, and ultimately crucifixion. Hebrews 11:36-39 references believers who faced persecution and mistreatment of all sorts.

Before Abraham's first son was born, he struggled with doubt and disappointment. God had promised to make of him a great nation, yet where was the child through whom the promises would be fulfilled. Even with the Lord's reassurance (Gen 15), Abraham struggled to believe. Many long years had passed, and still he and Sarah cradled no child. Abraham was seventy-five years old when he received God's initial promise. Abraham and Sarah must have experienced deep disappointment facing an uncertain outcome since they had to wait *twenty-five years* for Isaac's birth. Sue Monk Kidd observed, "We've forgotten about the slow, sometimes tortuous, unraveling of God's grace that takes place in the 'middle places.'[3] We live in an "Insta-" culture where faster is always better. "Growth germinates," however, "not in tent dwelling but in upheaval. Yet the seduction is always security

---

2. Get help at https://www.mentalhealth.gov/get-help/immediate-help

3. Kidd, *When the Heart Waits*, 26.

rather than venturing, instant knowing rather than deliberate waiting."[4]
Kidd warned that "we're becoming a nation of quickaholics . . . avoiding
what is deep, difficult and therefore growth producing."[5]

Sarah and Abraham could not bear to wait, so they took matters into
their own hands. In Genesis 16, Sarah devised a plan to produce the promised child on her own; she told Abraham to wed her Egyptian slave, Hagar—
and he acted on the suggestion. Hagar conceived Ishmael. Just like Abraham
and Sarah, we too desire to control outcomes when we are disappointed and
struggling through a season of waiting. We tend, as Kidd says, "to see that
waiting time as a wasteland. . . . We think that the 'real thing' is concentrated
in the next moment, the next month, the next year. We can go on and on,
waiting for the next 'happening' of life, hurrying toward it, trying to make
it happen."[6] Allow me to point out, however, that God moves in mysterious ways. Numerous biblical stories demonstrate this. Thus, God presents
different faith challenges to different people in different scenarios. Just wait
until we get to Tamar's story. She took matters into her own hands and also
experienced an unexpected outcome.

When Abraham was ninety-nine years old, God issued his covenant
promise again. But what was their response? "Abraham fell facedown, he
laughed and said to himself, 'Will a son be born to a man a hundred years old?
Will Sarah bear a child at the age of ninety?'" (Gen 17:17). Wouldn't we also
consider such a thought inconceivable? Sarah scoffed at the prophesy (Gen
18:12). Henri Nouwen warned of our propensity to fall into cynicism or fatalism, which can hold us hostage "to a discouragement that insists that nothing
more can be done."[7] It's important to distinguish between fatalism, cynicism,
and faith during a period of difficult waiting and disappointment.

Fatalism believes nothing can be done to change a bad situation. One
must therefore be practical and accept reality. A fatalistic person views a
problem and asks a question like, "why even bother?" Being victimized by
fate "can easily lead to resentment, bitterness, hopelessness, and despair."[8]
Rather than focusing on God, solutions, or trying something different, we
can become paralyzed by our problems. "We may settle for finding satisfaction in dysfunctional, painful places, growing attached to our complaints,
symptoms, addictions," Nouwen wrote.[9] When this happens, we become

---

4. Kidd, *When the Heart Waits*, 25.

5. Kidd, *When the Heart Waits*, 30.

6. Kidd, *When the Heart Waits*, 36–37.

7. Nouwen, *Turn My Mourning into Dancing*, 50.

8. Nouwen, *Turn My Mourning into Dancing*, 49.

9. Nouwen, *Turn My Mourning into Dancing*, 50.

our own worst enemy. "Fatalism anesthetizes desire . . . their stance results in distance from others, lack of empathy, and a trivialization of their part in shaping the future."[10]

Faith, Nouwen suggests, opposes fatalism. "Rather than displaying passive resignation, faith leads us to hopeful willingness. . . . Trust in God allows us to live with active expectation, not cynicism . . . Faith is the deep confidence that God is good and that God's goodness somehow triumphs."[11] Such faith refers not to rose-colored optimism. The person you love may not feel the same. A cure for diabetes may not occur. The job opportunity or promotion may not transpire. Reconciliation with that estranged family member or old friend may not ever unfold. The cancer may worsen. The depression may always require medication. But faith rests not on the condition of future outcomes. It rests not on wishes, predictions, circumstances, people, or odds. Our faith and hope rest in God, and his goodness. Despite what is happening, faith trusts that somehow his goodness will triumph. As we observe in this story, and countless others, God does not prevent trials; he redeems them.

The faithfulness of God

In Genesis 21, we find out that God's faithfulness, indeed, did triumph with the birth of Isaac as promised. They had waited twenty-five years. Any newborn is worth celebrating, but especially one born to Abraham, who was then 100, and Sarah, who was ninety. Envision being in a hospital waiting room at the moment a loved one invites you in to see the baby. After nine months of waiting, the celebratory atmosphere would be filled with laughter and joyful tears. Now, imagine being present with Sarah and Abraham at the moment they grasped Isaac's small hand after waiting twenty-five years to meet him.

Isaac means, 'He laughs,' a purposeful connection with Abraham and Sarah's response to God's promise. "In this (the name of Isaac) God underscores that he is quite capable of fulfilling his promise, in spite of Sarah's barrenness, in spite of their tampering, and even in spite of their doubts,"[12] wrote Dr. Michael Williams. In response to this long awaited and sacred moment, Sarah burst forth again with laughter—though, this time, with a tender and transformed heart: "God has brought me laughter, and everyone who hears about this will laugh with me" (Gen 21:6). Isaac's birth

---

10. Allender, *The Healing Path*, 11.

11. Nouwen, *Turn My Mourning into Dancing*, 51.

12. Williams, *Far As The Curse Is Found*, 128.

gave reason for "laughing with joyous amazement" because God's grace had worked "against and above the forces of nature."[13] Sarah's heart leaping with jubilant laughter this time emerged not out of some cynical and fatalistic view, but rather because of God's goodness and faithfulness to his promise. Isaac's name itself would serve as an ongoing reminder to them of God's goodness, love, and faithfulness.

Germination and growth of faith

For Isaac, perhaps no event marked his life like the one recorded in Genesis 22. God had made it clear to Abraham that Isaac would be the one through whom his covenant promises would extend (Gen 21:12). Yet God tested Abraham's faith again when he said to him in Genesis 22:2, "Take your son, your only son, whom you love—Isaac—and go to the region of Moriah. Sacrifice him there as a burnt offering on a mountain I will show you." Note the emphasis on Abraham's love for his *one and only* son. Though this story is most often reflected upon from the perspective of Abraham, I think it also is worth considering from Isaac's viewpoint.

The text does not tell us if Isaac was aware of what was going on as Abraham gathered what he needed for the journey. Similarly, as we are going about our lives, we too are often unaware of what we are about to face. Fear of the unknown can keep us stagnant and comfortable, giving us a false sense of security. "God, life, destiny, suffering have to give us a push—usually a big one—or we will not go."[14] To build on this idea a little more, Allender wrote, "God's sacred path leads us away from safety, predictability, and comfort. Any attempt to fly over the dangerous terrain or make a detour to safer ground is doomed because it will not take us to God."[15]

At this point in Abraham's life, he appears at peace even though faced with an uncertain outcome. He cut the wood, and off they went. After the third day of travel, Abraham said to his servants, "Stay here with the donkey while I and the boy go over there. We will worship and then we will come back to you " (Gen 22:5). Did you catch the subtle confidence in Abraham's words? "*We* will come back to you." Abraham believed that despite what God was asking him to do that he would return to that same spot *with* Isaac. Hebrews 11:17–19 says:

---

13. Keil and Delitzsch, *Commentary on the Old Testament*, 1:155.

14. Rohr, *Falling Upward*, xvii.

15. Allender, *The Healing Path*, 19.

"By faith Abraham, when God tested him, offered Isaac as a sacrifice. He who had embraced the promises was about to sacrifice his one and only son, even though God had said to him, 'It is through Isaac that your offspring will be reckoned.' Abraham reasoned that God could even raise the dead, and so in a manner of speaking he did receive Isaac back from death."

Off they went, father and son, to worship God together. As they were walking, it occurred to Isaac that something was missing. According to verse 7, he asked his father where the lamb was for the burnt offering. Perhaps such a question reminded Abraham of the times he asked in his own mind, "where is the child God promised me?" Abraham did not waver in unbelief this time as he assured his son God would provide the lamb. Though the biggest test of his life, Abraham remained confident in the Lord's goodness.

When they reached their destination and Abraham built the altar, what must have gone through Isaac's mind? The passage does not indicate if they spoke even a word to each other. Some commentators suggest that we can interpret that Isaac permitted "himself to be bound and laid upon the altar without resistance."[16] This interpretation is hard to imagine. What normal person would willingly go along with this? The text does not indicate Isaac put up a fight. Perhaps Isaac implicitly trusted his father's words that God would provide the lamb even as he was being laid on the altar. Surely Isaac knew about those twenty-five years his parents had waited for his birth. Surely, he knew about the time God said to his father, "Yes, but your wife Sarah will bear you a son, and you will call him Isaac. I will establish my covenant with him as an everlasting covenant for his descendants after him" (Gen 17:19). Nonetheless, Isaac must have been overcome with anxiety, doubt, and fear in the moment. Was God backing out on his promise? Were God and his own father abandoning him? All he could see was a sacrifice about to occur, and he was the offering. *But why?*

So much happens in life that we will not ever understand. During December 1975, and for a few days in the following March, John Kavanaugh was in Calcutta doing the "long experiment of humble ministry"[17] that Jesuits undertake during their last year of formation. During that time, he had several conversations with Mother Teresa. Shortly before he left Calcutta, he asked her to pray for him.

For what? she said.

For clarity, he pled, but she immediately refused. Kavanaugh complained, begging for her clarity and certitude.

16. Keil and Delitzsch, *Commentary on the Old Testament*, 1:161.
17. Kavanaugh, "Godforsakeness: 'Finding one's heart's desire,'" line 37.

I've never had clarity and certitude, she said. *I only have trust. I'll pray that you trust.*[18] Clarity was the last thing to which he was clinging. "By craving clarity," wrote Brennan Manning, "we attempt to eliminate the risk of trusting God. Fear of the unknown path stretching ahead of us destroys childlike trust in the Father's active goodness and unrestricted love."[19]

At the climactic moment when Abraham with a raised arm was about to thrust the knife into his own son, the angel of the Lord called out: "Abraham, Abraham! . . . Do not lay a hand on the boy. Do not do anything to him. Now I know that you fear God, because you have not withheld from me your son, your only son" (Gen 22:12). Immediately Abraham looked up and saw a ram caught in a thicket to be used as the burnt offering instead of his son. "So Abraham called that place, 'The Lord will provide" (Gen 22:14). Note where the story leads the reader to focus:

> "Ultimately the episode is more revealing about God than it is about Abraham. The climax of the whole episode is the angel stopping Abraham from carrying out the sacrifice of his son, and providing a substitute, which is why 'Abraham called the name of that place The Lord will provide' (v. 14). The name draws attention to God, not Abraham. The focus of the passage is not, 'Abraham-has-performed,' but rather 'God-will-provide.'"[20]

The Lord closed out the scene between Abraham and Isaac with a reassurance of his covenant promises: "I will surely bless you and make your descendants as numerous as the stars in the sky and as the sand on the seashore. Your descendants will take possession of the cities of their enemies, and through your offspring all nations on earth will be blessed" (Gen 22:17–18). Why did God repeat his promises? Perhaps for the same reason we find these messages of God's love repeated for us throughout the Bible. We who are children of Abraham by faith, also forget God's promises. We easily are overcome and overwhelmed by our own difficult circumstances and seasons of waiting. We forget God loves us. Because we forget, we are vulnerable to becoming fatalistic and cynical. After all, we are human. So, we need to be reminded over and over of truth.

I originally read about that story involving Mother Teresa in Brennan Manning's book, *Ruthless Trust.* Reflecting on her words of wisdom, Manning said, "We often presume that trust will dispel the confusion, illuminate the darkness, vanquish the uncertainty, and redeem the times. But

---

18. Kavanaugh, "Godforsakeness: 'Finding one's heart's desire,'" lines 26–40, 45–48.

19. Manning, *Ruthless Trust,* 6.

20. Hamilton, *Handbook on the Pentateuch,* 109.

the crowd of witnesses in Hebrews 11 testifies that this is not the case. Our trust does not bring final clarity on this earth. It does not still the chaos or dull the pain or provide a crutch. When all else is unclear, the heart of trust says, as Jesus did on the cross, 'Into your hands I commit my spirit' (Lk. 23:46).'[21] Yoga can be a fantastic exercise in breathing and releasing the tension in our bodies. Exercising our faith often means releasing the anxieties we are experiencing about any uncertain or unwanted future into God's caring hands. It means breathing in the life-giving truth that God loves us. It's not a one-and-done practice, by the way. Abraham's faith was not all at once set in stone upon being given an initial promise by God. Isaac must have experienced tremendous anxiety in his journey.

Mari-Helen's condition and Drew's diabetes have been challenging for them and us, for sure. But Drew grew accustomed to the maintenance required to stabilize his blood sugars and developed independence early on in taking care of himself. He gets annoyed with it from time to time. Yet diabetes has not prevented him from doing anything he has wanted to do. At the time of this writing, he is twenty-three years old and a recent college graduate. We are so proud of who he is and the direction he is headed. Diabetes and his relationship with Mari-Helen have played a huge role in shaping his unfolding story and growth as a human being. I have mourned plenty of times Mari-Helen's inability to do certain things like sing in a choir, act in a play, go to the prom, play a sport, drive a car, or take a road-trip with friends. But I will tell you with utmost conviction that her life—like special-needs persons all over the world—has not been a burden, but rather an indescribable gift. Her beautiful life, on which I will elaborate in chapter nine, has brought unspeakable joy to my life and impacted me in more ways than you could imagine. Jorja, Caroline, and Drew would attest to the same thing. Caroline, for instance, chose a career path as a licensed professional counselor. At the time of this writing, she works with people who have eating disorders. After high school and during college, she invested two summers in Jinja, Uganda, working through a nonprofit organization committed to empowering vulnerable, abandoned women and children to live sustainably within their communities. Caroline is a fierce advocate for those who are vulnerable. I'm sure she would say her relationship with her younger sister, Mari-Helen, had the most significant impact in shaping her compassionate heart and future career.

As we go through life facing all sorts of unwanted and uncertain outcomes, what we need more than anything is the assurance of God's love . . . that he is with us, for us, on our side, and working all things together for

---

21. Manning, *Ruthless Trust*, 6.

good. This powerful rendering of excerpts from this rich passage in Romans 8:31–39 (MSG) can help us as we pray:

- *With God on our side like this, how can we lose?*

- *If God didn't hesitate to put everything on the line for us, embracing our condition and exposing himself to the worst by sending his own Son, is there anything else he wouldn't gladly and freely do for us?*

- *Do you think anyone is going to be able to drive a wedge between us and Christ's love for us? There is no way! Not trouble, not hard times, not hatred, not hunger, not homelessness, not bullying threats, not backstabbing, not even the worst sins listed in Scripture.*

- *None of this fazes us because Jesus loves us. I'm absolutely convinced that nothing—nothing living or dead, angelic or demonic, today or tomorrow, high or low, thinkable or unthinkable—absolutely nothing can get between us and God's love because of the way that Jesus our Master has embraced us.*

In those waiting seasons and days when we are struggling deeply, I pray we would remember this, and perhaps even recall that Isaac's name means, "He laughs!" I know it is hard, and this is much easier said than done. Buried seeds of redemption in the ground of our struggles take time to break through and grow. But it is precisely in these deep and difficult seasons of waiting that growth germinates in ways we cannot see or understand in the moment. Such growth roots out toxic fatalism and cynicism. Such growth emerges as a deeper confidence that God is good and somehow his goodness triumphs—even though future outcomes are uncertain or even unwanted. Such growth leads to hopeful willingness and active expectation. So, on those days we find ourselves believing with much conviction, that *Yes!* God does love us, may that *yes* "*be a Yes that's choked with confession and tears and . . . great laughter.*"[22]

---

22. Buechner, "What Believing Means," line 12.

Liberation from Hidden Bondage

Jacob

"When we want to be something other than the thing God wants us to be, we must be wanting what, in fact, will not make us happy."[1]—C.S. Lewis

*T*he *Inferno*, the first part of Dante's *Divine Comedy*, is an allegory that describes Dante's journey through hell, illustrated as nine circles of suffering guided by Virgil, a Roman poet.[2] Gustave Dore illustrated the fourth circle, greed, by drawing nine physically robust, but exhausted men straining to push money-laden bags up an incline but buckling under their weight. They had attained what their souls craved. Yet the fulfillment of their ambitions had yielded slavery instead of freedom; burdens instead of ease; and emptiness instead of fulfillment. In this fourth stage Virgil advises Dante not to speak to people obsessed with hoarding or squandering their possessions. They are too absorbed to listen.

What about us? What might be the driving motivation underneath our decisions and actions? What might we be so obsessed with that we are too absorbed to listen? Other people may see what we do, but they cannot see why. We probably can't either! Some of us are driven by our desire to obtain and maintain power and control over others. *People who are free do not need to control others.* Some of us may be driven by an underlying motivation to be liked or gain the acceptance and approval of others. Henri Nouwen said, "Many things we think we do for others are in fact the expressions of our drive to discover our identity in the praise of others."[3]

---

1. Lewis, *The Problem of Pain*, 46.
2. Alighieri, *Divine Comedy*.
3. Nouwen, *Turn My Mourning into Dancing*, 72.

People who are free do not need the approval of others. Some of us might be driven in our desire to be right or perfect.

God affirms the "self" as good. He tells us to love our neighbor *as we love ourselves.* Let us not, therefore, confuse *self* with *sin.* We are to love ourselves through basic care, education, and nurture of our bodies, souls, and minds. "The Bible is never opposed to human experience as such; to experience life includes touch and taste, work and play, love and beauty."[4] So what might indicate the difference between healthy self-love and self-centeredness? Whereas healthy self-love enhances neighbor love, it seems self-centered people typically are looking out only for their own interests and turn down opportunities or requests that require sacrifice or discomfort. They can't see how so many poor life choices are made based on what feels good in the moment as opposed to what would be better later.

Though we are to love ourselves, we are each vulnerable to becoming enslaved to self-centeredness, selfish ambition, and/or self-glory. Left unchecked, an underlying bondage can lead us down a path of unknowingly harming ourselves and others as well as depriving life "of all ultimate significance."[5] James 3:16 says, "For where you have envy and selfish ambition, there you find disorder and every evil practice." An executive, for example, resigned from a firm after several years of employment there because the culture had changed. What he characterized initially as a culture of integrity and humility had decayed into a culture of doing whatever was necessary to make the most money possible. Frederick Buechner said we are in danger of listening to the:

> [G]reat blaring, boring, banal voice of our mass culture, which threatens to deafen us all by blasting forth that the only thing that really matters about your work is how much it will get you in the way of salary and status. . . . [T]he world is full of people who seem to have listened to the wrong voice and are now engaged in a life's work in which they find no pleasure or purpose and who run the risk of suddenly realizing someday that they have spent the only years that they are ever going to get in this world doing something that could not matter less to themselves or to anyone else.[6]

With only one life to live, is it not worth taking time, then, to self-reflect and evaluate what we are doing and why we are doing it? Thomas Merton once observed, "He who attempts to act and do things for others or for the world

---

4. Macauley and Barrs, *Being Human,* 119.
5. Stott, *The Message of the Sermon on the Mount,*157.
6. Buechner, *Secrets in the Dark,* 38.

without deepening his own self-understanding, freedom, integrity, and capacity to love, will not have anything to give to others. He will communicate to them nothing but the contagion of his own obsessions, his aggressiveness, his ego-centered ambitions . . . his doctrinaire prejudices and ideas."[7]

Jacob's hidden bondage

Jacob lived and worked many restless years driven by his own selfish ambition. Read through his part of the story in the book of Genesis and you will discover a toxic family characterized by deceit, jealousy, hatred, bitterness, desire for revenge, murderous plots, and betrayal. Jacob's story holds a mirror to our own hidden motivations underlying so much of what we say and do. But his story also reminds us of the unconditional love of God which liberates and transforms us out of our desire to be the center of our own universe into the true, full, and beautiful humanity he intends.

Genesis 25:22 says Isaac's wife, Rebekah, was deeply disturbed regarding the struggle she felt within her womb between her two sons, Jacob, and Esau. Jacob received his name from having held Esau's heel as they emerged out of her womb. Figuratively, to hold another's heel was "to outwit, just as in wrestling an attempt may be made to throw the opponent by grasping the heel."[8] His name served as a sign of things to come.

Years after their birth, Esau, famished after laboring in the fields, pleaded with Jacob for some stew that his brother had cooked. Eager to capitalize on the moment, Jacob exploited Esau's hunger by convincing him to trade his birthright for food. Jacob craved the birthright because it meant receiving a double portion of their father's inheritance (Deut 21:17). Having the birthright meant being crowned as the family's chief ruler (Deut 27:29) and keeper of the blessing of promise (Deut 27:4, 27–29). The promise itself would grant him future possession of Canaan and covenant fellowship with God (Deut 28:4).[9] Jacob—an opportunist driven by his own selfish ambition—indeed outwitted his own brother to obtain this coveted birthright.

But he did not stop there. Jacob also conned his father with the help of his mother. When his father, Isaac, had grown old and blind, Jacob and Rebekah deceived him into granting the firstborn blessing to Jacob. Culturally, a father's final blessing to a firstborn son was the most powerful of all, and irrevocable. "Great importance was attached to the ceremony in which the father formally gave his "blessing" to his children. It carried the authority

---

7. Merton, *Contemplation in a World of Action*, 178–79.

8. Keil and Delitzsch, *Commentary on the Old Testament*, 1:172.

9. Keil and Delitzsch, *Commentary on the Old Testament*, 1:172.

of a will, and involved, especially in religious matters, a sort of prophecy or foretelling of their place in the future. The father's pronouncement of greatness for the future naturally would be coveted by young Jacob."[10] Jacob and his mother duped Isaac by preparing his favorite food, dressing Jacob in Esau's best garments, and applying the skins of young goats on Jacob's hands and neck so that he would feel hairy like Esau. Isaac naively fell for it all and bestowed the firstborn blessing upon Jacob.

Upon discovering the monumental betrayal, Esau boiled over with rage. He may have tossed some furniture, punched a hole in the wall, screamed, and gotten right up in Jacob's face. Consumed with vengeful anger, Esau vowed upon his father's death he would murder Jacob. Rebekah, fearful of Esau's desire for revenge, urged Jacob to flee to her brother, Laban's house, until Esau's fury subsided.

In the United States, our culture applauds and values upward mobility, achievements, status, and possessions. God has indeed richly blessed us with all good things to enjoy. "Scripture nowhere forbids private property. . . . Scripture praises the ant for storing in the summer the food it will need in the winter. . . . We are not to despise, but rather to enjoy, the good things which our Creator has given us richly to enjoy. So neither having possessions, nor making provision for the future, nor enjoying the gifts of a good Creator are included in the ban on earthly treasure storage"[11] (found in Matt 6:19). The trouble comes when our hearts have moved way beyond enjoyment to enslavement.

Because of the values we've inherited and celebrate, the enslavements can be well hidden. At the beginning of the 1800s, Alexis de Tocqueville, a French sociologist and political theorist, observed some traits of democratic cultures during his visit to America:

> "Most of the people in these (democratic) nations are extremely eager in the pursuit of immediate material pleasures and are always discontented with the position they occupy and always free to leave it. They think about nothing but ways of changing their lot and bettering it. For people in this frame of mind every new way of getting wealth more quickly, every machine which lessens work, every means of diminishing the costs of production, every invention which makes pleasures easier or greater, seems the most magnificent accomplishment of the human mind. . . . [O]ne usually finds that the love of money is either the chief or a secondary motive at the bottom of everything the Americans

---

10. Hester, *The Heart of Hebrew History*, 97.

11. Stott, *The Message of the Sermon on the Mount*, 154–55.

do. . . . [T]he prospect really does frighten me that (the Americans) may finally become so engrossed in a cowardly love of immediate pleasures that their interest in their own future and in that of their descendants may vanish, and that they will prefer tamely to follow the course of their own destiny rather than make a sudden energetic effort necessary to set things right."[12]

For Jacob, the ends justified the means. He got what he wanted. His manipulative behavior, however, caused a deep family divide and put his own life in danger. Blind enslavement to money, achievement, approval, power, or some other selfish ambition can result in unintended consequences such as loss of love, meaning, and a diminished "capacity for appreciating the beauty and magnificence of the world."[13]

Jacob escaped from a revenge-seeking brother to Haran, a 550-mile journey. No matter how far he traveled, however, he did not escape his own bondage. On his way, Jacob rested at a certain spot. During the night, Jacob dreamed of a ladder that reached heaven. Above it, the Lord graciously revealed himself to Jacob, reaffirming his covenant promises and assuring him of his blessing and continual presence: "I will give you and your descendants the land on which you are lying. Your descendants will be like the dust of the earth, and you will spread out to the west and to the east, to the north and to the south. All peoples on earth will be blessed through you and your offspring. I am with you and will watch over you wherever you go, and I will bring you back to this land. I will not leave you until I have done what I have promised you" (Gen 28:13–15). This is quite shocking when you consider all Jacob has done. God reinforces here that the covenant he made with Abraham, Isaac, and now Jacob, is based on *his* character and not ours.

Jacob's liberation

Being enslaved to a hidden bondage muffles the voice of God. Jacob, even after this memorable event, reverted to self-interest. He continued seeking ways to outwit others to control outcomes. He schemed to marry Rachel and build wealth while working for his uncle Laban over the next several years. Rather than suffering consequences for his deceitfulness, Jacob profited from it.

> "[T]he shrewd and ambitious man who is strong on guts and weak on conscience, who knows very well what he wants and

12. Tocqueville, *Democracy in America,* 462, 615, 645.
13. Gay, *Cash Values,* 74.

directs all his energies toward getting it, the Jacobs of this world, all in all do pretty well. Again, I do not mean the criminal who is willing to break the law to get what he wants or even to take somebody's life if that becomes necessary. I mean the man who stays within the law and would never seriously consider taking other people's lives, but who from time to time might simply manipulate them a little for his own purposes or maybe just remain indifferent to them.[14]

Eventually, however, Jacob's past came back to haunt him. He strove to control outcomes. He achieved success, married the woman of his dreams, and desired to return home. This time, however, circumstances emerged that rendered Jacob helpless. Esau, along with four hundred men, were on their way to confront Jacob. Recalling Esau's vow to murder him, Jacob fell into a state of fear and distress, threw together a survival strategy, and began to pray.[15] Calling upon God by his personal name, *Yahweh,* Jacob confessed his unworthiness and pleaded for deliverance. God would answer Jacob's prayer, but not without accomplishing a deeper work in Jacob's heart.

The writer of Genesis 32 documented a bizarre story. After Jacob began implementing his survival strategy which involved sending his herds, servants, possessions, and family members ahead of him, he remained alone in the dark. He would have heard the constant noise of water flowing over pebbles from the nearby stream all night. This soothing sound, however, would not have served him as a source of comfort like a modern-day sound machine. A night alone outside under any circumstances would frighten most of us. But Jacob also battled the terrifying prospect of death. This night might be his last. Yet a seed of redemption was buried in this dark night of Jacob's struggle. Recall this quote from an earlier chapter. "New life starts in the dark. Whether it is a seed in the ground, a baby in the womb, or Jesus in the tomb, it starts in the dark."[16] God was at work. During the night, a stranger appeared. We have no idea what he looked like or where he came from. All we know is Jacob wrestled with this stranger until daybreak. Is the meaning of Jacob's name as explained earlier not so ironic here? Unable to overpower Jacob, the stranger injured Jacob's hip, leaving him with a limp. As it turned out, the stranger was God himself. In a pivotal climax in the story, God wounded him, transforming his identity and name from Jacob to Israel. But it was a sacred wound!

---

14. Buechner, *Secrets in the Dark,* 5–6.

15. Genesis 32:7–9.

16. Taylor, *Learning to Walk in the Dark,* 129.

Dr. Ashley Null, a leading authority on the English Reformation, explained the difference between *unconditional affirmation* and *unconditional love*. Unconditional affirmation never challenges our right to be the center of our own universe. This is what our dogs provide. We may board our dogs while we travel for three weeks, but when we return, our dogs do not bite us or question why we left them for so long. They just wag their tails, jump all over us, bark with excitement, and lick our faces. Unconditional love, on the other hand, is about relationship. Unconditional love seeks to woo out of the beloved an equally selfless self-giving. Unconditional love challenges our right to be the center of our own universe.[17] Does Jesus in his unconditional love not challenge our right to be the center of our own universe, and woo us to be transformed in following him? Genuine unconditional love restores us to a liberated, full, true, and beautiful humanity, which is what Jesus embodied, taught, and demonstrated.

God had challenged Jacob's right to be the center of his own universe. James Houston asserted, "We may have to be similarly broken, to be wounded by the God of Jacob."[18] Being wounded tends to reveal hidden bondages we are clinging to. As a result of this wounding event, Jacob's ambitions appear to turn Godward, a posture reflected in his name changing to "Israel." He wept and reconciled with Esau, grasping his brother in an embrace. His twelve sons evolved into the tribes of Israel—and through Jacob's lineage the Messiah would bring blessing to all nations. In the Gospels, God would be known as the "God of Abraham, the God of Isaac, and the God of Jacob."

Liberation from our own bondage

Earlier in the book, I referred to the story of Jean Valjean and the bishop in Victor Hugo's *Les Misérables*. The bishop was described as one who exhibited an excess of love: "There are men who work for the extraction of gold; he worked for the extraction of pity. The misery of the universe was his mine. Grief everywhere was only an occasion for good always. Love one another; he declared that to be complete; he desired nothing more, and it was his whole doctrine."[19]

While eating dinner with the bishop, Valjean, confused by the kindness the bishop was showing him, kept trying to make sure the bishop knew who he was according to his yellow passport—a criminal. The bishop touched his hand and said, "'You need not tell me who you are. This is not

17. Null, "Thomas Cranmer's Gospel of Divine Allurement."

18. Houston, *Joyful Exiles*, 121.

19. Hugo, *Les Misérables*, 59, 64.

my house; it is the house of Christ. It does not ask any comer whether he has a name but whether he has an affliction. You are suffering; you are hungry and thirsty; be welcome. . . . Whatever is here is yours. What need have I to know your name? Besides, before you told me, I knew it.' Valjean opened his eyes in astonishment: 'Really? You knew my name?' 'Yes,' answered the Bishop, 'your name is my brother.'"[20]

That night, Valjean expected the worst—to be treated as a criminal. Instead, the bishop astonished him with extravagant love. That night all alone beside a stream, Jacob expected the worst—to be killed the following day. Instead, God astonished him by demonstrating steadfast love and faithfulness to his covenant promises despite Jacob's actions. The Bishop knew Valjean's name. God knew Jacob's name. Are we expecting the worst? Are we astonished at the extravagant love of God? Do we realize God knows our names? John 3:17 says, "This is how much God loved the world: He gave his Son, his one and only Son. And this is why: so that no one need be destroyed; by believing in him, anyone can have a whole and lasting life. God didn't go to all the trouble of sending his Son merely to point an accusing finger, telling the world how bad it was. He came to help, to put the world right again" (John 3:16–17, MSG).

Consider for a moment Jesus's motivation for entering the world? *Before* he ever accomplished anything, the Father expressed his delight in and approval of his son: "This is my Son, chosen and marked by my love, delight of my life" (Matt 3:17, MSG). Jesus did not have anything to prove to the Father. He did not have to perform to justify his existence while on earth and gain his Father's acceptance and applause. He *already* was the delight of his Father's life. In Jesus, we are the beloved of God. God already is delighted with us! Zephaniah 3:17 says: "The LORD your God is with you, the Mighty Warrior who saves. He will take great delight in you; in his love he will no longer rebuke you, but will rejoice over you with singing." So what voice are you listening to that has you convinced you must be, have, or do something to justify your existence? Again, it is so difficult to hear we are so loved in Christ because "we are too prone, too conditioned to listen for all the other voices that insist on success or results."[21]

Do we see ourselves as the beloved of God? Do we believe God delights in and rejoices over us? A counselor once said something like this to her client, *You have believed yourself to be unlovable and have set out to prove it. Furthermore, what goes deepest into the heart is what goes widest to the world.* What is deepest in our hearts? What is it that we feel we must be,

20. Hugo, *Les Misérables,* 83.

21. Nouwen, *Turn My Mourning into Dancing,* 78.

possess, attain, or achieve for our existence to be justified? How might that be affecting others in our lives?

I, like most people I know, care about my appearance. In the spring of 1997, I was playing basketball with some friends. During a break, one of them noticed my legs were practically hairless, and asked with a disturbed sound in his voice, "Dude, what happened to the hair on your legs?" I had not taken the hair loss seriously, so I didn't have an answer. The next week, I set an appointment with a dermatologist. I never will forget standing in a patient room when he walked in the door and looked me over. In a few seconds, he said, "You may want to sit down." He proceeded to tell me that I had alopecia, which is a hair loss disease. "It's possible your hair may grow back, or you could lose all the hair you have within a matter of weeks or months or a few years." Sure enough, over the next four or five years, I gradually lost more hair all over my body. Bald spots appeared and increased on the sides and back of my head. Even my eyelashes and eyebrows began to fall out. Every few months between 1997 and 2002, I went to the dermatologist for steroid injections into those bald spots. Eventually the dermatologist decided to try an irritant cream on the bald spots, but it burned the skin on my head so badly that I finally couldn't tolerate it anymore. I shaved my head completely. That season of life directly challenged my heart's attachment to my appearance.

In chapter 2 I reflected some on my failures in the business world from 2008 to 2016. Before that time, although I had faced some painful hardships, I had not been accustomed to failure. I had achieved academic success. I had married a beautiful and amazing woman right out of college. By the time I was thirty, I was the director of a growing campus ministry organization. During my twenties and early thirties, I was zealous to change the world. Yet during those years, my heart was overly attached to accomplishing a vision. I was set on devising strategies, accomplishing goals, achieving objectives, managing calendars, completing projects, reporting numbers, and raising money. Status quo was not an option. Working hard, organizing, and achieving results are good things of course. But what underlying motivation behind it all was driving me? Must I accomplish things and achieve results, or gain the approval of others to justify my existence? I'm confident various people I was involved with during those years felt genuinely cared for by me; yet, others, I'm afraid, felt as if I objectified them like projects or agendas. Perhaps the most significant event that jarred me awake to this damaging tendency was the day the pediatric neurologist told us we needed to get used to the term 'mentally retarded.' Rather than canceling everything else for that day after hearing such news, I stuck to my agenda, driving two hours out of town to meet with staff and speak at a late-night meeting, leaving my wife to grieve alone.

So deep was my bondage to goals, agendas, and image justifying my worth that the business failures I endured later sent me hurtling back on my heels, back against the ropes. The pain of failure runs deep when your heart is attached to proving your worth by keeping it together, seeking perfection, gaining the approval of others, or trying to accomplish things and then don't. We often are tempted to curse God in such moments of pain and suffering, but desert-wounding moments are sacred ground. Seeds of redemption lie buried within that sacred ground of struggle because God is present and at work. Jesus, I realized, did not live his life, die on the cross, and resurrect from the dead for our visions, objectives, goals, strategies, institutions, agendas or achieved results. He did all of that for us—you and me. God loves persons. Jesus came in the flesh to be with *us*. Struggles, therefore, can serve as means of making us more aware of our hidden bondage and opening our hearts more to the truth that we are accepted and the delight of God as his beloved children. Those struggles can serve as means of getting us to the point of letting go of the need to accomplish things, hold it all together, gain approval, or perfect ourselves to justify our existence. I certainly have not arrived. *Far* from it. None of us will in this lifetime. We each will struggle with certain tendencies and bondage throughout life. And guess what? We don't have to overcome our struggles to justify our existence. For Christ has overcome the world and released us from our bondage already. We are loved. We are forgiven. We have been liberated. We are delighted in. We are rejoiced over.

Hardships did not end for Jacob after the sacred wound, and neither have they ended for us. In the next chapter, we will be reminded of Jacob's heart-shattering loss of his beloved son, Joseph. But God was moving in ways Jacob could not see or understand. Dr. Ashley Null said, "what the heart loves, the will chooses, and the mind justifies. The mind doesn't direct the will. The mind is actually captive to what the will wants, and the will itself, in turn, is captive to what the heart wants."[22] And what is deepest in the heart goes widest to the world. Consider this insightful thought from Brian McLaren.

> "There's nothing wrong with desire. The question is, whose desires are you imitating? To be alive is to imitate God's generous desires . . . to create, to bless, to help, to serve, to care for, to save, to enjoy. To make the opposite choice—to imitate one another's

22. Zahl, "What the Heart Loves, the Will Chooses, and the Mind Justifies," lines 8–15.

desires and become one another's rivals—is to choose the path of death. If we imitate our way into that rat race, we will compete rather than create, impress rather than bless, defeat rather than protect, dominate rather than serve, and exploit rather than respect. As a result, we will turn our neighbor first into a rival, and then an enemy, and then a victim."[23]

May God in his mercy, as he did with Jacob, liberate us from hidden bondage that leads us down the path of death by captivating our hearts with the truth that we are indeed his beloved and delight. May this liberation and acceptance be what goes deepest in our hearts and widest to the world.

23. McLaren, *We Make the Road by Walking*, 17.

CHAPTER 5

Grace of Exposure

———— *Judah* ————

"We're only as sick as our secrets."—a common
Alcoholics Anonymous adage

"The man who lies to himself and listens to his own lie comes to a point where he does not discern any truth either in himself or anywhere around him, and thus falls into disrespect towards himself and others. Not respecting anyone, he ceases to love."[1]—Fyodor Dostoevsky

"His secret life is being exposed, and it needs to be. He's worked hard to keep the lids on things, but those lids have blown off. This will end up being the best thing for him and everyone involved." A wise man shared this perspective about someone whose self-deception had caused his own self-destruction and damaged others. The sobering lesson is that we all need to be exposed. But this is difficult. People caught in a web of self-deception are prone to be defensive. Confronting the reality of our human condition often can be a painful experience. Here is a small example with which you might relate: Your spouse sees a roach. You kill it, and throw it away. Your partner asks you to contact pest control. The next afternoon, another roach scurries across the floor. You totally forgot, so you're tempted to lie. If you tell the truth, the two of you may argue. You may feel ashamed as a result. You don't like to be blamed. You hate upsetting your spouse. So, you lie and say you left a voice message, or that you were just about to call them.

---

1. Dostoevsky, *The Brothers Karamazov*, 44.

Self-deception

It sometimes feels like lying is the best option in these situations to maintain peace and avoid any pain associated with blame and shame. Dr. Diane Langberg, who has decades of experience as a practicing psychologist and international speaker working with trauma survivors, caregivers, and clergy, said that self-deception "essentially functions as a narcotic because it protects us from seeing or feeling that which is painful to us."[2]

Think about it. If such a trivial event can tempt us to lie, consider how much more we would feel compelled to lie or conceal a matter when the issue is quite large. The conscience and soul of a habitual liar gradually die even as their confidence grows in their own delusions. People who live consistently this way can end up creating a living hell for themselves. M. Scott Peck in his book, *People of the Lie,* said that healthy persons are easiest for psychotherapists to treat because their thinking patterns are least distorted. In other words, they are honest. "Conversely, the sicker the patients—the more dishonest in their behavior and distorted in their thinking—the less able we are to help them. . . . When they are very distorted and dishonest, it seems impossible."[3] He went on to confess, "We literally feel overwhelmed by the labyrinthine mass of lies and twisted motives and distorted communication into which we will be drawn."[4] Dr. Langberg said deception is about "hiding, pretending, ignoring, camouflaging, and covering."[5] Let this sink in if you've been working hard to keep the lid on things—we are *all* vulnerable to self-deception. So, beware. If we engage in such deception long enough, we can "lose our taste for the good *and* our power to loathe evil. We eventually silence the voice of God and our response of fear to that voice."[6]

The proverbial frog in the kettle is placed initially in water at a comfortable temperature. The water is then heated one degree at a time while the frog adapts to the rising temperature . . . until it's boiled to death. The movie, *Good,* serves as an effective example. John Halder, played by Viggo Mortensen, is a respectable, laid-back, and seemingly scatterbrained literature professor in Germany during the rise of Nazism. He had written a novel around the theme of mercy killing. Because that theme was a matter of a degree of difference from the final solution—the Nazi agenda to annihilate the Jewish people—Nazi leadership valued Halder's book as propaganda. A high-ranking

2. Langberg, *Suffering and the Heart of God,* 198.
3. Peck., *People of the Lie,* 63.
4. Peck., *People of the Lie,* 64.
5. Langberg, *Suffering and the Heart of God,* 199
6. Langberg, *Suffering and the Heart of God,* 199.

Nazi official seduces Halder by flattering him with the praises of the party's inner circle. Intoxicated with recognition, promotion, and acceptance among the elite, Halder increasingly gets sucked into this web of deception. He passively accepts Hitler's agenda, justifying it as a passing fad. Another factor influencing Halder is Anne, a beautiful, vivacious student who sympathizes with Nazi beliefs, but also is crushed out on him. Over time, Halder caves to the attraction. Self-absorbed and deceived, Halder neglects and mistreats his aging and miserable mother. Somehow able to ignore the clear indications of the impending Holocaust, Halder callously watches his Jewish friend lose everything. As his friend pleads for help, Halder—too concerned about his own welfare—betrays him repeatedly. It is not until Halder personally enters a concentration camp, faces the friend he dehumanized, and encounters the horrific sights, sounds, and smells of mass annihilation that he finally awakens to reality. But it is way too late. What seemed to Halder a step up into a better life ended up being a step off a cliff into death. By deluding himself, he compromised his beliefs, betrayed his best friend, abandoned his wife, allowed his mother to suffer, and helped to enable the suffering and brutal killing of millions of innocent lives.[7]

Admittedly, this is an extreme example. But hopefully the story awakens us to our susceptibility. Second Corinthians 11:14 says: "Satan himself masquerades as an angel of light." Hebrews 3:13 urges us to encourage one another daily that we might not be hardened by sin's deceitfulness. Over time, deception makes a person's distortions appear true. The movie, *The Big Short*, opens with this quote: "It ain't what you don't know that gets you into trouble. It's what you know for sure that just ain't so."[8]

Descent into self-deception

One day while putting up groceries, I noticed water on the floor next to the refrigerator. Suspecting a leak, I pulled the refrigerator away from the wall. Immediately, I gagged at what I saw had accumulated underneath: little pieces of potato chips, cheese, crackers, bits of bread, grapes, and who knows what else. Now, what had been hidden was exposed.

Judah, our next character in the genealogical lineage of Jesus, eventually was exposed. You would think out of all Jacob's children, Joseph would have been the next person recorded in the lineage of Jesus. From Genesis 37 through the end of the book, the story centers around Jacob's family and the circumstances which lead to their move into Egypt. More specifically,

7. *Good*
8. *The Big Short*

the story focuses on Joseph. But he would not be the next child in line. Instead, the one in the lineage after Jacob was "Judah the father of Perez and Zerah by Tamar." Note the theme of this chapter is quite like the previous one. It's meant to be a sobering reminder that a parent can pass his or her struggles on to the next generation.

Just prior to Genesis 38, we read about Judah's participation in the deceptive cover-up regarding his brother Joseph's disappearance. The brothers, eaten up with jealousy, had intended on killing Joseph. Then, to save Joseph's life, Reuben, the eldest brother, suggested they throw him into a cistern and leave him, but all the while he had intended on taking Joseph back home to their father. Apparently at a time when Reuben was absent, the other brothers followed Judah's suggestion that they sell Joseph into slavery to a caravan of Ishmaelites passing by on their way to Egypt. Instead of telling the truth to their father, Jacob, they created a false narrative of how a fierce animal had devoured Joseph. Jacob loved Joseph more than any of his other sons. This news upended his life. Jacob was so distraught he tore his clothes. He cried for many days and could not be consoled by anyone. He vowed to continue mourning until he joined his son in the grave. Judah would collude with his brothers for many years to keep the truth buried.

The evil actions of Judah, along with his guilty brothers, directly enslaved Joseph to Potiphar—Pharaoh's captain of the guard (Gen 37:36)—and traumatized their father. This evil segues right into Genesis 38:1: "At that time, Judah left his brothers and went down to stay with a man of Adullam named Hirah." Don't miss this! Remember self-deception is often our drug of choice to protect against experiencing pain. This is not explicitly stated in the text, but I believe Judah could not bear the pain of watching his father suffer so severely. If he stayed anywhere near Jacob, Judah would constantly be reminded about the evil he had done. The pain of the guilt and shame was too much, and he fled. Judah is the frog in the kettle. He is losing his taste for good and the power to loathe evil, which is resulting in an increasingly dead soul.

Judah ended up meeting and marrying a Canaanite woman, Shua. They had three sons, Er, Onan, and Shelah. His marriage to a Canaanite woman would have been considered a serious compromise because of the corrupting influence and customs inherent in Canaan. After several years passed, their firstborn son, Er, married Tamar, also likely to have been a Canaanite woman. Yet Er was wicked and the Lord put him to death (Gen 38:7). As a result, Judah, according to Jewish custom, appointed Er's younger brother, Onan, to marry Tamar. (Deut 25:5–10). This custom insured the perpetuation of Er's family name. Yet whenever Onan had sex with Tamar, he wasted his semen on the ground knowing the children would be heirs of

Er. This was significant. A son born of Tamar deemed the heir of Er would be able to claim Er's double share of inheritance since he was the firstborn. Onan, however, did not want to lose the inheritance he would have if Tamar remained childless. This was considered betrayal against Er and the marriage. Therefore, Onan's actions were considered evil in the sight of God as well. The Lord also struck him dead.

Judah could not accept fault with his sons. Self-deception, once again, functioned as a narcotic to protect him from feeling pain. He blocked out any notion of his sons being the problem and secretly blamed Tamar for their deaths. Fearing a similar pattern with his youngest son, Shelah, Judah instructed Tamar to remain a widow in her own father's house until Shelah grew up. Tamar had not done anything wrong. Full blame belonged to Judah's sons. Furthermore, Judah was misleading Tamar. For time demonstrated he had no intentions of ever giving Shelah to her in marriage. He was willing to allow her to live as a destitute widow without children rather than to obey the law of God. In that culture, Tamar did not have an option to find another man to marry. Furthermore, we cannot fathom how much of a disgrace it was back then for a woman to die childless. So, it seemed as if Tamar would wait in vain.

During Tamar's waiting, Judah's wife died. Sometime following her death, Judah journeyed to a place called Timnah to shear his sheep. He was accompanied again by his friend Hirah of Adullam. What kind of friend was Hirah for Judah? Do we have the kind of friends who encourage us in such a way that we are not hardened by self-deception, or do we have the kind of friends that enable us to remain walking down that path? Upon hearing of her father-in-law's journey, Tamar contemplated the reality that she would never marry Shelah. If no brothers were left for the childless widow, then the obligation fell to the father-in-law to sire a child. If he could not or would not, then the obligation fell to the next nearest male relative. Consider Ruth and Boaz, for contrast, which we will cover in a future chapter. Tamar had been the victim of Er's evil behavior, Onan's reckless selfishness, and then Judah's deception. By now she realized that she could not expect or simply ask Judah to fulfill his obligation. Therefore, Tamar believed she had to act since Judah would not. She planned to disguise herself as a prostitute (I recognize how crazy this sounds and will elaborate more on this in the next chapter). Judah's departure to Timnah provided Tamar with the opportunity to execute her plan. Perhaps she knew something about Judah's prior behavior that made her believe her plan would succeed. Sure enough, along his journey, Judah saw a prostitute, but did not recognize her as Tamar because her face was covered. Judah indeed handled this situation as if he had prior experience. He knew what needed to be done. He requested sex.

He was not surprised by her demand for some guarantee of payment. Therefore, he handed her his staff, cord, and signet as temporary security for a goat he promised later to use as payment. These elements would have had distinctive characteristics recognizable to the owner.

Tamar wisely had collected his signet, a seal or stamp used to identify his property; a cord, a wrap with which he covered himself, or bound things together; and a staff, an object with which to help him walk and/ or shepherd, as a pledge in exchange for sex until he sent her the young goat. Later, Judah sent his friend, Hiram, with a kid goat to pay the woman and retrieve his personal items. But she was nowhere to be found. Judah decided it was not worth the effort to find her. Why bring any attention to the matter? For the sake of his reputation, he was willing to cut his losses and let go of the whole matter.

Three months after Judah's encounter with the prostitute, word got back to him that Tamar was pregnant by an immoral act. Ironically, Judah— knowing the Law and his own moral failure—ordered she be burned. As the pledged bride of his youngest son, Shelah, the news of Tamar's immorality not only would have embarrassed Judah, but also brought shame upon the family name. Under Mosaic law, the penalty for a woman who broke a pledge in such a way was death by stoning. "Judah's sentence, therefore, was more harsh than the subsequent law."[9] He clearly did not care about Tamar. How easy it was for him to pass such a severe judgment on her without passing the same judgment on himself.

Judah's choice revealed the depth of his self-deception. It's as though he issued a sentence to avenge the death of his first two sons for which he blamed Tamar. He remained in denial regarding the evil actions of his sons, and he refused to accept how their own deplorable behavior resulted in their own deaths. Perhaps by sentencing Tamar to be burned, he finally could be rid of her altogether. See the pattern? To alleviate his own shame and responsibility, Judah was shifting blame onto Tamar. He was making decisions based on his own distortions, and Tamar continued to be the victim. It was morally outrageous that Judah had issued such a death sentence. But over time, he had lost the taste for good and the power to loathe evil.

Escape out of self-deception

Tamar, anticipating this moment, seized the opportunity to expose Judah. Returning his signet, cord, and staff, she sent word to him *privately* (note that she did not do so publicly): "'I am pregnant by the man who owns

9. Keil and Delitzsch, *Commentary on the Old Testament*, 1:220.

these.' And she added, 'See if you recognize whose seal and cord and staff these are'" (Gen 38:25). Judah was exposed. Game over. But get this—exposure was the grace of God. For as long as he kept industriously concealing matters and living out his distorted thinking, he would have continued inflicting damage to himself and others. Something that remains hidden cannot be redeemed or healed.

Many people who are exposed still refuse to own up to the truth, accept responsibility, apologize, and seek to make things right. To avoid shame, they continue denying, minimizing, defending, or twisting reality to fit their own delusional narrative. They blame others. If it involves an institutional cover-up, the level of complexity compounds. Dr. Langberg has observed that institutional exposure creates a crisis, and that crisis "will reveal the heart of the structure or organization that is threatened by the truth."[10] "Instinctively we will move to protect (or so we think) our family, our organization, or our community."[11] The movie, *Spotlight*, based on a true story, won the Academy Award for Best Picture in 2015. In 2003, the *Boston Globe* won the Pulitzer Prize for Public Service because of the investigative work of its spotlight team. This team exposed a systemic pattern of sex abuse of children by Catholic priests in Massachusetts and an ongoing cover-up by the Boston Archdiocese, as well as complicit participants and advocates of the Catholic church. The exposure emboldened many victims to come forward with their stories.[12] I will address the topic of abuse of power in the next chapter on Tamar, and evil in the chapter on Manasseh and Amon later. Self-deceived persons that twist reality to fit their own delusional narratives are capable of damaging everyone in their path, like tornadoes decimating buildings on the prairie.

Judah, however, was clearly awakened to reality at the sight of his own staff, cord, and signet. Imagine his reaction to being exposed like this. Did his hands tremble as he gripped the staff again? Did tears drip from his face into his hands as he slid the signet back on his finger? Did a rush of guilt suddenly breakthrough the deadbolted door imprisoning his calloused heart? Truth indeed appears to have penetrated through the hardened soil of his self-deception. Exposed, Judah repented: "'She is more righteous than I since I wouldn't give her to my son Shelah.' And he did not sleep with her again" (Gen 38:26). He accepted responsibility, and he acquitted Tamar in an effort to make things right. He did not repeat his wrongdoing. Judah, in the context

10. Langberg, *Suffering and the Heart of God,* 222.

11. Langberg, *Suffering and the Heart of God,* 226.

12. *Spotlight*, directed by Tom McCarthy (2015; Los Angeles, CA: Open Road Films, 2016), DVD.

of this patriarchal society, held all the power in this relationship. For him to admit she was righteous and he unrighteous was extraordinary.

How can we know someone who's been self-deceived is authentically repentant once exposed? Any internal moral compass does not point true north at the moment of exposure. Tears may merely indicate barometric data about rapidly moving storms. "Repentance is long, slow, consistent change over an extended period of time because it is from the heart outward."[13] Someone, for instance, "can stop an addiction or an affair and still be injecting the narcotic of deception."[14] Judah's change of heart seems to be demonstrated by the fact he never slept with Tamar again. In the latter chapters of Genesis, Joseph, the other victim of Judah's past hidden secret exposes him along with his brothers. The next time we read of Judah, he is reunited and reconciled with his father and brothers, a sign perhaps of spiritual renewal in his life. According to Genesis 42, on the occasion of their initial visit to Egypt on account of the famine, Reuben acts as the family's spokesman before Joseph, now a powerful ruler, though they did not recognize him. In Genesis 43–44, however, Judah courageously leads in selfless humility. Still not knowing it was Joseph, Judah risks his own life, offering himself up in the place of his younger brother, Benjamin. Genesis 45 describes the climactic and dramatic reconciliation of Joseph with all his brothers. In Genesis 49, we read of Jacob's final words to each of his sons. A prolonged dominion is assured Judah's offspring. Part of this dominion is manifested in his offspring becoming a tribe, and then later as a nation distinguished from Israel. Only one judge, Othniel, ever arose from the tribe of Judah over Israel. It would be King David and Solomon, however, and eventually the anointed Messiah, Jesus, who would descend from the line of Judah through one of his twin sons born of Tamar. Does that not blow your mind?

The famous hymn, *Amazing Grace*, includes a powerful line about having been blind, which is an abbreviated way of saying caught in a web of self-deception. Yet, because of God's amazing grace, the songwriter, John Newton, testifies to God lifting the veil of deceit. Newton was born in 1725 about a mile down river from the Tower of London. His father was a sea captain and consequently a mostly absent parent. His mother taught him to read and exposed him to Christianity early on but died of tuberculosis when he was about to turn seven. At age eleven, he embarked on his first sea voyage with his father. He soon became a capable sailor in his own right, but he spent his youthful years living a licentious and debauched lifestyle. It was said his profanity was so horrible that even the most hardened sailors kept their distance

---

13. Langberg, *Suffering and the Heart of God*, 225–226.
14. Langberg, *Suffering and the Heart of God*, 264.

from him. Eventually, he became involved in the slave trade. Early on during his involvement, his father dispatched a sea captain to locate and bring his son home. Newton, in his early twenties, was in Africa when that sea captain found him. During Newton's return voyage to England, he came across Thomas à Kempis's *Imitation of Christ*, which prompted him to ask questions. He experienced the beginning of his conversion to Christianity when the ship almost sank due to a severe storm. Newton found himself praying and putting his faith in God, acknowledging his life had been a wreck.

That was a beginning, but he most certainly had a long way to go. For he continued working in the slave trade even though he had gained sympathy for slaves during his time in Africa. In 1750, he became a ship captain, the responsibilities of which included the gathering and trading of slaves. He held this post for three different voyages over a four-year period. During the 1750s, most English citizens, including Christians, accepted the slave trade as a respectable form of commerce. Afterall, they had no video footage or social media to shine a spotlight on where or under what conditions slaves produced cotton, brandy, and sugar for them. This made it quite easy for them to embrace their state of ignorance and denial with a toast of brandy, a cube of sugar in their afternoon tea, or stepping out in their finest clothes. Keep in mind, self-deception functions like a drug because it shields us from seeing or feeling that which is painful. Deception includes our efforts to ignore and pretend. We instinctively move to protect our systems rather than victims. The people of England did not start grappling with the immorality of slavery until the 1770s, with the debate lasting for decades.

Newton later wrote how increasingly unsettled he felt with this life of shackles, chains, and leg irons. His conscience was awakened to the false human narrative he had embraced. Later, as an ordained priest in the Church of England, he developed a reputation as being a loving and warm pastor. During his ministry years, he penned many hymns. A seed of redemption germinated and grew out of his earlier involvement in the slave trade. As a result of the evil having been exposed in his own life, he himself exposed and preached against the slave trade, calling it blood money. He exhorted his congregation, which included some men who made their living based on the slave trade, to have nothing to do with it.

In 1788, Newton published an influential pamphlet entitled, *Thoughts Upon the African Slave Trade*. The publication exposed the horrific conditions of the slave ships based on his firsthand knowledge. He knew his confession had come way too late; his active participation in that which now caused his heart to shudder would always be a humiliating reflection to him. Another significant way the seed of redemption grew and bore fruit through Newton's life was through his relationship with William Wilberforce, a leader of the Parliamentary campaign to abolish the African slave trade. Being a close mentor to Wilberforce, Newton exerted political influence. He lived to see the British passage of the Slave Trade Act of 1807, and he died in December of the same year.[15]

C.S. Lewis provided this profound insight. "Of course, I quite agree that the Christian religion is, in the long run, a thing of unspeakable comfort. But it does not begin in comfort, it begins in the dismay I have been describing, and it is no use at all trying to go on to that comfort without first going through that dismay. . . . If you look for truth, you may find comfort in the end; if you look for comfort you will not get either comfort or truth— only soft soap and wishful thinking to begin with and, in the end despair."[16] Those who have participated in Alcoholics Anonymous are well aware of the adage that we are only as sick as our secrets. So, let me challenge us to look for truth and go through the dismay. We all need to be exposed. Like Judah hiding the truth about what he did to Joseph, have we kept some skeletons buried? Like Newton's participation in slave commodities, or Judah's belief in a false narrative about his sons and Tamar, and consequent harm to Tamar because of those distortions—might we be believing and/or participating in false narratives that, directly or indirectly, may be damaging other people? For what reasons and in what ways are we hiding, pretending, or ignoring? This can be difficult to answer or confess because *inherent in self-deception is lack of self-awareness.* The patterns of our desires and thinking are so habitual that we can be blind to them. Nonetheless, do we believe it is possible that an unknown freedom and comfort, as Lewis stated, await us on the other side of the dismay of facing and walking through and out of our false narratives? Do we believe it is possible that exposure of such concealed matters and distorted thinking could significantly contribute to our own healing as well as the healing of others?

How can the journey of dismay and exposure begin? Relationships of all kinds—such as between parents and children, spouses, siblings, and friends—expose in us traits or tendencies we cannot otherwise see. We need community. Sometimes, it takes a willingness on our part to ask others to show us what we ourselves cannot see. Perhaps we may find value in processing some things in confidence with a professional counselor, trusted friend, or mentor. As I will discuss in an upcoming chapter, Nathan exposed David. Tamar exposed Judah. "Better is open rebuke than hidden love. Wounds from a friend can be trusted" (Prov 27:5–6a).

In the next chapter, I will discuss how God uses the vulnerable to expose us. The killing of George Floyd, among others, in 2020 exposed implicit American racial biases, for instance. We don't naturally want to experience the dismay associated with exposure. Who wants to end up

---

15. *John Newton*
16. Lewis, *Mere Christianity*, 32.

exposed like Judah? Sure, painful consequences can result. This is part of the dismay to which Lewis referred. But what remains hidden cannot be redeemed or healed. We can't treat a cancerous tumor if we don't know it exists; it must be exposed.

A helpful resource in developing self-awareness is the Enneagram. In a positive way, I have found it to be a profoundly beneficial tool in helping learn more about myself and do interior work. There is no better or worse Enneagram type. Its best feature is providing key insights into our best qualities and driving motivations. The Enneagram also can help reveal our patterns of struggle and how we can feel and act when functioning in our weaker moments. An aspect of self-deception is a weakened or unhealthy conscience which struggles to discern right from wrong. What some of us need exposed is an unhealthy conscience that is extremely self-critical and inaccurate. People who are held captive by an unbiblically harsh internal judge feel they are transgressing when they are not. This is characteristic of the struggle of an Enneagram type one, for example. If you are interested in learning more about the Enneagram, you might check out enneagramin-stitute.com or *The Essential Enneagram: The Definitive Personality Test and Self-Discovery Guide* by David Daniels and Virginia Price.

Whatever we choose—from personality typing tools to the honesty of our closest friends—we must never fear seeking the truth! Romans 5:20 (MSG) says, "But sin didn't and doesn't, have a chance in competition with the aggressive forgiveness we call grace. When it's sin versus grace, grace wins hands down. All sin can do is threaten us with death, and that's the end of it. Grace, because God is putting everything together again through the Messiah, invites us into life—a life that goes on and on and on, world without end." The grace of God delivers us from our compulsion to deny, minimize, defend, or justify ourselves in the face of truth. God knows everything about us and loves us. So, we can stop lying to ourselves. Our self-deception no longer has to imprison us. May seeds of redemption arise out of our own stories of self-deception. May God restore our taste for what is good and our power to loathe evil. May our ears once again hear the voice of God. May God enliven our deadened souls. May we not hide from the truth, but rather eagerly seek it. Like Newton's efforts to eliminate the slave trade, may we be the light God has called us to be, and seek to join him in making things right.

---------- CHAPTER 6 ----------

Power of the Vulnerable

---------- *Tamar* ----------

"Isn't it obvious that God deliberately chose men and women that the culture overlooks and exploits and abuses, chose these 'nobodies' to expose the hollow pretensions of the 'somebodies'"
—1 Cor 1:26–27, MSG

I n *The Lord of the Rings: The Two Towers*, Théoden, the King of Rohan, had grown ill, weak, and delusional. Others around the king were oblivious to how his advisor, Grima Wormtongue, had manipulated the king's mind over time. Théoden had been cast under the spell of Saruman, the powerful and evil wizard who sought to seize control of Rohan on behalf of Sauron, the story's main antagonist. Sauron, ruler of Mordor, ambitions to rule the whole of Middle-earth. Gradually, Saruman's power increased as Théoden's mind weakened, succumbing to Wormtongue's relentless and poisonous brainwashing and web of deception.[1]

Abuse of power

This term was not used in either the book or movie, but Wormtongue had succeeded in *gaslighting* Théoden. Gaslighting is a manipulative behavior people employ to control the feelings, thoughts, and behaviors of their victims. In the movie, *Gaslight*, Gregory manipulates his wife, Paula, by attempting to convince her and others that she is crazy. For example, he removes a picture from a wall in their house but persuades her that she is the one who took it down. Eventually, Gregory succeeds in isolating her from the outside world, convincing her that he is doing so for her own

1. *The Lord of the Rings: The Two Towers.*

safety.[2] People who gaslight lie. They deny saying or doing things that they in fact said or did. They accuse their victims of what they themselves are guilty. A pathological liar, for instance, accuses his victim of lying. They might make false threats or attack what they perceive to be their victim's most vulnerable weakness. They sabotage relationships by attempting to control how others view their victims. For instance, they might try to persuade others that their victim is crazy, dangerous, or unstable.[3] They have no capacity to feel shame. So, if confronted, they typically will react by gaslighting the one confronting them.

Victims of this sort of abuse often feel minimized, worn down, and perhaps even depressed, crushed, or smothered by the relentless attacks. They feel confused, constantly second-guessing themselves . . . their feelings, perceptions, and memories.[4] They may wonder if they *are* going crazy. Victims often remain silent out of fear of the abuser's retribution, which is what the abuser wants. This sort of abusive person is dangerous because his or her behavior can ruin not only a victim's life, but an entire family, organization, broader community, or even nation depending on his or her level of leadership and influence. How does this happen?

Author Carolyn Custis James wrote, "Combine individuals possessed of authority and power with individuals . . . conditioned to submit to authority. Then add devotees/enablers who . . . turn a blind eye to the abuse and may even defend it. Suddenly you have ideal conditions for . . . abuse to bluster up and thrive unchecked."[5]

"Abuse of any type occurs when someone has power over another and uses that power to hurt."[6] Abuse can include physically, emotionally, psychologically, or spiritually wounding one who is vulnerable. Abuse "deceives and confuses victims. The one abusing power is also clearly deceived and confused"[7] because their ability to discern good and evil has been deadened. Therefore, for the abuser, "truth and lies become confused or often even reversed."[8]

---

2. *Gaslight*

3. Sarkis, "11 Warning Signs of Gaslighting," Lines 17, 22, 27, 69–70.

4. Sarkis, "11 Warning Signs of Gaslighting," Lines 33, 51, 53.

5. James, "The Perfect Storm," lines 15–20.

6. Blue, *Healing Spiritual Abuse*, 12.

7. Langberg, *Suffering and the Heart of God*, 204.

8. Langberg, *Suffering and the Heart of God*, 204.

Environments where abuse thrives

During ancient biblical times, conditions existed which made women and different ethnicities especially vulnerable to abuse. In a patriarchal culture, fathers held supreme authority in the family, clan, or tribe, and descent followed the male line. Genealogies did not follow the lineage of mothers, although exceptions can be found.

During the time of Jesus, women possessed no power. They were not counted as full members of a congregation much like when African Americans did not count as full persons in the United States. They were discouraged, even forbidden, from pursuing education. Men refrained from speaking to them in public places. Their testimony was not admissible in court.[9] Women were considered as inferior to men. During all periods of Israel's history, women were legally subject to men, which also was the case in the rest of the ancient world. In such a patriarchal society, polygamy and concubinage were legal. Fathers could sell their daughters as slaves. Men could divorce their wives for trivial reasons, while women could not divorce their husbands. Many restrictions existed regarding women's religious roles as well.[10] A "woman had no legal rights; she was regarded, not as a person, but as a thing. She was merely the possession of her father or of her husband, and in his disposal to do with as he liked."[11]

Power in and of itself is not wrong. Afterall, God is all-powerful, good, and all-wise. Having been made in the image of God, each of us has some degree of power to act upon or influence others. "Blessing, power, or favor," writer Brian McLaren says, "is not given for privilege over others, but for service for the benefit of others."[12] The problem occurs when power is misused or abused. Ken Blue, in *Healing Spiritual Abuse*, states:

> "Jesus was so focused on the problem of *spiritual* abuse that it was the only social evil against which he ever developed a platform. It was the only cultural problem that he repeatedly exposed and opposed. This is amazing when we recall that his culture was plagued by a host of serious social ills. Jesus took no public stand against slavery, racism, class warfare, state-sponsored terrorism, military occupation, or corruption in government. He spoke not a word against abortion or infanticide, homosexuality or the exploitation of women and children."[13]

9. Bromily, *The International Standard Bible Encyclopedia,* 4:1094.

10. Bromily, *The International Standard Bible Encyclopedia,* 4:1091–92.

11. Barclay, *The Gospel of Matthew,* 1:17.

12. McLaren, *We Make the Road by Walking,* 34.

13. Blue, *Healing Spiritual Abuse,* 18.

Spiritual abuse is quite harmful and deadly. I touched on this in chapter one. "Legalism is the great weapon of spiritual abuse. Multiplying religious rules to gain control over followers is authoritarianism's primary tool. Legalism is an expression of a person's compulsion to seek security and predictability. If they can enforce an exhaustive list of dos and don'ts, they think they will gain that security and predictability they crave."[14] The Pharisees, learned in the Law and "devoted to hair-splitting legalism, carried on lengthy debates about the commandments, arguing whether any particular one was great or small, heavy or light."[15] It was natural, therefore, "that they often debated the question, 'Which—of the 613 commandments was . . . the greatest,' one."[16] Allender made this keen observation and conclusion about legalism: "Most people are more comfortable in a rule-driven culture where behavior is prescribed, and uncertainty largely eliminated. The resulting loss of freedom is rewarded with a greater distance from the prospect of shame. Such striving to avoid ambivalence and shame is the motivating force that shapes the soul of a Pharisee and the culture of legalism."[17] Legalistic communities tend to retreat from others who are different and exclude, or even punish, those who don't comply to their rules. Instead of building bridges to connect, they erect walls to separate.

Spiritual abuse thrives in communities where a central goal is to have control over the thinking and behavior of others. Leaders in such systems are abusive when they weaponize the Bible to threaten and manipulate. They do so when their missions, processes, policies, and agendas are more important than the real needs of people. They do so when they seek to shame, condemn, and intimidate. I attended a large father-son gathering once during which the guest speaker berated and shamed the fathers for their failures in front of their sons. While spiritual abusers "rarely *intend* to hurt their victims," Blue points out, their narcissism veils their eyes from noticing the wounds they inflict on others.[18]

Spiritual abuse can thrive if the image, success, or mission of an institution or organization becomes more important than the people for whom the institution or organization exists. James Houston observed, "The institutional bell curve forms when the original call of God is overtaken and suffocated by demands for professionalism and efficiency. . . .The original vision is eclipsed by money-making projects. What may have begun as a simple community

---

14. Blue, *Healing Spiritual Abuse,* 44.

15. Hendriksen, *Matthew, New Testament Commentary,* 809.

16. Hendriksen, *Matthew, New Testament Commentary,* 809.

17. Allender, *The Healing Path,* 106.

18. Blue, *Healing Spiritual Abuse,* 12–13.

dedicated to spiritual education and nurturing ends up an idolatrous environment of professional careerism."[19] Houston goes on to say:

> Moral failure occurs when original personal sacrifice is replaced by more worldly ambitions motivated by the reputation associated with a 'successful' enterprise. . . . [I]nstitutions are often blind to sin because they are designed never to be wrong. The majority vote is always right. The bigger the institution, the less likely it is to be challenged. Indeed, statistical growth is seen as evidence that it is doing things right. Institutions are not set up to repent, nor to redress personal wrongs, nor to know themselves intimately. Rather they are designed to believe and trust in themselves politically rather than to believe and trust in God. They become idols rather than instruments for worshiping the living God."[20]

Blue placed spiritual abuse on a continuum, and chose not to include the occasional rudeness, arrogance, or thoughtlessness committed by a leader. We can all be guilty of such occasional behavior. At the bottom of the continuum would be "when a leader pretends to be a friend and uses this illusion to dehumanize and manipulate his followers."[21] At the top of the continuum is the "deliberate exploitation and domination of the weak by a grandiose, authoritarian spiritual dictator. Almost any kind of abusive behavior may be found at this level: threats, intimidation, extortion of money, demands for sex, public humiliation, control over private lives, manipulation of marriages, elaborate spying and similar practices."[22]

How can we tell if we are involved in such an institution or organization where spiritual abuse is systemically occurring? People entrapped in a legalistic system are prone to not be authentic and vulnerable about their own failures. They work hard to avoid shame. They live more out of fear. They conceal matters. Masks and pretense emerge as normative. "Don't talk" rules emerge. Any wrongdoing is covered up, denied, minimized, defended, or blame-shifted onto others. Genuine community—characterized by compassion, humility, open communication, trust, vulnerability, acceptance, and accountability—is replaced by artificial community, the hallmarks of which are pride, secrecy, distrust, lies, and fear. Confusion and paranoia permeate the atmosphere. People's souls wither and die a slow death in such toxic cultures. Hidden problems fester as untold stories and unnoticed hurts

---

19. Houston, *Joyful Exiles*, 86.
20. Houston, *Joyful Exiles*, 93.
21. Blue, *Healing Spiritual Abuse*, 13–14.
22. Blue, *Healing Spiritual Abuse*, 14.

go untreated. If someone is courageous enough to confront abuses, leaders and their enablers may find ways to attack, discredit, and marginalize the whistleblower(s). Those who break silence are accused of causing trouble. William White wrote, "Whistleblowing often involves calling attention to actions that are either illegal or that could involve harm to innocent parties. Because whistleblowers are rarely protected from retribution by the company, whistleblowing is one of the purest and highest-risk forms of activism . . . That an act of whistle-blowing is morally and ethically justified does not serve as a protection from organizational retribution."[23] It's mind blowing! The Pharisees attacked Jesus as the troublemaker when *they* had it all completely backwards. They were the dangerous ones harming the people. Eventually, they played the key role in crucifying Jesus.

The vulnerable

For those of us who have endured abuse, perhaps the story of Tamar will provide a fresh lens through which we can view our own struggle. Tamar was not only a woman, but also likely of a different ethnicity—a Canaanite. Although the specifics of Er's evil behavior were not disclosed, we must wonder what kind of husband Tamar had to deal with.

When Er died, Tamar, according to Levirate law, had no choice but to marry his brother, Onan. When Onan died, then Judah assumed the position of power. Lest we forget, Judah had been the one to suggest to his brothers that they sell Joseph as a slave to the traveling Ishmaelites. He also scandalously concealed their actions, which in turn was horribly abusive to their father. In this situation with Tamar, he blamed her as the cause of his sons' deaths. No documentation exists to show that Judah sought out Tamar to understand what she had witnessed or experienced with his sons (remember, even when Jesus ministered much later, a woman's testimony was not admissible in court). Instead, Judah dismissed Tamar to her own father's house, falsely promising he would give her his youngest son when he was old enough. But he clearly never intended on following through. He defrauded Tamar. He was going to allow her to suffer like that for life.

The flip side of power is vulnerability. "A vulnerable person is susceptible to attack or injury."[24] Dr. Langberg during an address at the 2019 Caring Well Conference said that our response to the vulnerabilities of others exposes who we truly are.[25] She used the example of parents and babies. The

23. White, *The Incestuous Workplace*, 208.

24. Langberg, *Suffering and the Heart of God*, 194.

25. https://www.netgrace.org/resources/diane-langberg-clinical-psychologist -author-and-grace-board-member

hearts of parents who are unresponsive to their helpless crying babies are revealed as callous and hardened. Tamar is the helpless, crying vulnerable one with no power in this story. Judah's calloused and hardened heart is exposed when he does not use his power to understand, empathize with, protect, and advocate for her. Instead, he abused his power by wrongly scapegoating her and protecting his own self-interest and delusional narrative.

Now, take this same line of thought and apply it today. Observe how persons in positions of power respond to the vulnerabilities of others. Do they seek to nurture, protect, and serve those in the vulnerable position? Or do they callously ignore the vulnerable, or even scapegoat, abuse, and/ or exploit them? A doctor, for instance, has the power in the doctor-patient relationship. Church leaders have the power in the church governance-membership structure. Police have the power in the officer-citizen relationship. There are all kinds of other examples: parents and children; coaches and players; teachers and students; counselors and clients; bosses and employees; politicians and citizens; those with money and those without; those in the majority and those in the minority; those with powerful connections and those without. Nothing is inherently wrong with having power. But we can ask ourselves, how do we or those in power respond to or treat those in vulnerable positions?

At some point, Tamar awakened to her position of vulnerability and the fact that Judah had severely mistreated her. We can admire her courage, then, to choose to no longer be victimized. She accepted that Judah was never going to fulfill his obligation to God's covenant, so she decided to act. She devised a way to continue the line of Judah since he was forsaking his own responsibility. She planned to disguise herself as a prostitute. What are we to think of this? She must have known the death penalty would be her likely consequence. Judah was so angered upon learning about her alleged immorality that he ordered her to be burned to death. Why would she risk her life this way? Before we make the same mistake of drawing our own conclusions regarding Tamar's actions, let's allow the Scriptures to inform our thinking.

R.T. France points out that "in Jewish tradition Tamar, Rahab, and Ruth were regarded as heroines."[26] Judah, while admitting guilt, vindicated her of any wrongdoing and called her righteous (Gen 38:26). In Ruth 4:11–12, in celebration of the marriage of Boaz and Ruth, a Moabites whom we'll consider shortly, "the elders and all the people at the gate" pronounced this as a part of their blessing upon the couple: "Through the offspring the LORD gives you by this young woman, may your family be

---

26. France, *The Gospel of Matthew*, 37.

like that of Perez, whom Tamar bore to Judah." "If Tamar is some scandalous skeleton in the family closet, why would anyone bring her up on a holy
occasion like this?" James wrote. " . . . Yet Tamar is named without apology
in a statement intended to honor the bride and groom."[27] Later on, King
David named one of his beautiful daughters Tamar. David's son, Absalom,
also named one of his daughters Tamar.[28]

James's research has revealed the study of contemporary Old Testament
scholars has produced of the biblical texts "more precise translations in which
Judah takes full blame and not only acquits his daughter-in-law of wrongdoing but actually praises her by saying, 'She is righteous, not I,' or "She is in
the right, not I."[29] If this is a more precise translation, then we can throw out
theories that Tamar was motivated by vindication or desperation for a child.
How could such a motive be called righteous? According to Judah, "something deeper drove his daughter-in-law to such radical measures."[30] Consider
the fact God struck down Tamar's two husbands for whatever it was they had
done. Yet he did *nothing* to Tamar for this act.

Power of the vulnerable

God had made covenant promises to Abraham, and to his seed, including
Judah. Judah and his sons had blown it! Yet Tamar courageously "regarded
his seed as sacred and risked her life to preserve it."[31] Tamar's stepping up
in this moment reminds us that God often empowers the vulnerable, the
weak, the struggling, and the wounded to act when powerful people do
not or will not.

In the midst of that patriarchal culture two thousand years ago, where
the voices of women and those of different ethnicities were not acknowledged,
Jesus empathized, relating to women and those of different ethnicities in such
a way that dignified their humanity, affirmed their value, invited their full participation, and brought attention to their faith. He esteemed them as human
beings created in the image of God, and thus worthy of genuine respect and
dignity. He invited and empowered them to pursue learning by following him.
He welcomed their voices and encouraged others to hear their testimony. He
extended his reach to include everyone—Jew and Gentile, slave and free, men
and women, masters and servants.

27. James, *Lost Women of the Bible*, 106.

28. 2 Sam 13:1; 2 Sam 14:27.

29. Waltke, *Genesis*, 513.

30. James, *Lost Women of the Bible*, 113–114.

31. James, *Lost Women of the Bible*, 114.

Matthew included scenes that highlighted this radical departure from the cultural norm. In addition to including Rahab, Tamar, Ruth, and Bathsheba in Jesus's genealogy, Matthew put a spotlight on the virgin Mary. In the conclusion of his gospel, Matthew documented two women as the first to witness the resurrected Jesus, and then, the first ones commissioned to share the news of his resurrection with his disciples. In between these bookends, Matthew highlighted various women who played significant roles in Jesus's earthly ministry:

- In Matthew 9, a woman, who had been marginalized because of a twelve-year hemorrhaging condition, displayed courageous faith to think to herself, *if only I touch his garment, I will be made well.*

- In Matthew 15, a Canaanite woman in faith cried out to Jesus to heal her demonically oppressed daughter.

- In Matthew 26, a woman poured expensive ointment on Jesus's head to the bewilderment of the disciples, who chastised her, believing it would have been better sold for money and used among the poor. Jesus rebuffed them: "Truly I tell you, wherever this gospel is preached throughout the world, what she has done will also be told, in memory of her" (v.13).

What seeds of redemption might lie buried in the ground of struggle of the vulnerable among us? This bizarre story of a vulnerable Tamar reminds me of what Paul wrote in 1 Corinthians 1:25–28 (MSG):

> "Human wisdom is so cheap, so impotent, next to the seeming absurdity of God. Human strength can't begin to compete with God's 'weakness.' Take a good look, friends, at who you were when you got called into this life. I don't see many of 'the brightest and the best' among you, not many influential, not many from high-society families. Isn't it obvious that God deliberately chose men and women that the culture overlooks and exploits and abuses, chose these 'nobodies' to expose the hollow pretensions of the 'somebodies.' That makes it quite clear that none of you can get by with blowing your own horn before God."

This tells me if we want to hear what God might be saying today, we must actively seek out and listen to the voices of the most vulnerable in our world.

How strange that the humble birth of Jesus in a stall in Bethlehem was "the world-historical event that ruptured the established structures of power. . . . In his crucifixion, Christ disarmed all forms of worldly power and in his resurrection, he triumphed over them."[32] Jesus took on the nature of a servant, being born in the likeness of humanity. He engaged in the degrading and demeaning act of washing feet. He experienced ultimate humiliation by submitting himself to torture and crucifixion like a criminal. Compassion, rather than domination, defined his power—manifesting itself in how he sacrificially gave of himself to the powerless. Recall his care for the sick, disabled, poor, demon-possessed, and those who were hungry and thirsty. For his triumphal entry into Jerusalem, he rode a beast of burden rather than a war horse. His kingdom, in contrast to the worldly power that sought dominion and control, manifested "the power to bless, unburden, serve, heal, mend, restore, and liberate."[33] This kind of power then and now seems weak and foolish. Christianity, in the early years, spread most rapidly among the powerless—those considered by the elite of society as riffraff or the lower classes. "God picked out the scum of the earth and made them kings and priests in his kingdom. . . . By using such methods God is overthrowing one of the false standards of the world, i.e. the notion that those who matter to him are the wise, the well-bred, the articulate, the gifted, the wealthy, the wielders of power and influence."[34]

To victims of abuse

If you are a victim of abuse, I am profoundly sorry. I weep for the wounds you have endured. I pray this chapter has in some way validated your story, renewed your hope that God's grace is sufficient as his power is made perfect in weakness, and enhanced your confidence that your voice matters. Jesus experienced the most cruel and evil abuse in his crucifixion at the hands of the highest levels of religious and political power . . . for us. God loves you. He is with you and on your side. In a later chapter on evil, I will discuss further the trauma abuse causes and how God redemptively exploits evil for complex good. Like Tamar, I pray you heal and find your voice. God has chosen to use the weak, foolish, and lowly things. If you recall, I said in an earlier chapter on Isaac that the faith challenge for Abraham and Sarah was to wait on God. They blew it by scheming to control the narrative and taking matters into their own hands. The faith challenge for Tamar, however, was not to wait around, but rather to step up and take initiative. For whatever situation in which you find yourself, I pray that God gives you wisdom and courage as you respond to your own faith challenge.

32. Hunter, *To Change the World*, 188.
33. Hunter, *To Change the World*, 193.
34. Prior, *The Message of 1 Corinthians*, 46.

A powerful scene in *The Lord of the Rings: The Two Towers* takes place when Gandalf arrives in Rohan, along with his friends, Aragon, Gimli, and Legolas. Gandalf sneaks his white staff into the Golden Hall. He leverages his power to free Théoden from Saruman's spell. Consequently, the veil of deceit lifts, and Théoden's mind and body are restored to health. With renewed energy, Théoden bravely goes forth to lead forces against Sauron's warrior Orcs in the Battle at Helm's Deep to protect his people, ultimately claiming victory.[35] I wish it were that easy to eliminate abusers' power and usher in immediate healing for victims. What I do appreciate about this part of the story is that these powerful, good men show up together to both advocate for the victim and confront the abuser along with his enablers all at once. May we who have not experienced abuse not rush to protect our organizations or institutions by ignoring, denying, or silencing victims. Instead, may God enable us to be redemptive listeners to the voices of the vulnerable and have a willingness to enter their stories as advocates. Such advocacy is costly. Healing can be a long process and requires gracious patience.

We also must remember that God remains at work in the lives of the perpetrators; when his evil was exposed, Judah repented and demonstrated fruits of that repentance. Yet we must not be naïve either. People who regularly abuse power often have no self-awareness, feel no shame, and are thus blind to the damage they inflict. Self-deceived, they view themselves as victims. If exposed, they may seek ways to attack, manipulate, control, and discredit the persons who exposed them. Sometimes they succeed in their smear campaigns. If we enter such confrontations, we risk being not only maligned, but also misunderstood. If such is the case, a wise friend once advised me to walk about with fists unclenched by my side among those whose minds have been poisoned with false information. If abusers and their enablers, however, will not listen and change their beliefs and behavior to align with what is true and loving, then we must do what we can to advocate for and protect the vulnerable. For further reading on the topic of abuse in the church, I highly recommend Diane Langberg's book, *Redeeming Power: Understanding Authority and Abuse in the Church*.

---

35. *The Lord of the Rings: The Two Towers*

CHAPTER 7

A Present Helper When Afraid

Rahab

"Ignorance is the parent of fear."[1]—Herman Melville

"O, what ridiculous resolutions men take when possessed with fear! It deprives them of the use of those means which reason offers for their relief.... Thus fear of danger is ten thousand times more terrifying than danger itself . . . and we find the burden of anxiety greater, by much, than the evil which we are anxious about."[2]—Daniel Defoe

Awareness of fear

To be afraid is part of being human. Fear in certain situations serves us well when it alerts us concerning potential dangers. So, we take certain wise precautions when we hear a tornado warning. We forbid our young children to walk out into the street; click our seatbelts; follow hurricane evacuation orders; and wear masks in public during a pandemic. Yet there is also the kind of fear that can unnecessarily paralyze us from taking a good and right course of action. How much does fear play into our daily decision-making? Are we shackled to fear?

Full of fear

We are afraid of getting hurt. Perhaps you can remember the first time you tried something new like riding a bike or doing a flip off a diving board.

1. Melville, *Moby-Dick*, 41.
2. Defoe, *Robinson Crusoe*, 111.

After failing and succeeding a few times, we gained confidence and grew from our experiences. Every summer growing up, our family usually went to Seagrove Beach, near Panama City Beach, Florida. My father would take me and my brothers to a bay or inlet to catch blue crabs. The first time we went, I was afraid of getting pinched by the crabs. But my dad helped me overcome my fear by wading through the water right beside me holding one hand, while I held a net in the other.

People are afraid of rejection. I had a crush on a girl in the fifth grade. Phones back then had rotary dials. I had paged through the thick printed phonebook and found her family's number. Slowly, I dialed the first six numbers, and then with my heart pounding out of my chest—I hung up. I repeated that sequence several times before finally dialing the entire number.

Hello? she answered.

I like you, is all I can remember saying. Silence. Then, *Well, do you like me?* She muttered something like, *I guess so,* and then I immediately hung up. I don't think I ever talked to her again. In all seriousness, haven't each of us experienced the deep heartache of rejection?

People are afraid of failure and feeling shame. It was varsity high school basketball game night during my senior year. It was our toughest home game of the season. During pre-game warm-ups, the coach approached me with a reassuring look. *Take the shot. Just shoot the ball,* he said. He had observed how my insecurities had frozen me before. And he was probably right. Football season had preceded basketball season—and two plays proved my coach's hunch. They happened during another home game during senior year. In the first play, our quarterback threw me a deep pass that I somehow caught guarded between two defenders. In the other play, I was unguarded on the field when my teammate threw me a perfect pass. Not only was I wide open, but also *no defenders* stood between me and the goal line. However, right before I hugged the ball to my chest, I turned my head to run and dropped an easy catch—on *our side* of the field, right in front of *our coaches* and *entire sideline.* I felt shame. My mother captured pictures of both plays. Guess which one I remember most? Like many athletes, my insecurities at times got the best of me in live competition. So, my basketball coach was wise; I needed to hear his affirming words. I also needed the implied message he was communicating—*I am with you! I believe in you. I have confidence in you. You can do this. I'm rooting for you!* Regrettably, I occasionally ignored his advice. But on that day, I scored more points than I had in any other.

People are afraid of loss. We lock our house and car doors. We have security passwords for various online accounts. We fear losing our jobs, or income-making ability. Such fear leads us to live under constant stress and anxiety to meet our ongoing work-related demands and expectations. We fear losing our reputation. We naturally seek to protect what we value.

People are afraid of losing power or influence. Rather than doing what is best or right, people who succumb to this fear can end up making decisions in light of what they perceive to be their own best interest. It occurs in politics, businesses, families, and organizations of all types. Our fear of what we might lose signals its value to us; thus, paying greater attention to our fears can help us to name our idols. It was Herman Melville who wrote, "Ignorance is the parent of fear."[3] It could also be said idolatry is another parent of fear.

> "One of the signs that an object is functioning as an idol is that fear becomes one of the chief characteristics of life. When we center our lives on the idol, we become dependent on it. If our counterfeit god is threatened in any way, our response is complete panic. . . . This may be a reason why so many people now respond to U.S. political trends in such an extreme way. When either party wins an election, a certain percentage of the losing side talks openly about leaving the country. They become agitated and fearful for the future. They have put the kind of hope in their political leaders and policies that once was reserved for God. . . . They believe that if *their* policies and people are not in power, everything will fall apart."[4]

People are afraid of losing their institutions, systems, or missions. Recall what I discussed earlier about how people are prone to protect their institutions over victims.

People are afraid of losing their privilege, control, or wealth. Kings and queens take painstaking efforts to fortify the moat around their castles, so to speak, with elaborate investment, insurance, retirement, tax, and estate planning. They do their part to finance and elect policymakers who will protect their interests.

People are afraid of losing relationships. So, they may say, do, or go along with something they don't feel good about in order to preserve a relationship. We will often not make decisions based on what is best or right if we are more driven by pleasing people.

People are afraid of their past. We come up with excuses why we will not do something. Perhaps we've made too many mistakes or lack enough education or experience. For the longest time, I did not take action to get this book published because I had never written a book before. Perhaps

3. Melville, *Moby Dick*, 41.
4. Keller, *Counterfeit Gods*, 98–99.

you are reluctant to think seriously about marriage because your parents divorced. Maybe you are afraid to seek out that new job opportunity because you were fired by a previous employer or lack the background or qualifications. Perhaps you are reluctant to venture into a new relationship because you were so hurt in a previous one. Maybe you do not want to risk again because you've failed before.

People are afraid of an uncertain future. Anyone going through a significant transition understands this fear all too well: students graduating college; persons losing their job or going through a divorce. Some may even describe the experience like jumping off a cliff. The pain of stepping out into no-man's land can be terrifying. At a much greater scale, imagine children separated from their parents at the border because of immigration policies who now cannot find their parents. The pandemic has caused millions to fear what lies ahead.

People are afraid of growing old, deteriorating health, suffering from illness, and dying. A vivid memory of my last interaction with my paternal grandmother remains locked in a special room in my mind that I open every once in a while. I went to see her a few days before she died in January of 1991. She was bedridden from failing health conditions. Towards the end of our visit, I leaned over to kiss her on the forehead. She grabbed my hand, held as tightly as she could, and would not let go. Her eyes opened wide and locked deeply into mine for what must have been a half minute. She knew this was her last moment to see me. Many of you are suffering from cancer, heart disease, arthritis, high blood pressure, Parkinson's disease, macular degeneration, dementia, multiple sclerosis, kidney disease, or some other illness. Dealing with hospitals, memory care centers, nursing homes, medical bills, prescription drugs, and insurance are some of the realities that accompany such conditions. Others of you are providing care for a loved one who is ill. No wonder we fear such things.

Let's face it. On a day-to-day basis, courage is required of us. For many, it takes courage simply to get out of bed in the morning and face the day. "The opposite of courage isn't only fear but security."[5] In reflecting on a sermon about Jesus telling a rich young ruler to sell his possessions and follow him (Mark 10:21), author Sue Monk Kidd wrote this challenging word: "Total security eliminates all risk. And where there's no risk, there's no becoming; and where there's no becoming, there's no life."[6] Fear cannot stop us from dying one day, but it can stop us from living. So, again, how

5. Kidd, *When the Heart Waits*, 108.
6. Kidd, *When the Heart Waits*, 109.

much does fear drive our decision-making? Let's consider if this university professor is correct in saying:

> "We are a people obsessed with security. Our imagination of what counts as a threat to our security is hyperactive and becoming more so all the time. . . . We have become a nation and a people that simply cannot abide risks. . . . America is now devoted to the protocols and the apparatus of security. We strip down at the airport; we worry about identity theft; we fret about having our passwords stolen. Every door we approach is a locked door. Every entry requires that we be checked and vetted. The metal detectors are everywhere; the man always wants to see your identification. . . . The cameras are on at the public event and the subway."[7]

Edwin Friedman, an ordained rabbi, family therapist, and leadership consultant, shared his belief that the chronic anxiety which exists in "contemporary American civilization influences our thoughts and our leaders toward safety and certainty rather than toward boldness and adventure."[8] He wrote, "American civilization's emotional regression has perverted the elan of risk-taking discovery and pioneering that originally led to the foundations of our nation. As a result, its fundamental character has instead been shaped into an illusive and often compulsive search for safety and certainty. . . . The anxiety is so deep within the emotional processes of our nation that it is almost as though a neurosis has become nationalized. . . . [This] has lowered people's pain thresholds, with the result that comfort is valued over the rewards of facing challenge."[9] Friedman referenced *The Nuremberg Chronicle*, written in 1493, which described Europe as depressed, a civilization with little vision or hope "in the wake of the plagues, the breakdown of the feudal order,"[10] and a corrupt church. Its scientists had not made a major scientific discovery for a thousand years. Then, suddenly, Europe's cheeks began to flush once more with oxygen, signs of life. The depression lifted, ushering in the Renaissance as "over the next half-century, more radical change occurred in every field of human endeavor than had ever happened before."[11]

Friedman argued that the Age of Discovery, championed by navigators and explorers into unknown lands sparked a chain reaction of

7. Edmundson, "One Nation Under Fear," lines 21–22, 33, 55–62.
8. Friedman, *A Failure of Nerve*, 37.
9. Friedman, *A Failure of Nerve*, 59.
10. Friedman, *Failure of Nerve*, 33.
11. Friedman, *Failure of Nerve*, 34.

imaginative breakthroughs during that time. "Europe's imaginative capacity was unleashed not by the discovery of learning . . . but by the discovery of the New World."[12] Furthermore, "Whether we are considering a toothache, a tumor, a relational bind, a technical problem, crime, or the economy, most individuals and most social systems, irrespective of their culture, gender, or ethnic background, will 'naturally' choose or revert to chronic conditions of bearable pain rather than face the temporarily more intense anguish of acute conditions that are the gateway to becoming free."[13] Marilynne Robinson, in an article entitled, *Fear*, stated a compelling thesis in two parts: "First, contemporary America is full of fear. And second, fear is not a Christian habit of mind."[14]

Courage of Rahab, the prostitute

According to several sources, Rahab, the mother of Boaz, was a person who fascinated the Jews, and was "lauded as the archetypical proselyte."[15] In other words, here was a non-Israelite, who converted and became a hero to be emulated. The Jews hearing Matthew's gospel would have been familiar with the story of Israel's deliverance out of Egypt, and forty-year wilderness wanderings. Moses had transferred the leadership baton to Joshua. This period marked a major milestone for Israel as a new generation following those delivered out of Egypt. In Joshua 5:9, God said to Joshua, "Today I have rolled away the reproach of Egypt from you." Although the Israelites had struggled with fear throughout their difficult journey out of Egypt, God repeatedly had demonstrated his steadfast love and faithfulness to be their God, to be present among them, and to fulfill his promises to them.

The Israelites now beheld the promised land. But a monumental risk lay before them in crossing the Jordan River. God had a pre-Jordan crossing talk with Joshua: "Moses my servant is dead. Now then, you and all these people, get ready to cross the Jordan River into the land I am about to give to them—to the Israelites. I will give you every place where you set your foot, as I promised Moses" (Josh 1:2–3). Then in verse five he reassures Joshua that he will be with him as he was with Moses and gives Joshua his own commissioning: "Be strong and courageous. Do not be afraid, do not be discouraged, for the LORD your God will be with you wherever you go" (v. 9). Would Joshua believe God? Would the Israelites? I would like to think

12. Friedman, *Failure of Nerve*, 36.
13. Friedman, *Failure of Nerve*, 67.
14. Robinson, "Fear," lines 18–19.
15. Davids, *The Epistle of James*, 132.

if God told me to do something and added such a pep talk that I would be filled with such courage and belief that nothing could stop me! Yet so often, are we not prone to be just like the Israelites? Despite experiencing God's sustaining presence—and despite his exhortations to fear not—the Israelites remained shackled to fear.

Before them was Jericho, a formidable and fortified city. Encamped across the Jordan River, Joshua secretly dispatched two spies to survey the land, especially the city. When they arrived, they "entered the house of a prostitute named Rahab and stayed there" (Josh 2:1). Rahab's name is accompanied consistently by the descriptor, "the prostitute." Even in Joshua chapter 6, when Israel surrounds Jericho's walls, Joshua refers to her as "Rahab the prostitute" (v. 22). The writer of this story clearly wanted this fact emphasized. Think about it. Wherever Rahab walked around Jericho, she probably heard a lot of whispers about who she was and what she did for a living. I think it's interesting to note that the name Rahab was also an Old Testament "poetic name for a powerful enemy of Yahweh. . . . In three passages (Ps. 87:4; Isa. 30:7; 51:9) Rahab refers to Egypt, one of Israel's traditional enemies."[16] A prostitute with a name that represents an enemy of God finds herself in this story of redemption! Tucked away here are significant clues, I believe, about the extravagant, scandalous love of God.

What must Rahab's life been like before she met Joshua's spies? The Bible does not explicitly tell us. We know that she traded sex for money, but did she do so of her own volition, or as a slave handing over profits to her owner? Baby girls whose parents deserted them to die "were frequently picked up and raised for the purpose of prostitution."[17] Free women, however, sometimes chose the profession as a means to grow rich, and they often lived together in houses, or brothels. Rahab lived in a house that was built into one of the outer walls of the greatly fortified city which seems to indicate she was not a slave.

Rahab not only showed charitable hospitality to the spies, but she also protected them when the king of Jericho demanded she hand them over. She hid the spies on her rooftop while sending a group of soldiers out on a wild-goose chase, and helped the spies to escape without detection. Before they left, she delivered a powerful testimony, saying: "I know that the LORD has given you this land and that a great fear of you has fallen on us, so that all who live in this country are melting in fear because of you. We have heard how the LORD dried up the water of the Red Sea for you when you came out of Egypt, and what you did to Sihon and Og, the two kings of the

16. Bromiley, *The International Standard Bible Encyclopedia*, 4:34.

17. Bromily, *The International Standard Bible Encyclopedia*, 2:616–17.

Amorites east of the Jordan, whom you completely destroyed. When we heard of it, our hearts melted in fear and everyone's courage failed because of you, for the LORD your God is God in heaven above and on the earth below" (Josh 2:9). Isn't this all so ironic? The opening chapter of Joshua documents God's exhortation to him and the Israelites to be strong and courageous, to remain devoted to him, and to be confident in his presence with them and his power to support them. Then immediately in chapter 2, a non-Israelite prostitute is the one who demonstrates the kind of faith God is desiring of the Israelites. The people with whom God had demonstrated his presence and power directly, fixated on the challenges ahead of them and all that could potentially go wrong instead of on God himself. Rahab dwelt in a house within an exterior city wall. The most important and safest homes would have been located toward the city center. If an enemy invaded, Rahab's home, along with others located within the perimeter wall, would have suffered first attack. She acknowledged her city's vulnerability to possible destruction yet fixated on the power of Israel's God. Though not an Israelite herself, Rahab somehow knew of *Yahweh* and believed that she must align herself with him even if she feared those who held power in Jericho. She risked her life to welcome and protect the spies. She did not wait for guidance or approval from family or fellow citizens. She did not request permission from institutions or authorities. What she knew of Israel's God drove her decisions and compelled her actions in this moment.

After demonstrating courage in protecting them, she makes a request of the spies: "Now then, please swear to me by the LORD that you will show kindness to my family, . . . that you will save us from death" (vv. 12–13). They agreed, telling her to mark her house with a scarlet cord, which they had used to escape from her window and down the side of the wall. As promised, God spared Rahab and her family.

In addition to her place in the genealogy, Rahab is referenced in the book of James, which states, "In the same way, was not even Rahab the prostitute considered righteous for what she did when she gave lodging to the spies and sent them off in a different direction?" (2:25). Her briefly recounted story is put there right beside Abraham's. We also read about her in the book of Hebrews, which says, "By faith the prostitute Rahab, because she welcomed the spies, was not killed with those who were disobedient" (11:31).

The Good Shepherd

When struggling with fears of all kinds, we can tend to fixate more on what we fear, rather than on God and who he is. First John 4:18 says, "There is no fear in love. But perfect love drives out fear." How does God love us? Let's consider the imagery from perhaps the most recognizable Psalm—Psalm 23:1–4: "The LORD is my shepherd, I lack nothing. He makes me lie down in green pastures, he leads me beside quiet waters, he refreshes my soul. He guides me along the right paths for his name's sake. Even though I walk through the darkest valley, I will fear no evil, for you are with me; your rod and your staff, they comfort me." Of all the fears we have examined, each of us shares the certainty of walking through the valley of the shadow of death at some point. God's love is demonstrated to us through his presence with us. Scholars have observed that perhaps the most repeated biblical command or exhortation is, "Do not be afraid." God understands that we *will be* afraid. In his compassion, he never tires to whisper perhaps his most repeated promise: *I am with you; I will never leave or forsake you.*

Jesus said, "I am the good shepherd. The good shepherd lays down his life for the sheep" (John 10:11). Good shepherds deeply care about the welfare of their sheep. Philip Keller, a career shepherd himself, talked about his first venture paying for his own flock with cash during what he called the "grinding years" of the Great Depression: "Sheep do not just take care of themselves," he wrote. "They require, more than any other class of live-stock, endless attention and meticulous care"[18] Good shepherds, Keller says, delight in their flocks, know what is best for them, and give all they have for their benefit. Sheep are "so timid and easily panicked that even a stray jackrabbit suddenly bounding from behind a bush can stampede a whole flock. When one startled sheep runs in fright a dozen others will bolt with it in blind fear, not waiting to see what frightened them. . . . As long as there is even the slightest suspicion of danger . . . the sheep stand up ready to flee for their lives. They have little or no means of self-defense. They are helpless, timid, feeble creatures whose only recourse is to run."[19] But Keller discovered "that nothing so quieted and reassured the sheep as to see me in the field. The presence of their master . . . put them at ease as nothing else could do."[20] This is especially true when having to guide a flock through a dark valley where they are vulnerable to predators, sudden storms, rockslides, or other disasters. The good shepherd always carries a rod, an instrument of protection, to safeguard the sheep. A good shepherd also carries a staff, an instrument used to draw the sheep together, to catch wandering sheep, to rescue sheep from walking off a cliff or getting stuck in some situation from which they cannot extricate themselves. A good shepherd also can use a staff to guide the sheep along an unfamiliar path or perilous route.

18. Keller, *A Shepherd Looks at Psalm 23*, 20–21.

19. Keller, *A Shepherd Looks at Psalm 23*, 36.

20. Keller, *A Shepherd Looks at Psalm 23*, 37.

Never, never, never forsaken

This last point of a shepherd guiding sheep with his staff—along unfamiliar paths and perilous routes—segues nicely to our next topic of taking risks. Rahab modeled for us how to take risks when we trust God is leading the way. She had faith that God was leading and was present with Israel. Eugene Peterson, who gifted the world with *The Message*, a paraphrased translation of Scripture, said in an interview, "The assumption of spirituality is that *always* God is doing something before I know it. So the task is not to get God to do something I think needs to be done, but to become aware of what God is doing so that I can respond to it and participate and take delight in it."[21]

I cannot say what the particulars are in your situation regarding what God is doing in which you might participate. But I can say that whatever it is, you will require courage. God's mission may be something as simple as introducing yourself to your neighbor or demonstrating kindness to a stranger. It may be something which requires a level of discomfort or sacrifice on your part like donating blood, volunteering at a homeless shelter, standing in solidarity with the vulnerable at a peaceful protest, supporting a friend or family member going through a difficult situation, working through a conflict, or employing your gifts and skills in service to your community. It may be complex and even dangerous like the time Rosa Parks sat in a certain seat on a bus or when Harriet Tubman escaped slavery, then returned multiple times to the South to rescue dozens of other slaves, including family and friends. You may get involved in addressing an injustice or advocating for the needy and vulnerable. Tough love is hard and messy. Count on resistance and backlash. Abiding in the love of God in such struggle will be critical in maintaining a tender and compassionate heart. Perhaps you sense an internal tug to do something. I sensed such a tug to write this book. The Good Shepherd has guided me on this unfamiliar path despite my fear. He has been connecting my life's many stepping stones, including an undergraduate degree in English, seminary studies, personal losses, books I've read, people I've known, difficult events I've experienced, and this book's themes in which I have been interested. And just like Rahab and the Israelites, I have a choice about what to do with all my fears—of inadequate writing, rejection, criticism, and failure. I could come up with all kinds of excuses. Can't we all? Now what about you? What will you do with your fear when you know who is leading the way?

Earlier I said that I would like to think if God told me to do something, and said, *Be strong and courageous, do not be afraid, for I am with you wherever you go,* that I would be filled with so much courage and belief that nothing could stop me. Well, he *has* told us this: "Keep your lives free from

---

21. Clapp, "Eugene Peterson: A Monk Out of Habit," 25.

the love of money and be content with what you have, because God has said, 'Never will I leave you; never will I forsake you.' So, we say with confidence, 'The Lord is my helper; I will not be afraid. What can mere mortals do to me?'" (Heb 13:5–6). God's powerful promises carry through in the English version; however, the wording understates the force of the original Greek. The Greek language, from which the English version is translated, uses a double negative. If translated literally into English, the text would read something more like, *Never not will I leave you; never not will I forsake you*. It sounds awkward to our ears. Bear with me here as I get grammatically technical for a few seconds. When two negatives are together in English, they tend to make a positive meaning. The combination of "never not" with "will I leave," or "will I forsake"—which are both written in the aorist verb tense and subjunctive mood—is referred to as an "emphatic negation." "This is the strongest way to negate something in Greek."[22] This type of negation is emphatic and denies something will occur in the strongest language possible. *Never-not* "rules out even the idea as being a possibility."[23] God is promising us in the strongest language possible that he will never, never, never, no, not ever depart from, desert, abandon, leave, or forsake us. Doing so is not even or ever could be a possibility. His presence will never, never, never fail. Then, continuing in verse 6, "So we say with confidence, "The Lord is my helper, I will not be afraid." With such an unbelievably forceful, emphatic negation, we can say with utmost assurance and deep-rooted conviction that the "Lord is my helper" (Heb 13:6). A helper is our protector, defender, or ally, bolstering us with provision and encouragement in times of hardship and distress.[24] This being the case, we can also say with confidence and deep conviction that we will not fear (when we are indeed afraid).

Are we seeking awareness of what already God is doing so that we can respond and participate in it? God would have us play a role in his redemption story—doing justice, loving mercy, and walking humbly with him (Mic 6:8). We can be assured that we will incur risk as we try to apply this in our families, among our friends, with strangers, at our workplaces, churches, and in our communities. C.S. Lewis offered this profound challenge:

> There is no safe investment. To love at all is to be vulnerable. Love anything, and your heart will certainly be wrung and possibly broken. If you want to make sure of keeping it intact, you must give your heart to no one, not even to an animal. Wrap it carefully round with hobbies and little luxuries; avoid all entanglements; lock it up safe in the casket or coffin of your selfishness. But in that casket—safe, dark, motionless, airless—it

22. Wallace, *Greek Grammar*, 468.
23. Wallace, *Greek Grammar*, 468.
24. Bromily, *The International Bible Encyclopedia*, 2:682.

will change. It will not be broken; it will become unbreakable, impenetrable, irredeemable. The alternative to tragedy, or at least to the risk of tragedy, is damnation. The only place outside Heaven where you can be perfectly safe from all the dangers and perturbations of love is Hell.[25]

A portion of Isaiah 43:1–3 (MSG) says, "Don't be afraid, I've redeemed you. I've called your name. You're mine. When you're in over your head, I'll be there with you. When you're in rough waters, you will not go down. When you're between a rock and a hard place, it won't be a dead end—Because I am God, your personal God, The Holy of Israel, your Savior." I want to remind you of something I wrote in the introduction. Seeds of redemption lie buried in the ground of our fear because that *moment* is pregnant with possibility. This is so because God is ever present and ever at work. Rahab in her moment determined to pledge her allegiance to God and who she knew him to be. Little did she know in that moment God would be including her in his unfolding story of redemption through a savior who would eventually come from her lineage. May God continually fill our hearts with his love and drive out fear so that we will have the courage to take the shot, risk, and love boldly! When journeying *through* the valley of the shadow of death, it is human nature to be afraid. Remember especially during those dark shadowlands, the Lord is our constant helper whose presence will never, never, never fail.

> "My Lord God, I have no idea where I am going. I do not see the road ahead of me. I cannot know for certain where it will end. Nor do I really know myself, and the fact that I think I am following your will does not mean that I am actually doing so. But I believe that the desire to please you does in fact please you. And I hope I have that desire in all that I am doing. I hope that I will never do anything apart from that desire. And I know that if I do this you will lead me by the right road, though I may know nothing about it. Therefore, will I trust you always though I may seem lost and in the shadow of death. I will not fear, for you are ever with me, and you will never leave me to face my perils alone.[26]

---

25. Lewis, *The Four Loves*, 121.
26. Merton, *Thoughts in Solitude*, 83.

CHAPTER 8

Healing When Grieving Loss

"Jesus wept."—John 11:35

". . . when pain is to be borne, a little courage helps more than much knowledge, a little human sympathy more than much courage, and the least tincture of the love of God more than all."[1]—C.S. Lewis

I was the first one to walk out the front door to go to school that morning. In my early days of elementary school, my community had no laws requiring dogs to be gated or leashed. Poco, our dalmatian, was lying on the ground just beyond the front porch. I called to her, but she didn't respond. I leaned down to pet her. It was not cold outside, so I asked my mom—who had just come out of the house—*Why is Poco frozen?* It was the first experience with grief I remember. Losing a pet as an adult does not get any easier. A few years ago, I wept while loving on our old dog, Buddy, as he was being put down.

Reflection on grief

We all experience grief multiple times during our lives. Grieving loss takes place in many ways for many reasons. We could lose a pet, move to a new town, change schools, forfeit the big game, flunk a test, get cut from the team, or lose a job. We could grieve because a chapter in our lives has ended. A child may go off to college or a romantic relationship may crumble. Perhaps we may grieve the lingering pain of past mistakes or missed opportunities.

---

1. Lewis, *The Problem of Pain*, XII.

Every loss—from infertility and financial ruin to addictions and chronic illness—can feel like a small death.

I wrote most of this book while I was married. Jorja and I journeyed together through so much since college. Although I describe a few challenges we've faced, I left out other important stories. We were already separated when I began rewriting and editing this book. Our divorce was finalized before I submitted a final manuscript to the publisher. Although our divorce was amicable and we maintain a good friendship, mutual respect, and genuine hope for the best for each other, a divorce is nevertheless a painful event to endure. I understand what it means to walk through a grieving process of initially feeling panicked, confused, and powerless; then going into a state of denial; then weeping over what once was and would now be no longer; then accepting the loss, letting go, and moving on with life.

Grief is intense emotional suffering. When grieving a significant loss, we may exhibit or experience one or more of the following in no certain order: shock, denial, numbness, distress, panic, exhaustion, anger, loss of appetite, despair, confusion, forgetfulness, loneliness, sleeplessness, and/or powerlessness. We might plead with God, feel disoriented, be utterly brokenhearted, struggle to carry on, desperately miss the one who is gone and/or the reality that once was. We might impulsively scream or at times feel like we are drowning in an ocean of sorrow. No one wants to go through this, yet we cannot tell grief what to do. For it comes with every ending. A widower once told me he was amazed at how utterly depressed he constantly felt months after his wife's death. "Grief is a process that takes time and helps us mend after a loss. It is painful and we want to avoid it, but if we do so, we get stuck and healthy mending will never occur."[2] So it is best to reach a point of admitting and accepting the loss—which in itself could take a long time. Once we have done that, we can then experience and express all the range of emotions and thoughts we feel, finally finding a way, little by little, to let go.[3] If you think about it, grief is an amazing manifestation of love. Grief reveals the preciousness of life itself. Grief screams, *This is not right!* Death, suffering, pain, sorrow, and loss should not be; they were not part of God's original design.

Painful journey of loss

If you are one who has lost something or someone important in your life and cannot bear to read this chapter right now, I understand. It very well may

2. Langberg, *Suffering and the Heart of God*, 176.
3. Langberg, *Suffering and the Heart of God*, 183–84.

be the case that some people in the midst of grieving at this moment are not
going to find any comfort in this story or other verses I will share later in
the chapter. And that is perfectly okay. Some grief will take a very long time
to heal. There are no set rules or boundaries for what you are supposed to
feel or for how long it should take. Every person is different. I am so sorry
for your loss and ongoing pain. I will not pretend that anything written here
will suddenly heal your wounds. "Frequently in the midst of suffering the
most comforting 'answers' are simple presence, help, silence, tears. Helping
with gardening or preparing a casserole may be far more spiritual an exercise than the exposition of Romans 8:28. The Scriptures themselves exhort
us to 'mourn with those who mourn.' (Rom. 12:15)."[4]

The story told in the book unfolds during Israel's history of the Judges.
Israel had conquered the inhabitants of Canaan and settled the land under
Joshua's leadership. But the coming of the prophet Samuel and Saul, the nation's first king, loomed on the horizon. "In those days Israel had no king;
everyone did as they saw fit" (Judg 21:25). Some of what the Israelites were
seeing fit to do was abuse their power, engage in sexual misconduct and
abuse, and worship idols. Israel's departure from her covenant relationship with *Yahweh* spiraled into systemic lawlessness, spreading at epidemic
proportions. The people of God boomeranged to evil and embraced Canaanite gods, which always lead them into ruin. Yet God mercifully raised
up judges to deliver them from their oppressors. Even the great judges,
however, listed in Hebrews chapter 11—Samson, Jephthah, and Gideon—
turned away from God in different ways.

At some point during this period, the book of Ruth documents a famine in Judah, which caused a man named Elimelech, his wife, Naomi, and
their two sons to leave their home of Bethlehem for Moab, an enemy of
Israel. A famine would be reason enough to grieve. The food scarcity in
Judah was so widespread that the family had to take the desperate measure
of leaving their home, their family members, their friends, and everything
else familiar to them to settle in a new, unfamiliar place among unfamiliar
people. The text does not say how many Israelites died or to what degree
they suffered during that famine.

During the twentieth century, "an estimated 70 million people died
from famines around the world."[5] Unless one has truly experienced hunger to this degree, it would be impossible to relate to such desperation. By
the middle of October in 2015, more than four million people had been
displaced from Syria because of ongoing civil war. The global conscience

---

4. Carson, *How Long O Lord?*, 249.

5. "Famine," *Wikipedia*, line 60. http://en.wikipedia.org/wiki/Famine

seemed especially awakened to the crisis as refugees took desperate measures in fleeing to Europe by crossing the choppy Mediterranean Sea in makeshift crafts. Famished and exhausted from the dangerous journey, and cold from the winds and waters, the surviving men and women, children and babies—wearing all they owned—climbed onto foreign soil not knowing what tomorrow would bring. Perhaps such a contemporary example can help us visualize the hardship facing Naomi and her family as famine twisted their bellies and forced their hand.

After remaining in Moab for a period, Naomi's husband, Elimelech, tragically died. We are not told why or how. Now a widow living outside her homeland with no parents, siblings, or other family members for support, Naomi was left alone in the world to care for her two sons. The text does not tell us how old she or her sons were at the time of Elimelech's death. At some point later, Naomi's two sons married Moabite women—Orpah and Ruth. Then later, more tragedy struck. After a decade of riding out the famine in Moab, Naomi's sons also both died (Ruth 1:4–5)—and, apparently, without having had any children of their own. In that culture men provided the support and stability for family life. To be widowed and childless plunged Naomi, along with her daughters-in-law, into an unstable and uncertain position. The text states these facts in quick summary fashion. But just imagine what you would have felt like as a vulnerable and impoverished widow who had not only lost her spouse, but also her sons and homeland.

Jerry Sittser wrote a book in 1995 called, *A Grace Disguised*, in which he shared his own journey through grief as well as his perspective on how the soul can grow through loss. In 1991, while beginning to drive home from a daylong trip, the Sittser's van was struck head-on when a drunk driver going eighty-five miles per hour jumped its lane. Jerry's wife of almost twenty years, his mother, and four-year-old daughter were killed. He lost three generations of his family—gone in an instant. He and his other three children somehow survived.

> "The initial shock gave way to an unspeakable agony. I felt dizzy with grief's vertigo . . . tormented by the loss, nauseous from the pain. . . . I was so bewildered that I was unable to voice questions or think rationally. I could not stop crying. . . . That initial deluge of loss slowly gave way . . . to the steady seepage of pain that comes when grief, like floodwaters refusing to subside, finds every crack and crevice of the human spirit to enter and erode. I thought that I was going to lose my mind. . . . The foundation of my life was close to caving in. . . . Tears came for forty days, and then they stopped. . . . It was only after those forty days that my mourning became too deep for tears. So, my tears turned to

brine, to a bitter and burning sensation of loss that tears could no longer express. . . . Of course, I had no way of anticipating the adjustments I would have to make and the suffering I would have to endure in the months and years ahead.[6]

When Naomi did return to Bethlehem, she declared herself to be afflicted of God, and urged those who knew her to no longer call her Naomi, which means *pleasant*, but rather, *Mara*, which means *bitter*. Her soul had been radically scarred. "'Don't call me Naomi,' she told them. 'Call me Mara, because the Almighty has made my life very bitter. I went away full, but the LORD has brought me back empty. Why call me Naomi? The LORD has afflicted me; the Almighty has brought misfortune upon me'" (Ruth 1:20–21). It is not uncommon for people grieving to experience intense anger. It is normal for people to feel forsaken and betrayed by God, descend into a state of hopelessness, and feel like any future is over.

C.S. Lewis wrote *A Grief Observed* as he sought to face the most shattering grief of his own life, the death of his wife, Helen Joy Gresham, whom he refers to as "H." in the book:

> "When you are happy, . . . if you remember yourself and turn to him with gratitude and praise, you will be—or so it feels— welcomed with open arms. But go to him when your need is desperate, when all other help is vain, and what do you find? A door slammed in your face, and a sound of bolting and double bolting on the inside. After that, silence. . . . The longer you wait, the more emphatic the silence will become. There are no lights in the windows. It might be an empty house. . . . Why is He so present a commander in our time of prosperity and so very absent a help in time of trouble? . . . Not that I am (I think) in much danger of ceasing to believe in God. The real danger is of coming to believe such dreadful things about Him. The conclusion I dread is not 'So there's no God after all,' but 'So this is what God's really like.'"[7]

Yet along the way, grieving people come to the realization they are still alive. Either the struggle will begin to bury them slowly, or they must learn to adapt to a new normal. Part of the healing process upon letting go is discovering a way to move forward, a way to put energies into new relationships and possibilities. At some point following her sons' deaths, Naomi learned that the famine in Judah was over, and she decided to return to Bethlehem. The first chapter of Ruth allows the reader to glimpse the bond

6. Sittser, *A Grace Disguised*, 18–20.

7. Lewis. *A Grief Observed*, 6–7.

she shared with her daughters-in-law. How hard she must have wrestled the strength of those bonds as she tried to say goodbye to them for good. Her history was over; no one was left to carry on the family name. She embraced, kissed, and wept with her daughters-in-law. Orpah departed to rejoin her family in Moab, but Ruth courageously accompanied her mother-in-law back to Bethlehem. At a time of tremendous personal grief, an uncertain future, and when Israel had spiraled into apostasy, Ruth demonstrated the kind of faith and covenant commitment that the Israelites should have had when she begged Naomi to go with her: "Don't urge me to leave you or to turn back from you. Where you go I will go, and where you stay I will stay. Your people will be my people and your God my God" (Ruth 1:16). Ruth turned away from her home, her religion, her family, her community, and her culture—forsaking her own Moabite heritage—to live as a foreigner in the land of Judah, and to be a part of Naomi's people.

God's mysterious ways

While struggling through poverty back in Judah during harvest time, Ruth, by chance, went to the field of Boaz. Boaz, a relative to her deceased father-in-law, Elimelech, was a resident of Bethlehem and owned fields outside of town. Besides the fact he was related to Elimelech, what more do we know about Boaz? In Jesus's genealogy in Matthew, Boaz is identified as the son of Salmon and Rahab. (We will circle back around to that.) Under Jewish law (Deut 24:19–21), widows, orphans, and strangers were allowed to gather leftovers from fields not belonging to them. When Boaz arrived at his fields and greeted the harvesters, he asked the overseer in charge of the harvesting about Ruth. Pause a moment to read through the second chapter of Ruth to see for yourself how incredibly kind and gracious Boaz was to Ruth in providing her protection as well as generous privileges. Boaz had status; Ruth had the lowliest social station. Boaz was wealthy; Ruth was impoverished. Boaz belonged as a male Israelite with power; Ruth was vulnerable as a female foreigner. Ruth did not manipulate her way to this place in the story. She had no idea on whose field she was. Because of Boaz, Ruth kept working the fields in a privileged status until the end of harvest.

Later on, Naomi, knowing Boaz was a *kinsmen-redeemer*—one who delivers, rescues, or redeems property or a person on behalf of a relative in need—sent Ruth on a mission at night to boldly ask Boaz to marry her (Ruth 3:1–18). I know this sounds strange, but Boaz recognized what was going on. He first allowed a closer relative to Elimelech to have the opportunity to marry Ruth. When that relative declined, though, Boaz chose to become the kinsmen-redeemer—a decision that would require him to purchase Elimelech's property and marry Ruth.

Reading the story, we sense that behind the scenes, an invisible hand was at work. Through the most unlikely woman, Rahab—"the prostitute"— Boaz was born. I bet Ruth never in her wildest dreams as a child growing up in Moab could have imagined that she would one day be gathering leftovers as a destitute widow in a stranger's field . . . and then end up marrying that stranger!

Through the marriage of Boaz and Ruth—a foreigner from Moab, the enemy of Israel—God continued to unfold his redemptive story. For the couple had a son named Obed, who fathered a son named Jesse; who became the father of David; who became the king over all of Israel; through whom arrived the Messiah. Seeds of redemption buried in the sacred ground of grief were growing unseen. Ruth, Naomi, and Boaz had no clue at the time about their participation in the much bigger story that God had been unfolding since his covenant promise to Abraham. God's redemptive mission could not be thwarted by humanity's rebellion against him at Babel; by Abraham and Sarah's infertility or lack of faith; by Isaac's naivete; Jacob's self-serving interests and manipulative scheming; or Judah's culpability in Joseph's enslavement, the abandonment of his own people, and his unjust treatment of Tamar. By weaving Tamar, Rahab, and Ruth into the narrative, we further the thread of God's redemptive efforts to include marginalized people who were considered the least. We also see that God is ever present with us in our grief.

When the marriage of Boaz and Ruth took place, some women who must have been friends to Naomi said to her, "Praise be to the LORD, who this day has not left you without a guardian-redeemer. May he become famous throughout Israel! He will renew your life and sustain you in your old age" (Ruth 4:14–15). Naomi's bitter and sorrowful soul—who once declared her name to be *Bitter*—was restored to a state of peace, hope, and joy. No longer would she be in a state of instability and uncertainty. Boaz and Ruth would nourish, care, and provide for her needs. A beautiful story of love emerged after years of Naomi and Ruth walking through the valley of the shadow of death—and not just any love story.

Little did Naomi or Ruth imagine God would include them in the ancestry of Jesus, who would later come to redeem the world. But first, God would send Ruth a kinsman-redeemer in Boaz, through whose seed and their union came the eternal redeemer. All that belonged to Boaz now legally and fully belonged to Ruth. All that belongs to Jesus Christ, is now ours through our mystical union with him. Ephesians 1:3 says, "Praise be to the God and Father of our Lord Jesus Christ, who has blessed us in the heavenly realms with every spiritual blessing in Christ." Boaz's redemption was to Naomi, a restorer of life and nourisher of her old age. The redemptive grace of God in Christ is restoring and nourishing us, along with this broken world, until one day when he will make all things new (more on this later).

The path of healing

Grieving is normal and should not be considered a rejection of one's faith. In a forward to C.S. Lewis's book, *A Grief Observed*, author Madeleine L'Engle thanked Lewis for offering us permission to grieve and wonder aloud where God is in our loss as though it were normal . . . for it is. "It gives us permission to admit our own doubts, our own angers and anguishes, and to know that they are part of the soul's growth."[8] Do not portions of the Psalms voice such emotions? Psalm 42:9–11 says, "I say to God my Rock, 'Why have you forgotten me? Why must I go about mourning, oppressed by the enemy?' My bones suffer mortal agony as my foes taunt me, saying to me all day long, 'Where is your God?' Why, my soul, are you downcast? Why so disturbed within me? Put your hope in God, for I will yet praise him, my Savior and my God." Psalm 13:1–2 says, "How long, LORD? Will you forget me forever? How long will you hide your face from me? How long must I wrestle with my thoughts and day after day have sorrow in my heart?" As D.A. Carson so rightly said, "The bereaved Christian who suddenly starts lashing out with anger and resentment will not be written off as an apostate. The Christian who at this moment finds little comfort in the doctrine of the resurrection, so great is the sense of loss, is not to be berated and rebuked."[9] For each person, the process and timetable for grief is different. Recalling years of memories can also stir feelings of guilt and regret over missed opportunities or poor decisions. People in a state of grief may withdraw from relationships or activities they once enjoyed. They may experience shock and disbelief. Some even make it more difficult on themselves when they judge their own emotional processing.

God comforts us through his Spirit. Romans 8:16 says, "The Spirit himself testifies with our spirit that we are God's children." When we were hurt as children, to whom did we call out for help? Whenever we are reminded of God as being our good Father who loves us, delights in us, and is ever-present with us, it is the Spirit of God bearing witness with our spirit to affirm that we are his child.

God comforts us through his promises:

8. Lewis, *A Grief Observed*, xiv, xvi.
9. Carson, *How Long O Lord?*, 248.

- *I consider that our present sufferings are not worth comparing with the glory that will be revealed in us* (Rom 8:18).

- *Brothers and sisters, we do not want you to be uninformed about those who sleep in death, so that you do not grieve like the rest of mankind, who have no hope. For we believe that Jesus died and rose again, and so we believe that God will bring with Jesus those who have fallen asleep in him* (1 Thess 4:13–14).

- *I am the resurrection and the life. The one who believes in me will live, even though they die; and whoever lives by believing in me will never die* (John 11:25–26).

- *Do not let your hearts be troubled. You believe in God; believe also in me. My Father's house has many rooms; if that were not so, would I have told you that I am going there to prepare a place for you? And if I go and prepare a place for you, I will come back and take you to be with me that you also may be where I am* (John 14:1–3).

- *And I heard a loud voice from the throne saying, 'Look! God's dwelling place is now among the people, and he will dwell with them. They will be his people, and God himself will be with them and be their God. He will wipe every tear from their eyes. There will be no more death or mourning or crying or pain, for the old order of things has passed away.' He who was seated on the throne said, 'I am making everything new!'* (Rev 21:3–5).

God comforts us through people and the stories of others who have walked through similar suffering. "If God is the God of comfort, he, finally, must provide it—often through human agents, sometimes not, but he must do it."[10] For Naomi, God used Ruth as a human agent in her healing. Naomi had friends at home who cared deeply for her. Then, of course, God used Boaz as a healing agent in her life. Being in community is an essential part of our healing journey. The best comforters are those who are patient, nonjudgmental, refrain from providing pat answers, and who mourn with us throughout all stages of the grieving process. Naomi and Ruth allow us to see the ever-present, ever-redeeming invisible hand of God at work. Their story testifies to God's goodness, and that somehow, his goodness prevails. Again, Jerry Sittser:

> "The passage of time has mitigated the feeling of pain, panic, and chaos. But it has also increased my awareness of how complex and far-reaching the loss has been. . . . I have still not 'recovered.' I still wish my life were different and they were alive. . . . Much

---

10. Carson, *How Long O Lord?*, 252.

good has come from it, but . . . It remains a horrible, tragic, and evil event to me. . . . God is growing my soul. . . . My life is being transformed. Though I have endured pain, I believe that the outcome is going to be wonderful . . . the story God has begun to write he will finish. That story will be good. The accident . . . will remain a very bad chapter. But the whole of my life is becoming what appears to be a very good book.[11]

May God instill within us a steadfast hope in his desire and ability to heal us and weave a glorious story out of our sad chapters.

---

11. Sittser, *A Grace Disguised*, 198–99, 212.

CHAPTER 9

Significance When Feeling Small

Jesse

"They (hobbits) are little people, about half our height, and smaller than the bearded Dwarves . . . There is little or no magic about them, except the ordinary everyday sort which helps them to disappear quietly and quickly."[1] —J.R.R. Tolkien

"We are plain, quiet folk and have no use for adventures."[2] —J.R.R. Tolkien

"Yet it is clear that Hobbits . . . seemed of very little importance. But in the days of Bilbo, and of Frodo, his heir, they suddenly became, by no wish of their own, both important and renowned, and troubled the counsels of the Wise and the Great."[3] —J.R.R. Tolkien

In chapter three, I shared about my daughter, Mari-Helen. I was speaking to a group of college students on the topic of identity when Mari-Helen was about two or three years old. In describing her condition as we understood it at the time, I emphasized she would never be able to read or write sentences or solve a basic math problem, much less achieve academic honors. She would never attend college, compete athletically, play an instrument, have a career, be married, or raise children. Throughout her elementary, junior high, and part of her high school years, Mari-Helen did not have any close friends her age, except her siblings, Drew and Caroline, who always have loved her dearly. This does not mean she did not have friends or that her peers were unfriendly. We still are grateful and blessed for the kindness and

1. Tolkien, *The Hobbit*, 4.
2. Tolkien, *The Hobbit*, 6.
3. Tolkien, *The Fellowship of the Ring*, 2.

attention her neighbors, teachers, babysitters, family, friends, and classmates showed her in many ways. I'm just saying she did not have any particular friends who proactively and consistently invited her to do things and hang out. Such is the reality for so many special-needs kids.

Many high school yearbooks include superlative categories for students, including everything from *Most Likely to Succeed* and *Best Looking*, to *Best Entertainer* and *Most Likely to Be President*. Certain people stood out who would one day matter in the world. Unfortunately, high school can be brutal on those who might fall into the less flattering categories such as *Worst Hair, Most Boring, Least Athletic,* or *Least Likely to Succeed*. I remember days of pick-up basketball games or touch football, dreading occasions for the one chosen last. Some of my peers went unnoticed at best or were bullied at worst. In college, I rushed a fraternity—a process that happens yearly on college campuses across the country. For both fraternities and sororities, rush is a chance for members to handpick young freshmen to join their exclusive group. Each night during rush, members of these organizations hash out which rushees they should mark off the list and which ones they should invite back to the next evening's event.

The Lord of the Rings, written by Oxford scholar, J.R.R. Tolkien during World War II, has captivated and delighted the imaginations of millions of both readers and moviegoers. The central protagonist, Frodo Baggins, is the least likely hobbit hero who—with the help of his courageous friends and fellow travelers—embarks on a dangerous mission to destroy the ring that binds them all: the Dark Lord Sauron's ultimate weapon to conquer Middle-earth. In the prologue, Tolkien described Hobbits as "little people, smaller than Dwarves. . . . Their height is variable, ranging between two and four feet."[4] Who would have ever dreamed that a Hobbit, a little person who loved good food, socializing, and resting in the comfort and security of their cozy underground dwellings in the Shire, would be chosen for such a monumental task?

Runt of the litter

Just as Gandalf tapped Frodo for such a mission, God directed the prophet Samuel to find a successor to Saul, who had been Israel's first king. During this time in history, Israel clashed regularly with the Philistines. We are about to talk about David, and some of us already know the story of David and Goliath, the champion of the Philistine army. Because of their iron monopoly, the Philistines battled with superior weapons, and their troops were

4. Tolkien, *The Fellowship of the Ring*, 1.

also quite cohesive. Israel, on the other hand, had been functioning as a "loosely knit confederacy of tribes that had never needed to unite against a common foe," but now "badly needed a warrior leader who would unite the tribes against their powerful enemy."[5] Though old and no warrior, Samuel was Israel's revered priest-prophet leader. His sons, who he appointed as judges, acted corruptly and were broadly disrespected. The elders of Israel approached Samuel to request the appointment of a king to rule over them as did the surrounding nations. Although God viewed their request as another rejection of him by Israel, he informed Samuel to carry out their wish. Samuel appointed Saul, who is described "as handsome a young man as could be found anywhere in Israel, and he was a head taller than anyone else" (1 Sam 9:2). He was exactly who Israel thought it needed and wanted in a leader. Early on, Saul impressed. But later, Samuel came to regret Saul's leadership bitterly. For though he was indeed a courageous warrior and able to inspire others, Saul grew unfaithful to God, maniacally jealous of David, and irrationally paranoid.

God called Samuel to find Saul's successor not long into his reign and directed Samuel to Jesse—the great-grandson of Rahab and the grandson of Boaz and Ruth. Jesse also was a citizen of Bethlehem, mocked among the clans of Judah as a "runt of the litter" (Mic 5:2, MSG). Every year, Christians celebrate the birth of Jesus by singing the traditional carol, *O Little Town of Bethlehem* (emphasis added). In today's world, power, status, and wealth are concentrated in large cities more so than even the state, region, or country of which they are a part. New York City; Beijing; London; Paris; Washington, D.C.; Moscow; Berlin; Tokyo; and Seoul—are, for example, a few of the cities we might recognize as centers of power and influence. Yet Samuel was dispatched to the "runt of the litter"—the little, insignificant town of Bethlehem.

Jesse was a simple farmer, breeder, and sheep owner. Though likely a prominent resident of Bethlehem, Jesse would not have been a person of wealth or status. Readers get clues to his social capital later in the story when people refer to David only as the "son of Jesse."[6] This phrase "carried ridicule and scorn, as though Jesse were of no account in Hebrew society."[7] It was their way of viewing David as a nobody, even after he had slayed Goliath. For instance, when King Saul's anger was kindled against his son, Jonathan, for befriending David, he threatened Jonathan: "Don't I know that you have sided with the son of Jesse to your own shame and to the shame of the mother

---

5. Bromily, *The International Standard Bible Encyclopedia*, 4:345.

6. See 1 Sam 20:27; 22:7–9; 25:10; 1 Kgs 12:16.

7. Bromily, *The International Standard Bible Encyclopedia*, 2:1033.

who bore you? As long as the son of Jesse lives on this earth, neither you nor your kingdom will be established" (1 Sam 20:30–31).

When Samuel arrived in Bethlehem, he invited the elders of the town, including Jesse and his family, to be consecrated for a sacrifice. Samuel knew he had been sent to find someone who would replace Saul as king. Even though a prophet, Samuel had preconceived notions about what he was looking for. When regarding one of Jesse's sons, Eliab, Samuel assumed he was the LORD's anointed (1 Sam 16:6). Jesse also presumed he knew what Samuel was looking for. "Jesse had seven of his sons pass before Samuel, but Samuel said to him, 'The LORD has not chosen these.' So, he asked Jesse, 'Are these all the sons you have?'" (1 Sam 16:10–11). Jesse had not included his youngest son, David—the one out keeping the sheep—for Samuel to consider. As we discussed in the case of Jacob and Esau—being a firstborn son was of great significance. Jesse never imagined his *youngest* boy could ever be chosen king. So, when Samuel asked him if all his sons were there, Jesse was compelled to admit that one remained, but he immediately pointed out David's liabilities: his youth, and his sheep-herding vocation.

Neither Samuel nor Jesse had seen as only God could the makings of Israel's future king in the youngest son, a shepherd boy. Jesse himself never became a king. He remained a common farm owner, doing normal work for the rest of his days in that little runt of a town, Bethlehem. Yet contrary to the demeaning attitude David's enemies had towards his father's name, the prophets highly honored and esteemed it: "A shoot will come up from the stump of Jesse; from his roots a Branch will bear fruit" (Isa 11:1). In chapter 11 Isaiah goes on to prophesy regarding the coming Messiah: "In that day the Root of Jesse will stand as a banner for the peoples; the nations will rally to him, and his resting place will be glorious" (v. 10).

Before Isaiah foresaw this glorious resting place in chapter 11, he portrayed the destruction of a vast forest at the end of chapter 10, which served as a metaphor for the destruction of human evil. Isaiah was prophesying how bad things were going to get for Israel. Sure enough, as a consequence of their behavior, God eventually judged them through Assyria and Babylon. Even so, while Isaiah saw an almost complete destruction of the forest, symbolic of an almost complete death to the royal line of David, there remained a stump. Early in 2020, two large trees in our yard were cut down completely. All that remains are these two large stumps, no longer displaying life. But in the stump of Jesse, life remained. For a shoot would emerge—and out of this shoot would grow an everlasting and mighty tree. Why did Isaiah not prophesy about the stump of David instead of Jesse, that simple farmer of low social status from an insignificant little runt of a town. I love this picture of a shoot emerging from the stump. "Our salvation comes from something small, tender, and vulnerable, something hardly noticeable. God, who is the Creator of the Universe, comes to us in smallness, weakness, and hiddenness."[8]

Our identity and worth

Very, very few people who are reading this will ever make headline news. I don't care who we are, each of us is ordinary in light of the billions of people in existence, the amount of space we take up relative to the size of the world and universe, and the tiny amount of time we live relative to eternity. Only a handful of people in the future are going to remember our names or care about us after we are gone. In two hundred years, no one will care who we were, except for perhaps some curious family member researching genealogy. I am not trying to be discouraging, but am simply stating what I believe is obvious. Can any of us right at this moment name any of our descendants from two hundred years ago and tell something meaningful about them? We simply go about our daily routines of getting up, going to work, being involved with our kids if we are parents, playing some role in the community, engaging in a hobby and other interests, hanging out with friends, going to bed, and repeating a similar schedule the next day. We carry out mundane tasks like taking out the trash, studying for math, cleaning the house, mowing the lawn, raking leaves, running errands, doing taxes, taking a chemistry test, paying bills, hammering a nail, fixing a machine, trimming hedges, washing dishes, cleaning laundry, putting gas in the car, watching a show, sitting on the back porch, or spending all kinds of time looking at our phones. I will elaborate more in the chapter on Solomon about what then is the meaning of it all, but for now, let's think about this question: what is our worth?

I am not adopted, and I have never adopted a child. But from what I understand, adoption can be an emotionally, financially, physically, and psychologically draining process. Courageous and loving people expend themselves sacrificially to locate, and in many cases, rescue children who have been unwanted, abandoned, neglected, or abused. A price must be paid. Such action is required so the child gains legal status with a new name, and all the rights and privileges of being a part of his or her new family. Then, after the adoption process, the hard work of parenting sets in—for years into the future—guiding and shaping who that child will become. One mother described her experience of adopting her daughter as an intensive battle to gain legal custody. The biological parents were addicted to drugs,

8. Durback, *Seeds of Hope*, 156.

consumed with all sorts of issues, and had no desire or capacity to care for their daughter. The little girl, often unsupervised, was regularly forced to breathe whatever toxins might be airborne from the drug use. I will not describe any further details I remember other than to say it was a very bad situation. The state's Department of Human Resources was of no help. The system was so tied up under bureaucratic regulations that it cowered every time to the biological parents' wishes, which only harmed the child the system was designed to protect. The biological parents eventually split from one another. Compelled by an indescribable love, the adoptive mother fought for a long time and finally obtained legal custody. There was no pro-verbial mountain too high to climb or sea too wide to swim as far as she was concerned in her fight for that girl. Once the adoption was complete, the daughter had a new identity because she legally had a new name and a new family with all the rights and privileges that came with it.

Galatians 4:4–7 says, "But when the time arrived that was set by God, the Father, God sent his Son, born among us of a woman, born under the conditions of the law so that he might redeem those of us who have been kidnapped by the law. Thus we have been set free to experience our rightful heritage. You can tell for sure that you are now fully adopted as his own children because God sent the Spirit of his Son into our lives crying out, 'Papa! Father!' Doesn't that privilege of intimate conversation with God make it plain that you are not a slave, but a child? And if you are a child, you're also an heir, with complete access to the inheritance" (MSG). Instead of "Papa," other biblical translations use the term, "Abba." In the colloquial speech of Jesus's day, "'Abba' was primarily used as a term of informal intimacy and respect by children of their fathers."[9] It would be like my children calling out to me, "Daddy!" or like what we read here, "Papa!" Christ has removed all barriers for relationship with the Father. We've been rescued and adopted as beloved children of the Father. We are in the family of God with all the rights and privileges of being such.

> "The world says, 'Yes, I love you if you are good-looking, in-telligent, and wealthy. I love you if you have a good education, a good job, and good connections. I love you if you produce much, sell much, and buy much.' There are endless 'ifs' hidden in the world's love. These 'ifs' enslave me since it is impossible to respond adequately to all of them. The world's love is and always will be conditional. As long as I keep looking for my true self in the world of conditional love, I will remain 'hooked' to the world—trying, failing, and trying again. It is a world that fosters

9. Bromily, *The International Standard Bible Encyclopedia*, 1:3.

addictions because what it offers cannot satisfy the deepest craving of my heart."[10]

That evening back when I was speaking to those college students about Mari-Helen, I explained that in spite of all those realities of never being able to do or achieve this or that, she would end up being more secure with who she is and experience greater life satisfaction than any of us because she would never look for her true self in the world of conditional love. She would not be tempted to measure her value based on her looks, career, possessions, accomplishments, or the approval of others. She would not ever compare herself to, be envious of, or wish she was another person. And through the years, this has proven to be true. Mari-Helen loves people without expecting reciprocity. The thought never crosses her beautiful mind to feel sorry for herself. She loves to be with people, talking freely with no insecurity or awkwardness.

We will be sitting in the car at a red-light and she will roll down her window and say, "Hey," to anyone on the sidewalk. I will pull into a gas station and she will speak to the closest person pumping gas. In the checkout line of any store . . . same thing. I cannot begin to tell you how many people we have met by way of her introduction. And she does not stop with saying, "Hey." She follows up with multiple questions about their pets, children, work, and home. Her junior high teachers made up a private investigator award just for her at the end of her ninth-grade year because of her relentless quest to learn more about people. I have witnessed her on many occasions end a brief conversation with a perfect stranger by saying, "I love you." She has an amazing memory. If she knows someone who has been injured or sick, she will ask that person about it even two years after the fact. There is not a prejudiced bone in her body. To her, a human being is a human being. She does not care if someone is educated or not; rich or poor; Black or White; powerful or powerless; republican or democrat; gay or straight; religious or irreligious; pro-life or pro-choice; Catholic, Protestant, Muslim, or Jewish; American or foreigner. She does not process whether or not the person with whom she is initiating conversation could do something for her (unless it's the man in the ice-cream truck). She would never be kind to people as a means of manipulating or using them. Besides, if she wants something, she *will* let you know. Family members and close friends can all attest to this. It does not cross her mind to impress anyone. She says what she thinks. Power, money, fame, prestige, and possessions do not impress her. She treats every person she meets with dignity.

10. Nouwen, *Return of the Prodigal*, 42.

When we are secure in our identity as beloved, adopted children of God, we can be free of this notion of being little, insignificant persons. We can also be free of viewing our ordinary, mundane daily lives as insignificant. We are free from having to live up to something. We have nothing more to prove or protect. The question of our significance has been resolved once and for all. The person who is sorting through the mail, selling a product, folding clothes, organizing books on a shelf, crunching numbers, pouring concrete, teaching a spelling class to second-graders, changing a diaper, ringing at the cash register, presenting defense before a jury and judge, researching the tiniest cell or most distant galaxy, composing a piece of music, painting a canvas, assessing an x-ray, filling a prescription, carving wood, posting a blog entry, editing a film, removing debris, kicking a ball, creating a marketing strategy, organizing an event, or repairing a dryer can be doing something completely pleasing and honoring to the Lord. For God has made us each in his own image and given each person unique qualities and gifts to benefit the world. Each of us has a small location to occupy. He has given us a beautiful world indeed to take care of and enjoy in thousands of different ways.

Dallas Willard was a long-time professor of philosophy at the University of California in Los Angeles and is known for his writings on Christian spiritual formation. He pointed out that standing around Jesus as he spoke were "people with no spiritual qualifications or abilities at all."[11] Such people are those today who "would be the last to say they have any claim whatsoever on God. The pages of the Gospels are cluttered with such people."[12] Willard went on to say, "The Beatitudes are lists of human 'lasts' who at the individualized touch of the heavens become divine 'firsts.' The gospel of the kingdom is that no one is beyond beatitude, because the rule of God from the heavens is available to all. Everyone can reach it, and it can reach everyone."[13]

James Davison Hunter tells a story about a lady who bagged groceries. "Every day she greeted her customers with genuine enthusiasm, remembering customers' names and asking about their families. She would end every conversation by saying that she was going to pray for their family. Over time, this caused problems, for people wanted to get in her aisle, which resulted in long lines. People would wait though, because they enjoyed being with her, encouraged just by her presence. At her funeral, years after she retired, the

11. Willard, *The Divine Conspiracy*, 100.
12. Willard, *The Divine Conspiracy*, 101.
13. Willard, *The Divine Conspiracy*, 122.

church was packed to standing-room-only capacity, and she was eulogized again and again by people whom she had encouraged for years."[14]

No little people, no little places

Francis Schaeffer preached a sermon entitled, *No Little People, No Little Places*. He talked about the way God used Moses's rod, a stick of wood. When God appeared to Moses in the burning bush and commissioned Moses to deliver his people out of Egypt, Moses was skeptical. According to Exodus 3:11, Moses responded saying, "Who am I?" Or, said another way, "But why me? What makes you think that I could ever go to Pharaoh and lead the children of Israel out of Egypt?" (MSG). In Exodus 4:1, Moses continued to object: "They won't trust me. They won't listen to a word I say. They're going to say, 'God? Appear to him? Hardly!'" (MSG). In response, God brought attention to the rod or staff in Moses's hand, a stick of wood! According to Exodus 4:20, the rod of Moses had become the rod of God. Perhaps you may recall God telling Moses later in Exodus 14:16 to lift the rod in order that the Red Sea would be divided for the Israelites to escape the Egyptian army. Shaeffer made these points:

> Consider the mighty ways in which God used a dead stick of wood . . . Though we are weak in talent, physical energy, and psychological strength, we are not less than a stick of wood. But as the rod of Moses had to become the rod of God, so that which is me must become the me of God. . . . The Scripture emphasizes that much can come from little if the little is truly consecrated to God. There are no little people and no big people in the true spiritual sense, but only consecrated and unconsecrated people . . . as there are no little people in God's sight, so there are no little places. . . . Nowhere more than in America are Christians caught in the twentieth-century syndrome of size. Size will show success. . . . Not only does God not say that size and spiritual power go together, but he even reverses this (especially in the teaching of Jesus) and tells us to be deliberately careful not to choose a place too big for us. We all tend to emphasize big works and big places, but all such emphasis is of the flesh. To think in such terms is simply to hearken back to the old, unconverted, egoist, self-centered me.[15]

---

14. Hunter, *To Change the World*, 268–69.
15. Schaeffer, *No Little People*, 25–26.

Indeed, there are no little people, little deeds, or little places. I heard someone say once that his bucket list was doing small things well over a long period of time in the same place. This, he believed, seemed to be the way the kingdom of God grows. Practically that would mean, for example, learning the names of all his neighbors and making what he had as beautiful as possible. There is nothing wrong with small. If you would like help conveying this powerful message to your young children, I would strongly suggest the book, *Papa Put a Man on the Moon* by my friend, Kristy Dempsey. In 1962, President John F. Kennedy declared a vision of going to the moon within the decade. The federal government invested billions into the effort. Factories across the country played a part in developing each piece of equipment needed to bring the vision to reality. In the 1960s, a textile mill in Slater, South Carolina began producing Beta cloth, a fiberglass-thread fabric, which would become one of the layers in the Apollo spacesuits. Dempsey's own grandparents, parents, uncles, and aunts worked at the factory at one point or another. "At the time," she said, "the mill workers who made this fabric felt they were simply doing their jobs, making an honest living in textiles. But when the mission was finally accomplished and Neil Armstrong stepped onto the surface of the moon, they knew they had contributed to a monumental American achievement."[16]

So many people around the world view themselves as insignificant. They often feel invisible and easily forgotten. Perhaps you are one of them. But our significance rests in the fact that God created us in his image and adopted us as his beloved children, with all the rights and privileges as such. Each person has the potential through his or her life to make a unique contribution to the story of this world. "Mustard seed growth was an experience so common no one noticed it. Except Jesus. Jesus wants us to imagine a world in which our small actions are seen as significant actions. Offering someone a cup of cold water, opening the door of welcome, a short note of encouragement, a gentle word of help, a warm embrace . . . these are the little mustard seeds that can have large consequences. If we develop a kingdom vision, we will know our little actions swell into kingdom significance."[17] So, take it from a stick of wood. Take it from Jesse and his runt of a hometown. Take it from Frodo in the Shire. And, "Hey," take it from Mari-Helen. There are no little people and no little places. Tiny seeds buried deep in the ground are invisible; yet, unlimited potential exists within them to grow and reproduce.

16. Dempsey, *Papa Put a Man on the Moon*, Author's Note.
17. McKnight, *One Life*, 39.

CHAPTER 10

Forgiveness for the Guilty

— David, Bathsheba, and Uriah —

"Though your sins be as scarlet, they shall be as white as snow; though they be red like crimson, they shall be as wool."—Isaiah 1:18

"Water always falls and pools up in the very lowest and darkest places, just like mercy. And mercy is just grace in action."[1]—Richard Rohr

A lexandre Dumàs's *The Count of Monte Cristo,* tells the story of Edmond Dantès, an emerging young leader with impeccable character and everything going for him—a promising career as ship captain; peers who valued his friendship, yet devotedly followed his leadership; and Mercédès, a beautiful and intelligent bride-to-be. Yet tension roils under the surface as three of his associates—Danglars, who was envious of his role as captain; Mondego, who covets his relationship with Mercédès; and Caderousse, a drunk and greedy man—accuse him falsely of high treason. Gérard de Villefort, who initially seemed an honest, impartial young prosecutor in-clined to give Dantès the benefit of the doubt, quickly turns to self-interest for his name, reputation, and career would be at stake if he did not carry out a sentence. Captured by their own self-interest, reputation, image, greed, and lust, they cold-heartedly and permanently imprison Dantès, an innocent man, on a remote island within the impenetrable, dark, and cold rock dungeons of the Château d'If. For many years in that living hell, Dantès tragically suffers in isolation.[2]

Each of us at different times in our lives has played the part of Mon-dego, Danglars, Caderousse, or Villefort to one degree or another. Out of jealousy, greed, lust, pride, or overall self-interest, each of us has in some

1. Rohr, "A Santa Claus God," lines 28–9.
2. Dumas, *The Count of Monte Cristo.*

way injured another person by what we have done or not done. We are guilty of not loving our neighbor as ourselves. Also, each of us has experienced injuries like Dantès's wounds because of the harmful actions of others. We have not experienced neighbor love the way God intended. We have been on either or both ends of deception, betrayal, abuse, assault, neglect, manipulation, or mistreatment in some form or fashion. One of the Ten Commandments is "do not steal." But that is just the floor of God's intention. You might say that you have never stolen anything. If reworded positively, the command might read, "Be sacrificial and lavishly generous." Can we say we have sacrificially lavished the people in our lives with generosity not only with our belongings, but also with our words, time, and attention? And then as we look back over our lives, is there anyone who stands out who sacrificially lavished us with generosity? A few may come to mind. But most people from your past will not fit this description. Ultimately, all fall way short of such a standard and only Jesus has done so perfectly (We will talk about that later). When we wrongfully injure another person by what we have done or not done, a certain kind of death can occur. For instance, if we lie to or about someone, a certain kind of death to trust in the relationship occurs. If we do not restore through confession, repentance, reconciliation, and a demonstration of that repentance, then the relationship will die. For where there is deception, there is no relationship. Also, the liar will experience a partial death to his or her conscience. As the conscience dies, so does the soul with it. We all desperately need the merciful and gracious forgiveness of God. We also need the grace of God to enable us to forgive others. We need the story of David, Bathsheba, and Uriah.

Rise and fall of David

Second Samuel 1–10 reads like a biography of one of the greatest political success stories of all time. King Saul had been disgraced and removed from office. David was enthroned as king over the divided nation of Israel—first over Judah (2 Sam 1–2) and then over Israel (2 Sam 2—5). Chapter 5 documents David's establishment of Jerusalem as the capital by defeating the Philistines, their greatest enemy. Chapter 6 records him bringing the Ark of God back to Jerusalem. In chapter 7 God promises him an everlasting dynasty: "I have been with you wherever you have gone, and I have cut off all your enemies from before you. Now I will make your name great, like the names of the greatest men on earth. . . . And your house and your kingdom shall be made sure forever before me" (vv. 9, 16). More of David's great victories are recorded in chapters 8 to10. God was with David and gave him victory wherever he went. David consequently grew more powerful.[3]

Chapter 11 marks a tragic turning point as it documents one of the most scandalous stories in the Bible. David, a successful hero grievously falls. It is significant to note in the genealogy of Jesus that Matthew does not emphasize David's accolades such as defeating Goliath, being crowned king, or authoring numerous psalms. On the contrary, Matthew's brief mention of David brings attention to the scandal. "David was the father of Solomon, whose mother had been Uriah's wife."

The first part of Second Samuel, chapter 11 says David had not gone out to battle as kings normally would have at this time. For some reason he stays back and apparently has idle time on his hands. One evening he gets up from his bed and strolls on the rooftop of his palace. Aroused by the sight of a beautiful woman bathing, David sends someone to find out more about her. She is Bathsheba, wife of Uriah, one of his mighty soldiers. It matters not. David sends for her to be brought to him anyway. Surely David knew what Leviticus said about adultery: "If a man commits adultery with another man's wife—with the wife of his neighbor—both the adulterer and the adulteress are to be put to death" (20:10). His lust and impunity as king, however, overtake his sensibilities. He sleeps with her and she becomes pregnant.

Weighed down heavily by the magnitude of his colossal mistake, David strategizes to cover up the sexual encounter. He orders Uriah home to be with his wife. David wants Uriah, along with everyone else, to believe the baby Bathsheba is carrying belongs to Uriah. Uriah, however, is an honorable man. Knowing his commander and fellow soldiers are still at war, encamped in tents in open fields, he does not dare think of being with his wife. So instead of sleeping with Bathsheba, Uriah sleeps at the door of the king's house with all the servants. Desperate to conceal the matter, David attempts again to manipulate Uriah by getting him drunk. Each time, though, Uriah holds true to his convictions.

Resolute to hide the scandal, David's heart hardens to the point of arranging Uriah's murder. "We may see from this how deep a soul may fall when it turns away from God, and from the guidance of his grace. This David . . . was now not ashamed to resort to the greatest crimes in order to cover his sin."[4] David orders his general, Joab, to place Uriah in the most dangerous spot of battle, and have his other men withdraw so that Uriah would be killed. David has the gall to have Uriah himself carry back to Joab

3. 2 Sam. 8:14b and 2 Sam. 5:10.

4. Keil and Delitzsch, *Commentary on the Old Testament*, 2:626.

the kill order. The fact that Uriah is killed by the sword of the Ammonites, the enemies of the people of God, "added to the wickedness."[5] So Joab sends a messenger back to David with a report about the battle. The messenger had this to say to David: "The men overpowered us and came out against us in the open, but we drove them back to the entrance of the city gate. Then the archers shot arrows at your servants from the wall, and some of the king's men died. Moreover, your servant Uriah the Hittite is dead" (2 Sam 11:23–24). As a direct consequence of David's heinous crime against Uriah, other innocent men lose their lives. And how does David respond upon hearing the news he had been so anxiously awaiting?

He callously told Joab, *Don't let this upset you.*

Ugly truth exposed

Unfortunately, it often takes exposure, as was the case with Judah, or being confronted before we admit wrongdoing. The same is true of David when Nathan, the prophet, confronts him, saying, "Why did you despise the word of the LORD by doing what is evil in his eyes? You struck down Uriah the Hittite with the sword and took his wife to be your own. You killed him with the sword of the Ammonites" (2 Sam 12:9). Then, in verse twelve, Nathan takes one more honest swing: "You did it in secret." Before this confrontation, David appears to believe he had gotten away with it. Yet now, he is exposed. David has no wiggle room to deny the truth, make excuses, defend himself, minimize his actions, or act like the victim.

Because of the scandalous nature of the adultery and murder, it would be easy to miss another significant aspect of evil threaded throughout the story. It has to do with the verb, *sent*. After David saw Bathsheba bathing, he *sent* someone to find out about her. After finding out who she was, David *sent* messengers to get her. Once he found out that Bathsheba was pregnant, David *sent* word to Joab to *send* him Uriah the Hittite. Once he saw Uriah would not be with his wife, Bathsheba, David wrote a letter to Joab and *sent* it with Uriah. After Bathsheba heard of her husband's death, she mourned for a time, and then David *sent* for her and had her brought to his house, and she became his wife.

Sent recurs several times in this passage with David as the subject. Each time David *sent,* he *sought* to accomplish a purpose in mind. To *send* involves someone in authority commissioning someone of lesser rank to accomplish a task. So maybe it would help us to think about it phrased as 'gave an order' or 'issued a command.' David as king severely abused his power, and his actions

5. Keil and Delitzsch, *Commentary on the Old Testament*, 2:629.

were "evil in the sight of the LORD." We already examined abuse of power in the chapter on Tamar, so we will not belabor the point here; however, we should take note its role in this story as well.

People respond differently when their behavior is exposed. Darkness hates light. Some take a posture of silent denial, never admitting their guilt. This was the case with Hadler, whose story I shared in an earlier chapter, when his Jewish friend confronted him. Others expressly lie, saying aloud that they did not do it. Others may justify their actions in their own minds. Others may refuse to accept responsibility and blame circumstances or other people. Others may take some responsibility but downplay their actions. Or they may do a combination of all these. They deceive themselves, as it states in 1 John 1:8. Others may admit guilt, but are still more concerned about their own image, as was the case with King Saul: "I have sinned. But please honor me before the elders of my people and before Israel" (1 Sam 15:24–25, 30). Saul may have felt convicted about his wrongdoing, but he seemed mostly concerned about his reputation.

Cost and beauty of forgiveness

If we, like Bathsheba and Uriah, have been wrongfully sinned against in some way, what seed of redemption might lie as buried treasure in the sacred ground of our struggle? A distinction exists between reconciliation, consequences for wrongdoing, and forgiveness. Without elaborating too much, here are a few thoughts. You may forgive someone and not be reconciled in the relationship. This would be true if the transgressor never accepts responsibility for wounding you, apologizes, or seeks to demonstrate a change of behavior. You cannot solve a transgressor's side of a problem. Also, extending forgiveness does not necessarily translate into removal of consequences for the transgressor. If you do not study for a test, you will most likely fail it. If you break the law or a court order, you will most likely pay a fine or perhaps even go to jail. If you cheat on your spouse, your spouse may very well forgive you, but also leave you because trust has been too badly broken. David, as we find out in the story, experiences God's forgiveness, but faces consequences. "The child conceived in David's adulterous union with Bathsheba dies. Rape, murder, and rebellion erupt in David's own extended family. At last God's judgment on David reaches its climax with the death of David's beloved son Absalom, who has tried to usurp the throne."[6] Also, forgiveness does not ignore or negate the wrong done. "Christianity does not want us to reduce by one atom the hatred we feel for

6. Bartholomew and Goheen, *The Drama of Scripture*, 98.

cruelty and treachery. We ought to hate them."[7] Furthermore, forgiveness does not mean lack of boundaries or allowing offenders to do or get what they want. If trust has eroded, it can take time to rebuild. So, if a spouse has cheated and been forgiven, that does not necessarily mean he or she will be allowed to live at home, even if that is what he or she wants.

Forgiveness, a divine gift that should be received with overwhelming gratitude when extended, is costly and can be a painful journey. This is especially true if the transgressor never accepts responsibility, confesses, or seeks forgiveness, or worse, gaslights *you* with false accusations of being the wrongdoer. It seems to be human nature for us to want someone to pay for what he or she has done, which is why forgiveness must be divine. Forgiveness is so costly that it is no wonder so many people would rather die than extend it. I want to try using an analogy here. Consider for a moment something wrong done to you in the past. Then, consider all the anger, or perhaps rage, you felt towards that transgressor because of it. List what you wish would happen to that person. Now pretend you could take what happened, all that anger and rage, as well as the wish list and turn it into liquid and bottle it up. Then instead of giving the bottle of vengeance to the transgressor to drink, drink it yourself. Sometimes, it's like we can only take sips of the drink at a time. We might take a sip and even spit it right back out. But if taken in love towards the other person, God's Spirit transforms the drink into something palatable and uses it to enhance growth of love, peace, hope, and joy in our own heart and life. This analogy helps me visualize both the cost and beauty of forgiveness.

Cost and consequences of vengeance

Yet so many people refuse to take the drink themselves. They desire the transgressor to drink it all as a bottle of vengeance and poison. We find such a pathway of vengeance in *The Count of Monte Cristo*. Dantès, after years of imprisonment at the Château d'If, escapes. Then, he reappears, but in disguise, with plans of revenge as the wealthy Count of Monte Cristo. Dantès begins his elaborate plot to take revenge on the three men responsible for his unjust imprisonment. Mondego is now married to Mercédès, the woman Dantès was passionately in love with and to whom he was to be wedded at the moment of his arrest. Mondego also is now Count de Morcerf. Danglars is now a baron and a wealthy banker. Villefort is now prosecutor for the king. Dantès does not choose the path of forgiveness and justice. Unintended and unforeseen consequences beyond Dantès's plan

7. Lewis, *Mere Christianity*, 117.

or control transpire because of his revenge-seeking decisions.[8] In seeking vengeance, which is not the same thing as justice, we will still take a drink of something; sadly, it's often from a bottle of bitterness. And bitterness is a drink that poisons the soul, choking out love like weeds taking over a once beautiful garden. Bitterness also seems to grant those who have harmed us ongoing control of our future narrative.

Consider Jesus

Follow the narrative of Jesus: "Consider him who endured such opposition from sinners, so that you will not grow weary and lose heart" (Heb 12:3). The two verses prior to this one refer to running with endurance the race set before us as a metaphor for living out a life of faith. Athletes competing get exhausted. Each of us inevitably faces adverse circumstances which beat us down, which is especially true when we have been injured by someone else's wrongdoing. The weight can crush our hope, feed our fear, and zap our vitality. A woman of color was being interviewed on the news one evening after experiencing an attack by four white men while sitting in her car at a stop light. She described the effects she experienced afterward. She hurt physically. She was traumatized. She wept. She could not eat or sleep. In another situation, a disgruntled employee was fired for lashing out and threatening his manager. The manager suffered through emotional and psychological torment for days due to the threats. Sin against another person does real damage and causes real suffering.

The writer of Hebrews says, "Consider him" (Heb. 12:3). The word "consider" itself means to attentively observe and analyze; to think carefully about; to examine, review, study, and reflect on. What we are to give such careful thought to is Jesus, "who endured such opposition from sinners" (Heb. 12:3). Jesus, as the Son of God, was indeed the most innocent of victims, described as "a lamb without blemish or defect" (1 Pet 1:19). Jesus performed so much good in the world. He gave sight to the blind; made the lame to walk; cleansed lepers; made the deaf to hear; raised the dead to life; cast out demons; confronted evil; ministered and preached to the poor; taught his listeners to love their enemies, and to do good to those who hated them; to bless those who cursed them; and pray for those who abused them.

Yet this perfect lamb of God suffered and persevered through every form of hatred, aggression, and hostility. King Herod went to horrific lengths to kill him as a baby. The devil tempted him in the wilderness for forty days and nights. People where he grew up were filled with wrath over his teaching

---

8. Dumas, *The Count of Monte Cristo*.

and attempted to throw him down a cliff (Luke 4:29–30). Religious leaders questioned his teachings and perverted his sayings. They ridiculed his claims and lied about him, accusing him of being a blasphemous glutton and a drunkard. They condemned him for being a friend of sinners. They opposed his plans. Religious leaders, filled with fury over Jesus's healing on the Sabbath, conspired to destroy him. They sought to deceive, manipulate, and trap him. He was abandoned by his friends in his greatest moment of need, betrayed by one of his closest followers, arrested for no reason, denied by one of his closest friends, put on trial as a criminal, mocked, spat upon, flogged, nailed to a cross, and crucified beside criminals.

Yet even through the ongoing hostility and opposition, Jesus was not thwarted in his mission. Even foreknowledge of his crucifixion did not deter him. Death itself could not hold him back from bursting forth from the grave. Consider Jesus.

And consider Jesus when we ourselves are guilty of harming another person. David's response upon being exposed by Nathan was plain and simple: "I have sinned against the LORD" (2 Sam 12:13). David penned Psalm 51 as a prayer of confession and repentance, allowing us a window into his soul as he processed his actions: "Have mercy on me, O God, according to your unfailing love; according to your great compassion blot out my transgressions. Wash away all my iniquity and cleanse me from my sin. For I know my transgressions, and my sin is always before me. Against you, you only, have I sinned and done what is evil in your sight; . . . Hide your face from my sins and blot out all my iniquity. Create in me a pure heart, O God, and renew a steadfast spirit within me. Do not cast me from your presence or take your Holy Spirit from me. Restore to me the joy of your salvation and grant me a willing spirit, to sustain me."

What an expression of brokenness, confession, repentance and passionate pleading for cleansing, restoration, and renewal. He did not play the victim by shifting blame. He did not lash out in anger against Nathan. He did not deny, hide, defend, or minimize what he had done. He did not ask Nathan to lie on his behalf to perpetuate the cover up. He accepted full responsibility calling them, "my transgressions," "my iniquity," and "my sin." He acknowledged his wrongdoings as inexcusable, and, furthermore, "evil."

Repentance is not an act of trying to get one's act together. It's a term meaning a change of mind; of agreeing God's judgment of us is correct. Coming to that place, and grieving over his wrongful actions, David pleaded for God to wash him thoroughly, "a verb normally connected with the laundering of clothes, as if David is comparing himself to a foul garment needing to be washed over and over again."[9] He prayed, "purge me with hyssop, and I shall be clean." This "alludes to the cleansing of the leper." Leprosy was a malignant skin disease. If a person was diagnosed as having it, he or she was banished from society as a hygienic precaution. "Only if divine healing occurred (cf. Nu. 12:9–15) could the sufferer apply to the priest for a medical discharge. When his healing had been established, he still had to satisfy certain social and religious requirements to be pronounced clean."[10] David, as a result of his wrongdoing, must have deeply felt what it meant to be banished from the people of God as if he had leprosy. Not only did he long for forgiveness and cleansing, but also relational restoration. He no longer attempted to cover-up his misdeeds, but rather faced the truth, desiring to be restored to experience God's presence once more. Kidner summarizes well the significance of this prayerful psalm saying, "It comes from David's blackest moment of self-knowledge, yet it explores not only the depths of his guilt but some of the farthest reaches of salvation."[11]

In response to David's repentance, Nathan replied, "The LORD has taken away your sin" (2 Sam 12:13–14). God removed the adulterous affair, abuse of power, and murder off David. You will most likely not understand or feel the significance of this unless you yourself have experienced the life-giving freedom of forgiveness. But this would not be possible unless and until you have felt the weight of your own guilt from wrongdoing. Romans 4:7–8 says, "Blessed are those whose transgressions are forgiven, whose sins are covered. Blessed is the one whose sin the Lord will never count against them." Paul was quoting from Psalm 32:1–2, also penned by David. I'm going to be the grammar nerd again for a second. Do you recall in the chapter on Rahab when I talked about emphatic negation regarding God's promises to never leave or forsake us? Well, it shows up again in Romans 4:8. We might translate this as, "Blessed is the one whose sin the Lord will never not count against them." Again, "This is the strongest way to negate something in Greek."[12]. This type of negation is emphatic and denies something will occur in the strongest language possible. Never-not "rules out even the idea as being a possibility."[13] Make this personal. Recall something you've done or left undone. God is promising us he will never, never, never, no, not ever count our sins against us. Let that sink in.

Psalm 103:12 says that "as far as the east is from the west, so far has he removed our transgressions from us." Picture a globe, or spherical model of Earth. Place your finger at the equator and move it directly

9. Kidner, *Psalms 1–72*, 190.

10. Bromily, *The International Standard Bible Encyclopedia*, 3:105.

11. Kidner, *Psalms 1–72*, 189.

12. Wallace, *Greek Grammar*, 468.

13. Wallace, *Greek Grammar*, 468.

north. When you get to the Arctic Circle and keep going, you will start going South on the other side. Then when you reach the bottom or Antarctica you will have to start going North again. Now, place your finger at the beginning point on the equator where you started before. This time start going east. Keep going. Keep going around and around and around. Is there ever a time you start going west? Now, take your finger, and go west. Keep going. Keep going around and around and around. Is there ever a time you start going east? No! So as far as the east is from the west, so far has God removed our sins from us! It was true of David. It is also true for me and you. "We all, like sheep, have gone astray, each of us has turned to our own way; and the Lord has laid on him the iniquity of us all" (Isa 53:6). And "though your sins be as scarlet, they shall be as white as snow; though they be red like crimson, they shall be as wool" (Isa 1:18). Jesus took the drink for us in love. We are forgiven.

Power of forgiveness

In another story, we witness a completely different pathway than the path of vengeance Dantès chose. *The Mission,* starring Robert De Niro and Jeremy Irons, is based on historical events in the eighteenth century. A Spanish Jesuit priest, Father Gabriel, along with a team of missionaries, establish a gospel mission among a Guarani community located in the northeastern Argentinean and eastern Paraguayan jungle. This is a dangerous mission, because prior to Father Gabriel's arrival, the Guarani had tied another priest to a wooden cross and sent him over the Iguazu Falls. But as Father Gabriel's team lives among them, the power of Jesus's love transforms the community. Eventually, however, Gabriel's team stands in solidarity with the people as a protective shield from greedy western imperialists seeking to expand their power, control, and wealth.

Rodrigo Mendoza, a character played by Robert De Niro, serves as a mercenary and slave trader for the Spanish empire. Arrogant, greedy, and self-serving, Rodrigo uses all means available to kidnap natives from this and other communities to sell as slaves. After returning home from one of these slave-trading journeys, Rodrigo finds out an agonizing truth that rocks his world. The woman he deeply loves is in love with his brother Felipe. Enraged, Rodrigo takes the path of vengeance, challenges his brother to a duel, and kills him. The resulting guilt and shame cause him to spiral into a deep depression.

Later in the story, Father Gabriel meets with Rodrigo and challenges him to accept a suitable journey of penance back into the jungles where he had committed crimes. His self-inflicted punishment involves dragging a net weighted down with his own armor and sword among other things through the thick forest. Pulling this cumbersome bundle over rocks, through river currents, and up elevated slopes serves as a metaphor perhaps of how many of us live in bondage to our own failures, guilt, and shame. At the outset, Rodrigo is convinced that no amount of penance can make up for all his crimes. As his exhausted face and body evidence a tremendous degree of suffering, the team of priests accompanying him suggest Father Gabriel release him from his penance. But Gabriel knows that Rodrigo does not believe his suffering has been sufficient to pay for his past crimes. So, the self-punishment continues, but begins to climax with a grueling and dangerous climb up the rocks beside the water falls to the top of a cliff. It is there on the outskirts of the Guarani's territory where Rodrigo comes face to face with the natives whose loved ones he had murdered, kidnapped, and sold into slavery.

Covered in sweat and mud, barely crawling, Rodrigo lowers his head in shame and self-condemnation before the natives. In this tense and climactic moment, one of the chief Guarani leaders grabs a knife, approaches Rodrigo, and holds it to his throat. Rodrigo's submissive posture suggests he expects the justified vengeance for his evil deeds. Recall that the Guarani people had tied a priest to a wooden cross and sent him over the Iguazu Falls before. But now, instead of slitting his throat and sending Rodrigo over the falls, the leader cuts away the heavy bundle, delivering Rodrigo from both his physical and metaphorical bondage by casting the netted baggage over the cliff.[14]

This scene captures the beauty and power of God's forgiveness and removal of our sins from us. The Guarani and their leader had come not for retribution, but for redemption; not to hate, but to love; not to imprison, but to liberate; not to condemn, but to forgive; not to harm, but to bless; not to end his life, but to offer him a new life. They drank the bottle in love themselves. They embraced a broken down, beat-up sinner held captive to his own internal prisons of shame and guilt. Rodrigo sobbed uncontrollably with tears of joy and freedom in response to the forgiveness, mercy, and grace lavished upon him so undeservedly. Such has Jesus done for me and you. May he grant us grace and strength to extend such forgiveness and freedom to others.

14. *The Mission*

CHAPTER 11

Meaning in the Struggle to Survive and Succeed

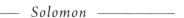

Solomon

". . . man's will to meaning is frustrated on a worldwide scale. Ever more people are haunted by a feeling of meaninglessness which is often accompanied by a feeling of emptiness . . ."[1]—Viktor Frankl

Shia LaBeouf has been a huge box-office star. Before its release, *Transformers: Revenge of the Fallen*, was expected to push the worldwide total of his film grosses over $3 billion. "I don't handle fame well. . . . Most actors on most days don't think they're worthy. I have no idea where this insecurity comes from, but it's a God-sized hole. If I knew, I'd fill it. Actors live dependent on being validated by other people's opinions. . . . The good actors are all screwed up. They're all in pain. It's a profession of bottom-feeders and heartbroken people."[2]

Sue Monk Kidd, author of *The Secret Life of Bees*, described facing struggles of midlife, including a stale marriage, stifling religious structures, and things that no longer mattered:

> "My life curled up into the frightening mark of a question. . . . I too sat in the midst of many selves. The Pleaser, the Performer, the Perfectionist. . . . I was learning how closely these old roles were connected to another powerful role . . . the Good Little Girl. She was the part of me that had little self-validation or autonomy, who tended to define life by others and their expectations, by collective values and projections. . . . I sometimes felt that I had been scripted to be all things to all people. But when I

---

1. Frankl, *Man's Search for Ultimate Meaning*, 139.
2. Rader, "The Mixed-up Life of Shia LeBeouf," lines 38–40, 43, 106–7.

tried, I usually ended up forfeiting my deepest identity, my own unique truth as God's creature. My Good Little Girl endured everything sweetly, feared coloring outside of the traditional lines, and frequently cut herself off from her real thoughts and feelings. She was adapted to thinking other people's thoughts and following the path of least resistance. . . . Who was this self inside of me who cried out to be?"[3]

Henri Nouwen, in his book, *In the Name of Jesus*, shared about his journey of working with Harvard's best and brightest to living in a home with individuals with special needs. They were not impressed with his resume of experience at Notre Dame, Yale, or Harvard. None of his skills and acquired knowledge were practical in this setting.

"I was suddenly faced with my naked self, open for affirmations and rejections, hugs and punches, smiles and tears, all dependent simply on how I was perceived at the moment. In a way, it seemed as though I was starting my life all over again. Relationships, connections, reputations could no longer be counted on. . . . This experience was and, in many ways, is still the most important experience of my new life, because it forced me to rediscover my true identity. These broken, wounded, and completely unpretentious people forced me to let go of my relevant self—the self that can do things, show things, prove things, build things."[4]

Ed Dobson, for eighteen years, was the lead pastor of a church in Grand Rapids, Michigan, preaching weekly to thousands. He loved his work. However, back around 2000, Dobson was diagnosed with ALS, or Lou Gehrig's disease. He knew the disease would abolish his ability to speak. Sure enough, within five years, he had to quit his job. When that day came, life suddenly went from a fast clip to a complete halt. Dobson described how he had been accustomed to his cell phone constantly ringing. Then the day after he quit, it did not ring once. He even called his wife and asked her to call his phone to make sure it was working. "When you are not needed, you lose part of your purpose in life,"[5] he said. This hit home the day after quitting. He entered his office—where he studied and prepared for sermons—but he had nothing to do. He felt lost. When he was younger, he never thought speaking and writing and doing those things he loved would ever come to an end. Week after week for many years, thousands of people looked to Dobson for answers to

---

3. Kidd, *When the Heart Waits*, 5–7.

4. Nouwen, *In the Name of Jesus*, 73–74.

5. https://www.cnn.com/videos/living/2012/02/11/eds-story-my-garden.cnn

life. Yet age and the challenges of his disease caused Dobson to confess, "The more I live, the fewer answers I have."[6]

A friend once vented at the end of a hard day: *I'm just having one of those days. I'm so over this damn job. So over the pettiness. So over the stress for so little pay. The 'situation' that is my manager. I'm just dragging and drained. There's got to be more to life than this.* It's an honest statement that I also have said in different ways. I sleep normal hours then head to work. Like most people, I'm a bit worn-out by the end of a workday. But then it's time to exercise, cook dinner, take care of personal tasks, occasionally participate in a volunteer opportunity, keep up with friends, neighbors, and other family members. When I am keeping her every other week, Mari-Helen requires extra assistance each evening with cleaning up her space, taking her medicine, and preparing for bed. Then I usually just want to rest on the couch, scroll social media for a minute, and watch another episode of some series I'm into. Then off to bed I go to read for a few minutes if I have enough focus and energy. Next day, repeat. Normal, right?

What is the meaning of life?

The repetition of daily living makes me think about the movie, *Groundhog Day,* or Sisyphus in Greek Mythology. Once King of Ephyra, Sisyphus—because of his greed and deceitfulness—was punished by Zeus, who forced him to roll a boulder up a steep hill. Right before reaching the top of the hill, the boulder was enchanted to roll away from Sisyphus back to the bottom of the hill. You can imagine how such a repetitive activity would cause perpetual frustration and sense of meaninglessness. At the end of a long week, have we not all felt the question deeply in our souls, *So, what's the point?*

Life simply doesn't turn out like we expected. A gap exists between what reality is, and what we want or think it should be. We live, breathe, work, play, and relate in this world wishing something will happen or come along or some relationship will finally bring that lasting sense of meaning and fulfillment we so crave. Occasionally, that something or someone does come along and fills that gap . . . temporarily. But if we look to those gifts to fill the gap in any lasting way, before too long, we find ourselves asking the same haunting question, *Is this really all there is?*

I believe Solomon eagerly sought the answers to such questions. Solomon was the son of King David and Bathsheba. He took over his father's throne as a teenager and soon became the wealthiest person of his

---

6. Merica, "Facing Death, A Top Pastor Rethinks What It Means to Be Christian," lines 12–13, 16, 20.

time. He had dreamed that God permitted him to request whatever he wanted. According to 1 Kings 3:6–9, he asked for wisdom, or a discerning heart, that he might rule over God's people well, understanding the difference between right and wrong. Indeed, God granted him wisdom. On top of this, God granted him additional blessings such as honor and wealth. Traditionally, scholars have ascribed authorship for the book of Ecclesiastes to Solomon. He most likely wrote it later in life. In Ecclesiastes 1:14, he says, "I have seen all the things that are done under the sun; all of them are meaningless, a chasing after the wind." He repeats this theme in chapter 2, verse 11: "Yet when I surveyed all that my hands had done and what I had toiled to achieve, everything was meaningless, a chasing after the wind; nothing was gained under the sun." Then he lists out a good many of his achievements. From this list, we can conclude that Solomon possessed valuable real estate and invested significant resources to develop those properties. He wielded enormous influence and possessed a vast amount of treasures. Solomon had more sexual encounters with women than perhaps any man who has ever lived with his seven-hundred wives and three-hundred concubines. He boasted that no one who preceded him could match his greatness. "I denied myself nothing my eyes desired; I refused my heart no pleasure. And whatever my eyes desired I did not keep from them. I kept my heart from no pleasure" (2:10).

He "exhibited great ability in a variety of fields; as a politician, diplomat, strategist, organizer, and administrator he excelled, and his poetry and proverbs apparently were equally admirable."[7] He wrote more than one-thousand songs and about three-thousand proverbs. Leaders traveled from all over to find out firsthand if what they heard was true regarding his wisdom. His forty-year reign amassed for himself as well as Israel vast wealth, the finest resources, and an unprecedented labor force, which toiled for seven years to fashion a glorious temple unto God. First Kings chapter 8 and 2 Chronicles chapter 6 record a magnificent prayer punctuating a public ceremony to celebrate the dedication of the temple—which the Lord visibly filled with his glory in front of the assembly. Truly, Solomon accumulated and achieved more than he could possibly have imagined.

Even though Israel experienced this golden age of peace and a flourishing economy during his reign, Solomon's "real undoing was his lack of moderation. His extravagance in his harem, court luxury, and building schemes laid an impossible burden on his subjects, and moreover served to emphasize the contrast between his happy position and their own increasing poverty. Because of these failings, Solomon brought his empire to the brink

---

7. Bromily, *The International Standard Bible Encyclopedia*, 4:568.

of disruption from which Rehoboam, his son and successor, was unable to rescue it."[8] For example, though it took seven years to build the temple, it took thirteen to build his own house, which was almost twice the size of the temple. He began well with a devotion to God, but compromise after compromise lead him down a path away from God. His path eventually divided the kingdom. From there, it was just a matter of time before Israel was invaded and conquered by the foreign powers of Assyria and Babylon. Although Solomon had guided Israel to this golden age of peace and political self-sufficiency, "along the way he lost sight of the original vision to which God had called them. . . . Success in the kingdom of this world had crowded out interest in the kingdom of God. . . . The more he enjoyed the world's gifts, the less he thought about the Giver."[9] Solomon summarized his material appetite and consumption as "meaningless, a chasing after the wind" (Eccl 2:11). In other words, even after attaining, achieving, building, and experiencing tremendous power, pleasure, and fame, Solomon's own conclusion was that it was all worthless and empty. Human enterprising in and of itself as a life pursuit and object of worship is ultimately fruitless.

Why is this? Continual stimulation of the senses and emotions is needed to stay happy in a materialistic way of living. Yet, as Barrs and Macaulay explain, "The stimulation of the senses leads only to the need for greater and greater stimulation till the senses are jaded and unable to appreciate anything. In this vacuum of human experience people look desperately for something that will inject meaning into reality."[10] So where will we find it?

Viktor Frankl, a preeminent psychotherapist during the twentieth century and a Holocaust survivor, wrote, "Meaning may be squeezed out even from suffering, and that is the very reason why life remains potentially meaningful in spite of everything,"[11] He went on to point out his findings. "The truth is that among those who actually went through the experience of Auschwitz, the number of those whose religious life was deepened—in spite, not to say because, of this experience—by far exceeds the number of those who gave up their belief."[12] If so many suffering prisoners who were tortured in Nazi concentration camps could find meaning, surely there is hope for me and you to find meaning in our own struggle to survive and succeed.

8. Bromily, *The International Standard Bible Encyclopedia*, 4:568.

9. Yancey, *Disappointment with God*, 84–5.

10. Macaulay and Barrs, *Being Human*, 31.

11. Frankl, *Man's Search for Ultimate Meaning*, 141–142.

12. Frankl, *Man's Search for Ultimate Meaning*, 152–153.

Augustine of Hippo famously said, "Thou hast made us for thyself, O Lord, and our heart is restless until it finds its rest in thee."[13] Colossians 2:3 says that in Christ "are hidden all the treasures of wisdom and knowledge." Note the plurality of treasures; note they are hidden and therefore must be sought. As part of that pursuit, allow me to reflect on some contrasts between Solomon's perceived glory and Jesus's genuine glory. Jesus possesses unlimited power, has the highest position of authority in the universe, and owns every inch of Creation. Yet although he rules over all Creation, he did not cling to his power as a person in the godhead. Philippians 2:5–9 tells us that Jesus—the second person of the Trinity, mediator of Creation, King of kings, and Lord of lords—emptied himself of his rightful place as ruler with all power. He did not "selfishly exploit his divine form and mode of being, but by his own decision emptied himself of it or laid it by, taking the form of a servant by becoming man."[14] That's not to say he quit being fully God. He was willing to forego his own privileges of divinity, while still being fully divine. We would think that—being fully God, though fully man—he would automatically assume the title of universal ruler and leader of all nations. We would think he would have been born in a palace of unmatched architectural structure and beauty. We would think that he would have risen to the highest level of fame, prominence, and fortune of any human in history. We would think that his presence alone immediately would have caught the attention of the masses. Yet Isaiah 53:2–3 depicts a completely different story. "He had no beauty or majesty to attract us to him, nothing in his appearance that we should desire him. He was despised and rejected by mankind, a man of suffering, and familiar with pain. Like one from whom people hide their faces he was despised, and we held him in low esteem."

I love the following parable by Søren Kierkegaard about a powerful and feared king who loved a humble maiden:

> "'How could he declare his love for her? . . . If he brought her to the palace and crowned her head with jewels and clothed her body in royal robes, she would surely not resist . . . But would she love him? She would say she loved him, of course, but would she truly? . . . How could he know? If he rode to her forest cottage in his royal carriage, with an armed escort waving bright banners, that too would overwhelm her. He did not want a cringing subject. He wanted a lover, an equal. He wanted her to forget that he was a

---

13. Augustine, *Confessions*1.1.

14. TDNT, III:661.

king and she a humble maiden and to let shared love cross over the gulf between them."[15]

Philip Yancey noted, "The king, convinced he could not elevate the maiden without crushing her freedom, resolved to descend. He clothed himself as a beggar and approached her cottage incognito, with a worn cloak fluttering loosely about him. It was no mere disguise, but a new identity he took on. He renounced the throne to win her hand."[16] Second Corinthians 8:9 says, "For you know the grace of our Lord Jesus Christ, that though he was rich, yet for your sake he became poor, so that you through his poverty might become rich."

"In order to make sense of our lives we depend on some story. . . . I can only answer the question, 'What am I to do?' if I can answer the prior question, 'Of what story do I find myself a part?' Our lives—the questions and events and decisions and relationships that fill it—take their meaning from within some narrative."[17] Frankl, when trying to define some sort of ultimate meaning, expressed a similar idea invoking the analogy of a movie: "It consists of thousands upon thousands of individual pictures, and each of them makes sense and carries a meaning, yet the meaning of the whole film cannot be seen before its sequence is shown. On the other hand, we cannot understand the whole film without having first understood each of its components, each of the individual pictures. Isn't it the same with life?"[18] This analogy is most helpful in conveying the whole of Jesus's genealogy. We cannot understand the whole meaning of Solomon's life, or any of the others in the genealogy, without understanding the larger story about Jesus and his purpose in coming. And we cannot comprehend the story of Jesus without understanding the stories embedded in the names of the people in the genealogy.

Let's consider Frankl's statement that there must be a meaning to life under *any* conditions, alongside what Colossians 2:3 teaches us—that in Christ are "hidden all the treasures of wisdom and knowledge." If we can find meaning in *any* condition, then it is because we can draw upon hidden treasure *in Christ* for that moment. Frankl himself does not make this connection, but I believe it's true. At the center of the biblical metanarrative is Jesus. Our stories will find meaning in him and his story of redemption.

15. Yancey, *Disappointment with God*, 107. (Yancey's footnote credits Kierkegaard, *Philosophical Fragments*. Translated by David Swenson. Princeton: Princeton University Press, 1962, 31–43).

16. Yancey, *Disappointment with God*, 108.

17. Bartholomew and Goheen, *The Drama of Scripture*, 18.

18. Frankl, *Man's Search for Ultimate Meaning*, 143.

You and I will have countless opportunities in life to dig for and appropriate some hidden treasure of wisdom and knowledge in Christ, whether it's watching an indescribable sunset at the beach, or taking the trash to the street; witnessing the birth of a baby or laying to rest a loved one in the grave; experiencing the euphoria of a wedding day, or grieving the devastation of divorce; being awarded a Grammy or singing in the shower; watching an Oscar-winning film, or witnessing your child perform in the school play; being honored at work, or being humiliated by being fired; celebrating with friends, or enduring a season of isolation during a pandemic; laughing hysterically over a funny thing that happened, or weeping over a profound loss; participating in some significant cause, or carrying out a mundane task like washing the dishes. In each and every single one of these moments, there is some hidden treasure in Christ to be found and experienced. "If we want to know what God is like and what the universe is about, we should pay attention to the logic, meaning, wisdom, and patterns found in the life of Jesus."[19] We must consider his life, death, and resurrection.

Since 2018, I have had the privilege of getting together with a small group of friends almost every Thursday evening. On many of these evenings, Kurt, our facilitator, asks each of us to take turns in sharing what was most significant to us that week and why. It's a simple yet profound exercise because it forces us, in a good way, to reflect and draw some meaning out of life as we're living it. Such is a worthy habit—to search for hidden treasures of wisdom and knowledge in Christ for the rest of our lives.

Recovery of what God originally intended

For starters in searching for hidden treasure in Christ, let's seek to understand why Jesus descended to our level by considering the beginning of the *movie* of Scripture. Then, let's briefly consider some treasure in the first beatitude. Colossians 1:16–17 says, "For in him all things were created: things in heaven and on earth, visible and invisible, whether thrones or powers or rulers or authorities, all things have been created through him and for him. He is before all things, and in him all things hold together." According to the first couple of chapters in Genesis, God made everything in the universe, and saw that it was all good. Jesus descended to live among us in the flesh, affirming our earthly bodies and this entire material world as not evil, but good. Jesus participated in everyday human activities like eating, working, socializing, and sleeping. Romans 12:1, 1 Corinthians 10:31, and Colossians 3:23–24 affirm all of life as being sacred. But just as an oil spill pollutes and

---

19. McLaren, *We Make the Road by Walking*, 12.

poisons clean water, people throughout history going all the way back to Adam and Eve have made decisions which have twisted and distorted what God made and intended for good. "Everywhere we turn, the good possibilities of God's creation are misused, warped, and exploited for sinful ends."[20] Thus, "wherever anything wrong exists in the world . . . there we meet the perversion of God's good creation."[21]

But Jesus, of the lineage of King Solomon, and referred to as the Lion of Judah, descended and broke into the narrative to redeem this world. First published in 1950, C.S. Lewis's book, *The Lion, the Witch, and the Wardrobe*, has fascinated readers for decades. A chapter opens toward the end of the book as Narnia—liberated under Aslan's merciful reign—feels the warmth of spring spreading across the land, breaking through the endless winter of the witch's wicked rule. Aslan's power to redeem and renew emerge in every realm and with everyone he touches. The stories of the children who broke into the world of Narnia through the wardrobe, along with the stories of all creatures living in the midst of utter brokenness, suddenly gain new life, meaning, and purpose as their stories merge into the story of Aslan, the lion-king.

As Aslan came to restore Narnia to its original state before the winter of the witch's wicked rule, so too, the "whole purpose of the Christian life is the recovery of the original image of God, in other words, the recovery of the kind of human experience which God intended Adam and Eve to have before the Fall."[22] Jesus did not come to "repudiate" the humanity that God created, but rather to "recover the original." The message of Christianity "gets played out in us, in our limbs and eyes, in our feet and speech, in the faces of the men and women we see all day long, every day, in the mirror and on the sidewalk, in classroom and kitchen, in workplaces and on playgrounds, in sanctuaries and committees."[23] We were created in God's image. "He made us to relate to him and express his likeness in all of life—body, mind, emotions, will."[24] God affirms the self as good. We are to love our neighbor *as we love ourselves*. Don't confuse self with sin. We should care for and nurture our bodies, souls, and minds. "The Bible is never opposed to human experience as such; to experience life includes touch and taste, work and play, love and beauty."[25] We were intended by God to enjoy his Creation and all of its

---

20. Wolters, *Creation Regained*, 45.

21. Wolters, *Creation Regained*, 46.

22. Macauley and Barrs, *Being Human*, 16.

23. Peterson, *Christ Plays in Ten Thousand Places*, 3.

24. Macauley and Barrs, *Being Human*, 36.

25. Macauley and Barrs, *Being Human*, 119.

profound beauty. Having been made in God's image, we also were intended to create within and manage this Creation ourselves. Each of us has unique gifts and abilities given by God to employ for the service and benefit of others and the material world itself. It is healthy and good, then, to work at becoming more knowledgeable of who we are, how we are wired, about what we are passionate, and develop our talents and skills. Consider the vast array of jobs, careers, and voluntary roles millions and millions of people engage in day after day which provide goods and services needed (and often enjoyed) by the rest of humanity. Does it not amaze us to witness, experience, and benefit from the unique abilities of others? An artist painting on a canvas; a musician composing, singing, or playing an instrument; a teacher explaining a difficult concept; an entrepreneur setting forth a vision and strategy, a landscape architect beautifying our yards; an attorney advocating for a client. I could go on and on. The incredible diversity of people on this planet—and their myriad of talents—can astonish us if we atune ourselves to those hidden treasures in Christ. Human beings are beautiful!

It is critical, though, to keep in mind the biblical storyline as we view the world around us. "God is the ultimate origin of everything, the one who gives significance to all of life."[26] Meaning gets lost when we, like Solomon, seek to "snatch at the world to use it for our own pleasure and glory."[27] Meaning gets lost when success in the kingdom of this world crowds out our interest in the kingdom of God. Meaning gets lost when we consider the gifts of God more valuable than the Giver. As Timothy Keller puts it, "[T]he human heart takes good things like a successful career, love, material possessions, even family, and turns them into ultimate things. Our hearts deify them as the center of our lives, because, we think, they can give us significance and security, safety and fulfillment, if we attain them."[28]

"The way down is the way up."[29]

Conversely, we verge on discovering and experiencing true meaning when we've reached the bottom, echoing the words of Solomon: "I have seen all the things that are done under the sun; all of them are meaningless, a chasing after the wind." But no one wants to continue what feels like a downward journey. Rohr says this is the "primary reason why many

26. Macauley and Barrs, *Being Human*, 119.

27. Wright, *Following Jesus*, 9.

28. Keller, *Counterfeit Gods*, xix.

29. Rohr, *Falling Upward*, xviii

people never get to the fullness of their own lives."[30] What we've worked so diligently to attain, accomplish, accumulate, and achieve "have to fall apart and show themselves to be wanting in some way, or we will not move further."[31] He goes on to say, "The human ego prefers anything, just about anything, to falling or changing or dying. The ego is that part of you that loves the status quo."[32] The way to succeed at finding meaning is to dwell on the descent of Jesus as discussed earlier in the chapter. Then secondly, follow him down the same path.

The pathway that leads to healing, transformation, and meaning is, for sure, a process of brokenness, but it's also a pathway of grace. No performance is needed to gain God's approval. We've got it all backwards. We think the answers to life are found on the ascent to the top. But the first beatitude Jesus taught in Matthew 5:3 says, "Blessed are the poor in spirit." The Greek word for *blessed* is *makarios*. It denotes a transcendent happiness of life. Blessed is a distinctive joy unique to the person described by Jesus in these verses. The Greek word for *poor* in this instance is not the working-poor person who struggles to put food on the table after a hard day's labor earning a low wage. Poor in this instance is referring to the kind of person who is completely destitute, unable to work, forcing him or her to seek the help of others by begging.[33] A beggar is out of options, and therefore desperate and shameless in seeking help. A beggar in spirit then is someone experiencing spiritual poverty, or emptiness, and whose soul is desperately hungry to be filled.

At the beginning of this chapter, LeBeouf described feeling he had a God-sized hole in his life that needed to be filled. Kidd testified that her life had curled up into a frightening mark of a question: "Who was this self-inside of me who cried out to be?"[34] Nouwen also questioned his meaning and identity without the prestigious roles, accolades, and other achievements he had attained. Dobson humbly admitted that he no longer had answers for life's biggest questions after experiencing the devastating effects of ALS. My friend woefully cried out, "There's got to be more to life than this," and Rohr said, "Most of us have to hit some kind of bottom before we even start the real spiritual journey."[35] Otherwise, we will not hunger and thirst

---

30. Rohr, *Falling Upward*, xix.

31. Rohr, *Falling Upward*, xix.

32. Rohr, *Falling Upward*, xxiv.

33. Bromily, *The International Standard Bible Encyclopedia*, 3:906.

34. Kidd, *When the Heart Waits*, 7.

35. Rohr, *Falling Upward*, 138.

or even bother with searching for all those hidden treasures of wisdom and knowledge in Christ.

And so why are those who are poor in spirit considered blessed? Because *theirs is the kingdom of heaven.* Jesus descended, but he also ascended! But the descent happened *before* the ascent: "And being found in appearance as a man, he humbled himself by becoming obedient to death—even death on a cross! Therefore God exalted him to the highest place and gave him the name that is above every name" (Phil 2:8–9). Resurrection follows crucifixion. Being poor in spirit places us on the edge of winter's surrender to spring.

CHAPTER 12

Justice in the Face of Evil

—— *Manasseh and Amon* ——

"When souls become wicked they will certainly use this possibility to hurt one another; and this, perhaps, accounts for four-fifths of the sufferings of men. It is men, not God, who have produced racks, whips, prisons, slavery, guns, bayonets, and bombs."[1]—C.S. Lewis

"To love righteousness is to make it grow, not to avenge it."[2] —George MacDonald

A biographer of George Washington Carver described how traders handled enslaved Africans upon capture: "[They] were branded with the merchant's initials by means of hot irons, their heads were shaved, and they were stripped naked, men and women alike. To the clanking of their leg irons they were stowed away."[3] Hundreds of thousands died, many casting themselves into the sea, on the long ocean voyage. "Only one out of six, captured in Africa, arrived in the New World."[4] Then the journey would end on the slave block.[5] Their labor as slaves served as the basis upon which prosperity was built, "but neither the land nor its fruits were their own."[6] In the post-Civil War context, leaders such as Booker T. Washington and George Washington Carver emerged to try to emancipate their "race from the ad-

---

1. Lewis, *The Problem of Pain*, 16.
2. MacDonald, *Life Essential: The Hope of the Gospel*, 24.
3. Holt, *George Washington Carver*, 134.
4. Holt, *George Washington Carver*, 134.
5. Holt, *George Washington Carver*, 134.
6. Holt, *George Washington Carver*, 137.

juncts of slavery and instruct them how to live like free men."[7] Following is a description of the kinds of challenges they faced in the deep South:

> In Macon County, as elsewhere in the deep South, were count-less unschooled men and women, recently slaves, whom Emancipation had thrown on their own with no knowledge of anything except taking orders and laboring in the cotton fields. These children of the scarred back and branded breast suddenly had no food, no clothes, no homes, and had never been taught to provide such things for the morrow; they had never owned anything which had to be protected. Families had been torn apart by sales, marriage had been forbidden, and their women had been subject to the command of white masters; hence they were as lacking in morals as in stability. Their religion preached submission, but even the comfort of the hope of a better land hereafter they could enjoy only at night in the woods by 'stealing away to Jesus.' Thus spiritually crippled by white men, they were entering upon merciless competition with those same men, who were set in the determination to keep them without lands, with-out votes, without schools.[8]

The Equal Justice Initiative in 2015 published a five-year study that found nearly four-thousand Black men, women and children were lynched in the southern states alone between 1877 and 1950.[9]

In a different country, a young boy—who for some time attended a Catholic school, sang in the choir, and considered becoming a priest—eventually dreamed of attending a classical school and becoming an artist. The boy, however, became neither a priest nor a painter, but a national zealot who orchestrated the murder of some six million Jews. The boy was Adolf Hitler.

Presence of evil

Evil is real. Sex trafficking—girls being kidnapped, enslaved, threatened, abused, drugged, and forced to work as prostitutes all day every day, seven days a week; genocide; racial injustices; the millions of children who are homeless around the world—just to name a few examples. Such evil pro-duces traumatized persons. Yet over time we can become desensitized and

---

7. Holt, *George Washington* Carver, 110.

8. Holt, *George Washington* Carver, 110.

9. Stevenson, "As Study Finds 4,000 Lynchings in Jim Crow South, Will U.S. Ad-dress Legacy of Racial Terrorism?", lines 5–7.

emotionally detached to all the harm inflicted upon our fellow human beings as well as to the earth itself.

Dr. Scott Peck in his book, *People of the Lie*, reflected upon evil committed during the Vietnam War by American troops against civilians in an area called My Lai. He discussed some of the psychology behind how humans respond to stress to help explain why such group evil occurred there. When we are in painful and unpleasant circumstances that are emotionally overwhelming, "we have the capacity to anesthetize ourselves. . . . The sight of a single bloody, mangled body horrifies us. But if we see such bodies all around us every day, . . . the horrible becomes normal and we lose our sense of horror. We simply tune it out. Our capacity for horror becomes blunted. . . . Unconsciously we have become anesthetized."[10]

When most think about evil, their thoughts go to Hitler, Bin Laden, or some serial killer. We also tend to associate evil with what I've mentioned. Yet wolves exist among us in sheep's clothing. Sylvia Fraser recounted the tributes paid at her father's funeral. He was a man "who didn't smoke or drink . . . who helped with the grocery shopping, who never took the Lord's name in vain."[11] Mr. Fraser was nice and neighborly. "He also sexually molested his daughter Sylvia from age four to twelve, threatening first with the loss of her toys (he'd throw them into the furnace), then with killing her cat, then with sending her away to an orphanage—all this if she were to disclose their secret."[12]

The Bible does not hide, minimize, deny, or sugarcoat any of the horrible history which took place. King Manasseh, for example, "did much evil in the eyes of the LORD, arousing his anger" (2 Kings 21:6). His son, Amon, also did what was evil in the sight of the LORD: "He forsook the LORD, the God of his ancestors, and did not walk in obedience to him" (2 Kings 21:20, 22). Unlike the faith heroines, these kings were remembered for their evil legacies. Manasseh's reign began at age twelve and lasted fifty-five years. Can you imagine one president in the United States holding office for that long? The people of Israel would not listen to or follow God. Second Kings 21:9 says, "Manasseh led them astray, so that they did more evil than the nations the LORD had destroyed before the Israelites." He "plunged his nation into gross idolatry unequaled in Palestine since the days of Ahab and Jezebel."[13] Jezebel, a Phoenician princess, married King Ahab of Israel, who ruled from 874—853 BC. Many of God's prophets were killed at her command. Under

10. Peck, *People of the Lie*, 221.

11. Fraser, *My Father's House: A Memoir of Incest and Healing*, 239.

12. Plantinga, *Not the Way It's Supposed to Be*, 46–47.

13. Bromily, *The International Standard Bible Encyclopedia*, 3:234.

Manasseh's leadership, astronomical worship was instituted, as well as the sacrifice of children to the Ammonite deity Moloch. He even sacrificed his own son in a fire. "Manasseh also shed so much innocent blood that he filled Jerusalem from end to end" (2 Kings 21:16).What an extraordinary statement summarizing his profound wickedness.

Amon, Manasseh's son, continued in his father's evil footsteps. Twenty-two years old when he became king. Amon also abandoned the Lord and served the idols that his father served. For another two years, he perpetrated the same atrocities as his father.

We wonder at times how one evil person with this much power can cause so much widespread destruction and death. What were the key advisors and leaders around Manasseh doing? Based on verses we just read, anyone disloyal was likely put to death. To help us make sense of this, consider on a small scale the power of negative peer pressure in groups. Too fearful of being ostracized, ridiculed, or attacked themselves, bystanders remain silent, or even act as if they approve. As a young boy, I was bullied in a men's locker room one summer day by older and bigger teenage boys. The ringleader grabbed my head, slightly banging it against the lockers. He laughed and taunted me as his friends gathered around and laughed as well. My mother, who had brought us to the pool for the day, somehow caught wind of what was happening and stormed in. *Oh, we were just having a little fun*, the ringleader said. Even with my mom present, I would not call him out for fear I would be viewed as a sissy or cause more trouble for myself if I encountered them again. But I've been guilty as well of not speaking out. In junior high, three of my classmates initiated a fight against two brothers from Iran for no reason. Many students, including me, gathered around the classroom to watch the drama unfold. When fists started to fly, we all just stood there watching until a teacher rushed in, and then we all scattered like the wind. Every year across the country, young men seeking to join college fraternities endure verbal, psychological, and, in many cases, physical hazing as the other members stand around and do nothing. Similar situations occur to rookies on athletic teams.

Evil behavior occurs and persists in many cases because of enablers who remain silent and/or align with and support the perpetrator of evil. Perhaps they do so out of fear as was the case perhaps with the leaders and advisors around Manasseh. They knew he would have them executed immediately if they showed even a hint of protest. In other cases, however, the enablers agree with and advocate for the perpetrator and his or her actions because they are entangled in the same web of deception and have adopted his or her sick narrative. Such support enhances the perpetrator's confidence. Enablers may be part of the family, system, organization, or institution in which the evil takes place. Rather than protecting and advocating for victims being harmed, enablers are more committed to protecting themselves and the family, system, organization, or institution of which they are a part. Perhaps they wish to protect the perpetrator from experiencing the consequences of his or her actions. If someone within such a group courageously speaks out against the evil, he or she likely will be punished by the leader or group in some way. I will share this quote again about whistleblowers from William White: "Whistleblowing often involves calling attention to actions that are either illegal or that could involve harm to innocent parties. Because whistleblowers are rarely protected from retribution by the company, whistleblowing is one of the purest and highest-risk forms of activism. . . . That an act of whistle-blowing is morally and ethically justified does not serve as a protection from organizational retribution."[14]

Evil is thematic throughout Scripture. Early in the story of humanity, "The LORD saw how great the wickedness of the human race had become on the earth, and that every inclination of the thoughts of the human heart was only evil all the time" (Gen 6:5). The word, *evil*, appears almost four hundred times in the Old Testament and over one hundred times in the New Testament. Jesus taught his disciples to pray for deliverance from evil. In Matthew 12, he called the Pharisees evil, a brood of vipers. "For out of the heart come evil thoughts—murder, adultery, sexual immorality, theft, false testimony, slander" (Matt 15:19). Jesus healed many people of evil spirits,[15] and referred to Satan as the evil one (John 15:17). In Romans 1:29–32, there are those described as being "filled with every kind of wickedness, evil, greed and depravity. They are full of envy, murder, strife, deceit, and malice. They are gossips, slanderers, God-haters, insolent, arrogant and boastful; they invent ways of doing evil." Jesus came to deliver us from this present evil age (Gal 1), where we fight ". . . against the powers of this dark world and against the spiritual forces of evil in the heavenly realms" (Eph 6:12).

Understanding evil

What is evil? Jesus said in John 10:10, "The thief comes only to steal and kill and destroy; I have come that they may have life, and have it to the full." One author defines evil as "any spoiling of shalom, whether physically, morally, spiritually or otherwise."[16] Shalom he defined as "universal

---

14. White, *The Incestuous Workplace*, 208.
15. See Luke 6.
16. Plantinga, *Not the Way It's Supposed to Be*, 14.

flourishing, wholeness and delight—a rich state of affairs . . . ."[17] Rather than seeking to enrich life, evil seeks to steal from or destroy it. Allender and Longman in their book, *Bold Love,* shared these insights about evil: "Evil is present when there is a profound absence of empathy, shame, and goodness. . . . Goodness involves a desire to see someone or something grow in strength, freedom, and beauty. An evil person seems to delight in stripping away purpose, individuality, and vitality."[18] Furthermore, "an evil person . . . simply will not allow himself to enter the heart of his victim as a person."[19] "An evil person, regularly and masterfully, portrays his motives and behavior as innocent. . . . He is deceitfully gifted in making the victim of his abuse feel like the perpetrator of the harm. . . . He portrays himself as the real victim, cruelly misunderstood and falsely accused."[20] "Evil is devoid of a conscience."[21] "Evil is bad. That is, it is persistently destructive. But it is also deceitfully subtle. . . . [I]t often portrays itself at times as helpful, open, kind. . . . Such kindness or generosity seems to entangle the victim deeper in the evil person's web. If one is in a relationship with an evil person for long, the signs of death will begin to show—anemia (a loss of self, vitality, and strength), despair (a loss of desire and hope), and disorientation (a loss of direction and purpose)."[22]

Peck points out that "evil is in opposition to life. It has, in short, to do with killing."[23] Spell *live* backwards to help you remember this. This killing doesn't have to be physical, but can be spiritual, emotional, or psychological. Evil behavior may include "the desire of certain people to control others—to make them controllable, to foster their dependency, to discourage their capacity to think for themselves, to diminish their unpredictability and originality, to keep them in line. . . . Evil, then, . . . seeks to kill life or liveliness."[24] Evil people are "chronic scapegoaters, . . . Since they must deny their own badness, they must perceive others as bad. They project their own evil onto the world. They never think of themselves as evil; on the other hand, they consequently see much evil in others."[25]

17. Plantinga, *Not the Way It's Supposed to Be,* 10.

18. Allender and Longman, *Bold Love,* 234.

19. Allender and Longman, *Bold Love,* 234.

20. Allender and Longman, *Bold Love,* 236.

21. Allender and Longman, *Bold Love,* 237.

22. Allender and Longman, *Bold Love,* 240–241.

23. Peck, *People of the Lie,* 42.

24. Peck, *People of the Lie,* 43.

25. Peck, *People of the Lie,* 73.

I strongly urge you to be careful about using this information to categorize certain people as evil. Each of us has been hurt by the actions of others, and each of us has hurt others. This does not mean we or they are evil persons. Romans 3:23 says, "[A]ll have sinned and fall short of the glory of God." King David's sins of adultery, abuse of power, and murder were evil actions. Yet he was referred to as a man after God's own heart according to Acts 13:22 and 1 Samuel 13:14. David wrote many of the Psalms. His sorrow and repentance appeared genuine. Always remember, *any* human being made in God's image is redeemable.

I share these stories and explanations of evil to awaken the conscience, raise awareness, and break us out of tolerating behavior that should not be considered normal or acceptable. For our own protection and for the sake of victims being harmed, we must not allow ourselves to become or remain anesthetized. Knowledge can play a huge part of the healing process and efforts to do justice. For example, if we understood the dynamics of gaslighting, we would be better equipped to protect ourselves and provide support for a friend being victimized by it. Our friend may be confused and feel a false sense of shame believing he or she is the problem. And that is exactly what the abusive person wants. Abusive persons can be deceitful, exploitative, manipulative and controlling, yet lack any guilt, shame or remorse. Victims who are often unaware of how they have been deceived, manipulated, and exploited need a caring voice of truth speaking to their beautiful hearts and minds.

How does evil grow in a person's heart? How do they become so hardened and impenitent? As a reminder, it begins with self-deception. If engaged in long enough, our internal moral compass erodes, and we cease hearing or listening to God's voice. Dr. Langberg says that as deception normalizes in a person's life, "evil can be easily practiced by an increasingly dead soul."[26] Evil people don't just destroy others, they destroy themselves. But they blame others for their own self-destruction because they believe their delusions to be reality. Evil unfolds as "temptation arises, self-deception or delusion joins in, evil is termed good or at least justified, the choice is habituated, and the prisoner is trapped, actively participating and barreling toward death."[27]

Evil actions of people cause trauma to victims. Trauma is like being taken under by a personal tsunami. "Trauma means living with the recurrent, tormenting memories of atrocities witnessed or borne."[28] Such

---

26. Langberg, *Suffering and the Heart of God*, 200.
27. Langberg, *Suffering and the Heart of God*, 200.
28. Langberg, *Suffering and the Heart of God*, 5.

trauma can result in ruined relationships, emotional suffering, horrific nightmares, and an inability to work or function normally. Trauma can destroy faith and leave a person feeling hopeless. If you have been traumatized, I am so sorry. Perhaps you will find some of the resources footnoted in the book helpful. I hope you have a trusted friend or friends, a safe church, mentors, and professional counselors who can walk with you through your healing journey. To have another demonstrate love by being present, listening with empathy, and offering timely encouragement and ongoing advocacy and support is an immeasurable grace. If you are going through something traumatic currently, the help you need is not reading or reflection, but rescue. A person pinned under a car because of a wreck does not need a book, counseling, or a rehab session at the point of impact. So, if this describes you—someone currently suffering trauma—I pray you're getting the help you *do* need to get to a place of safety.

Justice, redemption, and good overcoming evil

Do seeds of redemption lie buried in the ground of such horrible situations? Is there hope for healing? World War II was traumatic for millions of people around the world. C.S. Lewis wrote a lot within the context of that war. At one point, he wrote:

> We may distinguish (1) the simple good descending from God, (2) the simple evil produced by rebellious creatures, and (3) the exploitation of that evil by God for His redemptive purpose, which produces (4) the complex good . . . Now the fact that God can make complex good out of simple evil does not excuse— though by mercy it may save—those who do the simple evil. And this distinction is central . . . The crucifixion itself is the best, as well as the worst, of all historical events, but the role of Judas remains simply evil.[29]

Judas's actions contributed directly to the greatest unfairness in all of history—the brutal crucifixion of the most innocent of all men. Yet God exploited that evil for his own redemptive purpose. Another classic example is the story of Joseph, son of Jacob. As already discussed, he was sold into slavery by his own brothers, and then unjustly sentenced to prison for several years in Egypt because of a false accusation. Yet God exploited this evil for his own redemptive purposes. God raised up Joseph to a powerful position to oversee preparation and management of resource distribution

29. Lewis, *The Problem of Pain*, 111.

during years of famine. His oversight saved countless lives both inside and outside of Egypt. When he was reunited with his brothers after so many years of separation, his response was: "You intended to harm me, but God intended it for good to accomplish what is now being done, the saving of many lives" (Gen 50:20). Suffering, violence, abuse, and death are *not* good. But God can redeem the deepest injustices and hurts.

Be assured. God rages against evil and injustice. Tim Keller, in a sermon on Romans 3:21–31, said, "You don't pit anger and justice against love and goodness. It's the love and goodness that makes you angry at injustice."[30] Many are quick to protest that *God is a God of love, not a God of wrath.* Anger is not the opposite of love. Hate is. "God is angry because he is filled with love."[31] The final form of hate is indifference. If God didn't love us, he wouldn't care![32] Several other passages of Scripture address these themes.[33]

Justice is, according to N.T. Wright, "a shorthand for the intention of God . . . to set the whole world right."[34] He also explains that "God's coming judgment is a good thing, something to be celebrated, longed for, yearned over. . . . In a world of systematic injustice, bullying, violence, arrogance, and oppression, the thought that there might come a day when the wicked are firmly put in their place and the poor and weak are given their due is the best news there can be. Faced with . . . a world full of exploitation and wickedness, a good God must be a God of judgment."[35] He goes on to note: "The one through whom God's justice will finally sweep the world is not a hardhearted, arrogant, or vengeful tyrant but rather the Man of Sorrows, who was acquainted with grief; the Jesus who loved sinners and died for them; the Messiah who took the world's judgment upon himself on the cross."[36] "[God] is a king who wants not subservience, but love," Philip Yancey beautifully stated. "Thus, rather than mowing down Jerusalem, Rome, and every other worldly power, he chose the slow, hard way of Incarnation, love, and death. A conquest within."[37] George MacDonald said, "To love righteousness is to

---

30. Keller "By the Blood of Jesus Christ."

31. Keller "By the Blood of Jesus Christ."

32. Keller "By the Blood of Jesus Christ."

33. Matt 25:31–46; Luke 21:22–4; John 5:22, 27; Acts 10:42, 17:31; Rom 1:18, 2:5, 5:9, 12:19, 13:4–5, 14:10–12; 2 Cor 5:10; Phil 2:10; 1 Thess 1:8–10, 5:9; 2 Tim 4:1, 8; Rev 6:16, 14:10–11.

34. Wright, *Surprised by Hope*, 213.

35. Wright, *Surprised by Hope*, 137.

36. Wright, *Surprised by Hope*, 141.

37. Yancey, *Disappointment with God*, 123.

make it grow, not to avenge it . . ."[38] I'm reminded of Romans 12:21, which says, "Do not be overcome by evil, but overcome evil with good."

Dr. Langberg has had decades of experience sitting with victims of every kind of abuse and violence—from sexual assault and domestic violence, to combat and genocide. She says, "the trauma of this world is one of the primary mission fields of the twenty-first century."[39] Therefore, "we are not to respond passively. We are not to sit back and let evil, sin, suffering, or the Evil One have its way. We are called to do battle."[40]

During the time I was reviewing and editing this chapter, something happened that deeply convicted me. I received a bill from the power company for $428. I had recently moved, and the bill was for the old address. I was livid because I knew I was paid up on that account. So, I got on the phone with customer-service and inquired about the bill, expecting her to fix it. She kindly tried to explain why I had to pay it. I calmly pushed back, arguing that it made no sense and was unfair. I could feel my insides boiling, so I got off the phone. This was the power company. It's not like they have competition. If I did not pay it, they would shut my power off. Period. So, it infuriated me to be victimized like that by the power company. Then, a light bulb came on (had to). How is it that reading a bill for $428 triggers such anger within me, yet reading that two-hundred million children are homeless in this world does not? How is it that being victimized by the power company troubles me, but sex-trafficked slaves being victimized by those abusing power does not? How is it that I can be so resolved and swift to take action to try and solve my trivial, short-term problem, yet so unresolved and slow to address the pervasive, long-term suffering of those who are most vulnerable? And guess what ended up happening with the power company. There was a big misunderstanding. But overall, they were correct.

It is good to pause and return here to Micah 6:8—"He has shown you, O mortal, what is good. And what does the LORD require of you? To act justly and to love mercy and to walk humbly with your God." To do what is fair and just *to* our neighbors, to advocate for what is fair and just *for* our neighbors, to be merciful and compassionate towards and *on behalf of* our neighbors will require that we walk humbly with the Lord. Left to ourselves, we are prone to be concerned only with ourselves. In our own strength, we would not be able to persevere for long among the vulnerable traumatized by evil. The wounds are deep, the healing path is long, and therefore the

---

38. MacDonald, *Life Essential: The Hope of the Gospel*, 24.

39. Langberg, *Suffering and the Heart of God*, 9. Further resources available at http://www.dianelangberg.com, and at the website for the Global Trauma Recovery Institute: http://global-traumarecovery.org.

40. Langberg, *Suffering and the Heart of God*, 57.

costs are high. Evil persons are extraordinarily strong-willed and deter-mined to have their own way. The task is too burdensome to go at it alone. If not careful, bitterness, evil, and hate could unexpectedly take root in our own hearts and begin to consume us. We must therefore walk humbly with the Lord and seek his redemptive work in our own lives.

We also need the ongoing encouragement of a community. Sam and Frodo's climactic approach to Mount Doom provides a relevant depiction of the journey we face against evil:

> "So the desperate journey went on . . . For the hobbits each day, each mile, was more bitter than the one before, as their strength lessened and the land became more evil. . . . But far worse than all such perils was the ever-approaching threat that beat upon them as they went. . . . Nearer and nearer it drew, looming blacker, like the oncoming of a wall of night at the last end of the world. . . . All this last day Frodo had not spoken, but had walked half-bowed, often stumbling, as if his eyes no longer saw the way before his feet. Sam guessed that among all their pains he bore the worst, the growing weight of the Ring, a burden on the body and a torment to his mind . . . when his (Frodo's) eyes beheld the Mountain and the desert he quailed again. 'I can't manage it, Sam,' he said. 'It is such a weight to carry, such a weight.'"[41]

Let's consider one man's effort to love righteousness and make it grow. Bryan Stevenson as a young attorney founded the Equal Justice Initiative (EJI), a legal practice dedicated to defending the poor, the wrongly con-demned, and those trapped in the furthest reaches of our criminal justice system. His book, *Just Mercy*, tells the true story of Walter McMillian, a man sentenced to die for a murder he didn't commit. Stevenson defended him.

> "The book is about getting closer to mass incarceration and extreme punishment in America. It is about how easily we con-demn people in this country and the injustice we create when we allow fear, anger, and distance to shape the way we treat the most vulnerable among us. It's also about a dramatic period in our recent history . . . Today we have the highest rate of in-carceration in the world. The prison population has increased from 300,000 people in the early 1970s to 2.3 million people today. . . . For years, we've been the only country in the world that condemns children to life imprisonment without parole; nearly three thousand juveniles have been sentenced to die in prison. Hundreds of thousands of nonviolent offenders have

41. Tolkien, *The Return of the King*, 914, 916.

been forced to spend decades in prison. . . . There are more than a half-million people in state or federal prisons for drug offenses today, up from just 41,000 in 1980. . . . We've given up on reha-bilitation, education, and services for the imprisoned because providing assistance to the incarcerated is apparently too kind and compassionate."[42]

EJI, which is based in Montgomery, Alabama, creatively has provided a voice for African Americans who were lynched between the 1870s and 1950s. The National Memorial for Peace and Justice[43] gives a powerful voice to the legacy of enslaved Black people, people terrorized by lynching, "African Americans humiliated by racial segregation and Jim Crow, and people of color burdened with contemporary presumptions of guilt and police violence." Six million Black people fled the South as refugees and exiles because of racial terror lynchings. EJI staff have been able to "memorialize this history by visiting hundreds of lynching sites, collecting soil, and erecting public markers, in an effort to reshape the cultural landscape with monuments and memorials that more truthfully and accurately reflect our history."[44]

In what ways are we seeking to love and grow righteousness and push back evil with goodness? Often, the voices of victims end up serving as prophetic voices to expose and overcome a particular evil. Dozens of women, for instance, bravely came forward with allegations of sexual mis-conduct against a former and powerful American film producer in 2017. Their courageous voices helped empower many other victimized women to come forward with their own stories. In May 2020, the wrongful killing of George Floyd under the knee of a white police officer triggered public out-rage and mass protests against police brutality and racial injustice around the world. You may remember Elizabeth Smart who was kidnapped at the age of fourteen in 2002, and held captive for nine months before she was discovered eighteen miles from her home. Smart became an advocate for missing persons and victims of sexual assault. You may recognize the name Malala. In her region, Pakistani Taliban had banned girls from attending school. In October of 2012 after taking an exam while riding a bus, she and two other girls were shot by a Pakistani Taliban gunman as an act of retali-ation for her activism. A bullet hit her in the head, causing her to remain unconscious and in critical condition for a period. The event rocketed her to a global stage. She survived and now advocates for human rights—particularly for the education of women and children in that northwest

---

42. Stevenson, *Just Mercy*, 14–15.

43. Find more information at: https://museumandmemorial.eji.org/

44. https://museumandmemorial.eji.org/memorial

region of Pakistan. Her efforts have had an international impact. She is the youngest Nobel Prize laureate. What redemptive good could grow out of the seeds existing within the wounds of our lives?

Eventually, after Stevenson fought a laborious battle to prove Walter McMillian's innocence and win his freedom, the Alabama Court of Criminal Appeals finally ruled he had been wrongfully convicted. A judge pronounced McMillian a free man. They won! Today, suffering is prevalent. Evil is here. The planet is groaning for freedom. While we work hard to cope in this life, we must remember that the genealogy did not stop with Manasseh and Amon. The seed of redemption that God initially planted in the story of Abraham continued. Evil will not have the last word. Our hope remains in the one who said in John 16:33, "In this godless world you will continue to experience difficulties. But take heart! I've conquered the world" (MSG). Conquering denotes victory, superiority, winning, defeating, or overthrowing an opposing force.[45] It's true! Evil *will not* win. So, do not fear. "But let justice roll on like a river, righteousness like a never-failing stream" (Amos 5:24). May God exploit the evil we have faced, redeem it for his purposes and grow goodness from those seeds of redemption in the world.

45. TDNT, IV:942, 944.

CHAPTER 13

Future Hope While Longing for Home

Hezekiah & Josiah

"Like Adam, we have all lost Paradise; and yet we carry Paradise around inside of us in the form of a longing for, almost a memory of, a blessedness that is no more, or the dream of a blessedness that may someday be again."[1]—Frederick Buechner

"The more I considered Christianity, the more I found that while it had established a rule and order, the chief aim of that order was to give room for good things to run wild."[2]—G.K. Chesterton

I n case you have not watched *Game of Thrones* from beginning to end, you may want to skip over the next couple of pages. For purposes I will explain afterward, I want to share about a couple of key characters in the series. Season one introduces us to House Stark of Winterfell. Lord Ned Stark and his wife, Catelyn, have five children. Their fourth child is Bran. Early in the season, Bran as a young boy is climbing on the rock wall of an unused structure and works his way over to a large, open window where he witnesses an event he shouldn't see. He unintentionally catches Ser Jaime Lannister secretly together with his sister, Cersei, who is in a loveless marriage with King Robert Baratheon, a good friend of Bran's father, Ned. Immediately aware of the severe consequences if Bran makes known their incestuous affair, Jaime shoves Bran out of the window.[3] Bran does not die but remains in a coma for some time. When he awakes, Bran realizes he

---

1. Buechner, *The Magnificent Defeat*, 91.

2. Chesterton, *Orthodoxy*, 97.

3. *Game of Thrones*, Season 1, episode 1, "Winter is Coming," created by David Benioff and D.B. Weiss, featuring Isaac Hempstead, Wright, Lena Headey, and Nikolaj Coster-Waldau, aired April 17, 2011, in broadcast syndication, HBO.

is paralyzed. He later begins having mysterious dreams beckoning him to travel North beyond the great Wall as rumors grow about the White Walkers, ancient enemies who had been dormant for a thousand years. Eventually in his journey with other companions, he discovers he possesses unique powers and abilities. While other complex storylines evolve regarding who will take control of the Iron Throne to rule over the lands of Westeros, Bran's path takes him closer to a confrontation with the White Walkers and their leader, the Night King.

By the end of the series, Bran, as a paraplegic, is crowned king and thus rules on the Iron Throne.[4] He is good-hearted, demonstrates admirable courage and wisdom, and will act in the best interest of the people in the realms he rules. Bran was the victim of an evil act. Yet a seed of redemption lay buried in the ground of his horrific circumstances. Over time, this seed grew. An unlikely, but good, humble, and wise young man emerged to unify kingdoms, replacing what had been divided and destroyed by those greedy for power and control.

In one of the most dramatic scenes in season eight, Bran sits beside a weirwood tree during the night in the godswood of Winterfell as a fierce battle is raging. Bran is about to face the Night King as the White Walkers appear to have all but conquered the allied forces. A few guards surround Bran, including Theon Greyjoy, the heir apparent of one of the other kingdoms as son of Balon Greyjoy. Early on in his life, Theon had been taken in by the Starks and was raised in Winterfell. But when he grew older, Theon became cocky and turned on the Stark family. He was later captured, imprisoned, and tortured by Ramsay Bolton, illegitimate son of Roose Bolton, Lord of the Dreadfort and House Bolton. Ramsay severely abused and brainwashed Theon to the point of believing his name and identity was Reek, which of course means *stink*. The journey for Theon thus involved regrettable decisions on his own part as well as immense suffering at the hands of an extraordinarily wicked man. Yet here at the end, Theon, among other honorable actions, displays valiant courage in his willingness to sacrifice his life to protect Bran. Moments before the appearance of the Night King, Theon approaches Bran, who is seated in his wheelchair, to confess his misdeeds and to make things right—*Bran, I just want you to know, I wish the things I did . . . .* But before he could utter anything else, Bran interrupts him, saying, *Everything you did brought you where you are now, where you belong . . . home.*[5]

4. *Game of Thrones*, Season 8, episode 6, "The Iron Throne," created by David Benioff and D.B. Weiss, featuring Isaac Hempstead Wright, aired May 19, 2019, in broadcast syndication, HBO.

5. *Game of Thrones*, Season 8, episode 3, "The Long Night," created by David Benioff

Our good Father

In a way, this scene reminds me of the story of the prodigal son as told in Luke 15. The younger of two sons asks the father for his inheritance early. Luke 15:12–17 says, "It wasn't long before the younger son packed his bags and left for a distant country. There, undisciplined and dissipated, he wasted everything he had. After he had gone through all his money, there was a bad famine all through that country and he began to feel it. He signed on with a citizen there who assigned him to his fields to slop the pigs. He was so hungry he would have eaten the corn cobs in the pig slop, but no one would give him any. That brought him to his senses" (MSG). The pig slop was probably a messy, wet mix of various leftovers no human would ever want to smell, touch, or taste. The son, clearly at the end of his rope and filled with guilt and shame over his disastrous decisions, decides to journey back home in hopes his father will at least hire him to work. Here is how the Father responded upon seeing his son in the distance in Luke 15:20–24: "When he was still a long way off, his father saw him. His heart pounding, he ran out, embraced him, and kissed him. The son started his speech: 'Father, I've sinned against God, I've sinned against you; I don't deserve to be called your son ever again.' But the father wasn't listening. He was calling to his servants, 'Quick. Bring a clean set of clothes and dress him. Put the family ring on his finger and sandals on his feet. Then get a prize-winning heifer and roast it. We're going to feast! We're going to have a wonderful time! My son is here—given up for dead and now alive! Given up for lost and now found!' And they began to have a wonderful time" (MSG). Henri Nouwen's book, *The Return of the Prodigal Son,* is the product of his own personal experience of spending hours reflecting on this story while viewing a reproduction of Rembrandt's painting of this biblical scene. (I highly commend the book.)

The last chapter on evil was difficult and exhausting to write. We all can attest to our own experiences—or to the trials of people we know—who have walked through the valley of the shadow of death because of evil done to them. It is tragic and devastating. It makes us angry. It makes us sick. It makes us grind our teeth, clench our fists, and shake our heads in disgust and despair as we play the questions in our minds like: *How could something like this ever happen?*

Being in such a valley of death can directly influence how we view God. *He must not be good, powerful, all-wise, or loving. If God even exists, how could he possibly allow something like this to happen?* Such questions

---

and D.B. Weiss, featuring Isaac Hempstead Wright, Alfie Allen, and Iwan Rheon, aired April 17, 2011, in broadcast syndication, HBO.

are honest and understandable. Yet along the journey, are there not sign-posts and both normal and extraordinary experiences of wonder, beauty, justice, and goodness that resonate deeply in our souls and give us tastes and hints about a glorious kingdom we might refer to as home? Have we not had moments in our lives where our hearts screamed out, *Yes! This is how it's supposed to be! This is where I belong! I am in the right place!* I have experienced this witnessing our children being born; being caught up in the moment and music of a live concert; observing some beautiful aspect of nature; hugging someone I love; witnessing a spectacular achievement; engaging in an activity I have enjoyed or felt passionate about; or laughing with and participating in conversation with friends. It's as Frederick Buech-ner beautifully stated: "Like Adam, we have all lost Paradise; and yet we carry Paradise around inside of us in the form of a longing for, almost a memory of, a blessedness that is no more, or the dream of a blessedness that may someday be again."[6]

Dallas Willard provided this description of God, saying, "Undoubt-edly he (God) is the most joyous being in the universe. The abundance of his love and generosity is inseparable from his infinite joy . . . he is simply one great inexhaustible and eternal experience of all that is good and true and beautiful and right." He goes on to say:

> "Jesus himself was and is a joyous, creative person. He does not allow us to continue thinking of our Father who fills and over-flows space as a morose and miserable monarch, a frustrated and petty parent, or a policeman on the prowl . . . . So, we must understand that God does not 'love' us without liking us—through gritted teeth—as 'Christian' love is sometimes thought to do. Rather, out of the eternal freshness of his perpetually self-renewed being, the heavenly Father cherishes the earth and each human being in it. The fondness, the endearment, the unstint-ingly affectionate regard of God toward all his creatures is the natural outflow of what he is to the core."[7]

Homesickness

Is this explanation of God not what is so profoundly manifested in the story of the father's response to the return of his prodigal son as told by Jesus? At a global scale, do we not long for a world where all is finally well, good, beautiful, peaceful, and just? (Spoiler alert again: skip this

6. Buechner, *The Magnificent Defeat*, 91.

7. Willard, *The Divine Conspiracy*, 62–4.

paragraph if you intend to watch GOT). Through all sorts of chaos, evil, war, twists, and turmoil of every kind and at every turn . . . finally all plot lines in the *Game of Thrones* found their resolution in Bran crowned king of the six kingdoms. At the end of that series, we witness something new arise out of the ashes of much destruction and death. At a personal level, do we not each long for redemption, not unlike Theon's encounter with Bran? To hear and know with all our hearts that we have been forgiven, accepted, and are dearly beloved. That God in his goodness, wisdom, and power has somehow exploited the evil which has occurred and produced a complex good out of all that has happened in our lives and has brought us to the place we've longed for all along . . . *home.* "We are all exiles, always longing for home. We are always traveling, never arriving. The houses and families we actually inhabit are only inns along the way, but they aren't home. Home continues to evade us."[8]

One night, a woman kidnapped two little girls. She gave them new names. For the next many years, she moved them from place to place. Far away from home, the girls did not know from day to day when they would get to eat or sleep. One day they would find themselves in one school only to be moved to a new location the next. The system, ignorant and too lazy to investigate the true identities of these girls, failed them. The kidnapper—an abusive, evil, and habitual liar—refused to answer the girls' questions about their identity, home, or families, even as they grew older. When one of the girls became an adult, she persevered in her relentless search to discover her true identity and parents. When all hope seemed lost, and the search given up, a couple of critical facts fell into place. A birth certificate emerged, allowing this lost woman the opportunity she had longed for . . . the chance to find home. Knowing now her real name, and the names of her parents, she at last became reunited with them after decades of separation. The inspiration behind her hope to persevere was the love she felt confident her parents had for her out there somewhere.

Each of us has a God-given homing device that causes us to yearn for that ideal home. "We are both driven and called forward by a kind of deep homesickness."[9] Yet the way life happens with all its brokenness and loss, we wonder if we will ever arrive. So often in that journey home, we don't recognize the mysterious ways in which God is at work, especially when it's all going wrong. Like Theon's story, it's so counterintuitive to see how

---

8. Keller, *The Prodigal God,* 95.

9. Rohr, *Falling Upward,* 89.

"falling, losing, failing, transgression, and sin are the pattern," says Rohr. "Yet they all lead toward home."[10]

C.S. Lewis offered this keen insight about our desires:

> Indeed, if we consider the unblushing promises of reward and the staggering nature of the rewards promised in the Gospels, it would seem that Our Lord finds our desires not too strong, but too weak. We are half-hearted creatures, fooling about with drink and sex and ambition when infinite joy is offered us, like an ignorant child who wants to go on making mud pies in a slum because he cannot imagine what is meant by the offer of a holiday at the sea. We are far too easily pleased.[11]

We, like the Israelites, resist believing the truths about God as I just reflected on . . . that he is "simply one great inexhaustible and eternal experience of all that is good and true and beautiful and right."[12] That he cherishes the earth and us. And so, we have a hard time believing, therefore, that he is good and that his kingdom is like the offer of a holiday at the sea. We resist instead, insisting on the belief that surely making mud pies is as good as it gets. God's love for us is truly unfathomable and inexplicable. He passionately desires our good. So, when Jesus says the greatest command is for us to love God and love our neighbor as we love ourselves—could it be that intrinsic in this command is our greatest good? It is so simple, yet profoundly beautiful. Such love must be the core or essence of what it means to arrive finally at home. But the pathway to resurrection is through crucifixion. Like with Theon and the prodigal son, it often takes painful reality to come to our senses. Yet ironically, such is the pathway *home*.

Future hope

Weaved into the stories of the genealogy of Jesus are kings described as good. Not perfect by any stretch, but they are described as having done what was right in the eyes of God. Consequently, we are given a taste of a greater glory to come. Second Chronicles 30:26 provides a summary snapshot of what life was like for Israel in a season under such leadership: "There was great joy in Jerusalem, for since the days of Solomon son of David king of Israel there had been nothing like this in Jerusalem." Why all the celebration?

---

10. Rohr, *Falling Upward*, 67.

11. Lewis, *The Weight of Glory*, 26.

12. Willard, *The Divine Conspiracy*, 63.

Israel had needed a shepherd leader who would guide them back toward God and his ways. God had promised Abraham back in Genesis 17:6 that he would make him into a great nation and that kings would come from him. Numerous kings are listed in the genealogy starting with King David. Second Samuel 7 contains the covenant God made with David, which is an essential passage regarding the unfolding story of God's redemptive plan. The whole Davidic Covenant can be read in 2 Samuel 7:8–16. Here is some of what God tells David: "I will provide a place for my people Israel and will plant them so that they can have a home of their own and no longer be disturbed. Wicked people will not oppress them anymore, . . . I will also give you rest from all your enemies. . . . Your house and your kingdom will endure forever before me; your throne will be established forever." The last part of this covenant passage points toward an eternal kingdom that eventually is interpreted in Luke 1:31–33: "You will conceive and give birth to a son, and you are to call him Jesus. . . . The Lord God will give him the throne of his father David, and he will reign over Jacob's descendants forever; his kingdom will never end."

D.A. Carson says, "'Son of David' is an important designation in Matthew. Not only does David become a turning point in the genealogy (1:6, 17), but the title recurs throughout Matthew's gospel."[13] God swore covenant love to David (Ps. 89:29) and promised that one of his immediate descendants would establish the kingdom—even more, that David's kingdom and throne would endure forever (2 Sam 7:12–16)."[14] Isaiah prophesied concerning this coming king and kingdom: "For to us a child is born, to us a son is given, and the government will be on his shoulders. And he will be called Wonderful Counselor, Mighty God, Everlasting Father, Prince of Peace. Of the greatness of his government and peace there will be no end. He will reign on David's throne and over his kingdom, establishing and upholding it with justice and righteousness from that time on and forever" (Isa 9:6–7). In this, we come to the ultimate purpose of why Matthew starts out his gospel with the genealogy—"to show that Jesus Messiah is truly in the kingly line of David, heir to the Messianic promises, the one who brings divine blessings to all nations."[15]

Since the last chapter brought attention to evil kings, let's focus now on a couple of good ones. In these kings and their kingdoms, we get a foretaste of the glory to come. Hezekiah was the father of the evil king, Manasseh, and son of Ahaz, whose reign was also filled with idolatry and apostasy.

13. Matt 9:27; 12:23; 15:22; 20:30–31; 21:9, 15; 22:42, 45.

14. Carson, *Matthew*, 62.

15. Carson, *Matthew*, 63.

But Hezekiah placed his trust in the Lord and cared deeply about restoring his people to right relationship with Him.[16] This passage in 2 Kings 18:2–7 summarizes a lot about his reign:

> "He was twenty-five years old when he became king, and he reigned in Jerusalem twenty-nine years. . . . He did what was right in the eyes of the LORD, just as his father David had done. He removed the high places, smashed the sacred stones and cut down the Asherah poles. He broke into pieces the bronze snake Moses had made, for up to that time the Israelites had been burning incense to it. (It was called Nehushtan.) Hezekiah trusted in the LORD, the God of Israel. There was no one like him among all the kings of Judah, either before him or after him. He held fast to the LORD and did not stop following him; he kept the commands the LORD had given Moses. And the LORD was with him; he was successful in whatever he undertook."

He provided leadership that brought about the removal of idol worship and cleansing of the temple so that God could be worshipped, and appropriate sacrifices offered. As a result, Passover in Jerusalem was celebrated, and the law of God observed again.

Josiah, at age eight, believe it or not, became king when his father, Amon, was killed. Regarding his reign, 2 Kings 22:2 says that he also "did what was right in the eyes of the LORD and followed completely the ways of his father David, not turning aside to the right or to the left."[17] Under his young leadership, radical reform took place. Grieved over the nation's apostasy in his early years, Josiah turned away from the pervasive idolatry in Judah and turned his heart to serve and trust the Lord. Deep conviction drove him to deal ruthlessly with pagan practices, which "were abolished throughout Judah as well as among the northern tribes. Altars of Baal were broken down, Asherim were destroyed, and vessels dedicated to idol worship were removed. . . . The horrible practice of child sacrifice was abruptly abolished. The altars erected by Manasseh in the court of the temple were crushed."[18] Priests who engaged in idol worship were removed from their office. Josiah was committed fully to the Lord. These kings effectively served

---

16. An account of Hezekiah's rule can be found in 2 Kings 18:1–20:21; 2 Chronicles 29:1–32:33; and Isaiah 36–39.

17. A more detailed account of Josiah's reign can be found in 2 Kings 22–23 and 2 Chronicles 34–35.

18. Bromily, *The International Standard Bible Encyclopedia*, 2:1138.

as representatives of God's own kingship. Their rule over Israel was to be "an emblem of God's rule over all nations."[19]

These kings, along with David and others who sought to trust and obey the Lord, served as flickers of a greater king and kingdom to come. King Herod at the time of Jesus's birth, was troubled, and inquired of the leading chief priests and scribes where Christ was to be born. According to Matthew 2:6, they quoted Micah the prophet, saying, "'But you, Bethlehem, in the land of Judah, are by no means least among the rulers of Judah; for out of you will come a ruler who will shepherd my people Israel.'" Whether in synagogues, towns, or villages, wherever Jesus went he proclaimed the good news of the kingdom:

- *Jesus went throughout Galilee, teaching in their synagogues, proclaiming* the good news of the kingdom *and healing every disease and sickness among the people* (Matt 4:23, emphasis added).

- *Jesus went through all the towns and villages, teaching in their synagogues, proclaiming* the good news of the kingdom *and healing every disease and sickness* (Matt 9:35, emphasis added).

- *And this* gospel of the kingdom *will be preached in the whole world as testimony to all nations* (Matt 24:14, emphasis added).

Notice that in each case, it is the *good news* or *gospel of the kingdom* being proclaimed, accompanied by merciful deeds. The word, *kingdom*, can be found multiple times throughout Matthew's gospel.

My grandmother, Marion, grew up on a fifty-acre farm in Wilkes County, Georgia. The stock market crash in 1929 triggered the Great Depression. In 1930, when she was only nine, her thirty-one-year-old father died in a hospital after battling recurring headaches. Her mom, although helped by a small life insurance check, had never worked outside their home. Yet now she faced the reality of three young children to feed . . . again, during the heart of the Depression in the 1930s. Somehow, they survived. Marion married my grandfather when she was nineteen. When my grandfather died at age ninety-five in March of 2012, they had been married about seventy years. At almost age one hundred my grandmother still experiences moments of grief and depression over not having him home. A year after he passed away I wrote a song for her which acknowledges the struggles she must have faced as a young girl losing her father, and then losing her beloved husband toward the end of her life. The chorus says: *There's a home where love won't leave, where all that's good and beautiful*

---

19. Williams, *Far as the Curse is Found*, 242–243.

runs wild and free. And though this world is broken still, there's a hope that blossoms full and wounds that heal.

Genesis 1–2, the story of Creation, is intimately tied with the final two chapters of the Bible, Revelation 21–22, a description of when God will make all things new. These four bookend chapters of the Bible depict everything in a perfect state. The unfolding story in between those bookends is one of redemption. A glory is to be revealed which cannot be imagined. There is a home where love will never leave . . . where all that is good, glorious, and beautiful will run wild and free—forever. Revelation 21:4 says that "He will wipe every tear from their eyes. There will be no more death or mourning or crying or pain." A line in the chorus references a quote by G.K. Chesterton, an English writer, who said, "The more I considered Christianity, the more I found that while it had established a rule and order, the chief aim of that order was to give room for good things to run wild."[20] There's an image in Revelation 21, verses 21 and 25 about twelve gates never being closed or locked. Such an image conveys not only a sense of security, but this idea of all things good and beautiful being able to run wild and free. There will be no need for laws and regulations. For instance, "Thou shalt not steal." If we were to express our God-given humanity fully, we would not only *not* steal, but we also would be exceptionally generous! In this eternal home, can you imagine every being living out of a pure heart of generosity? All that is good will be running wild everywhere, all the time—liberation, beauty, generosity, and unbridled adoration of God will be the air we will breathe.

"A hope that blossoms full" is a reference to the tree of life in the garden of Eden in Genesis 2:9, as well as in Revelation 22:1–2, where it says, "[O]n either side of the river was the tree of life, bearing twelve kinds of fruit." Numbers in Revelation are mostly symbolic. For instance, Jacob had twelve sons. Those twelve sons formed the twelve tribes of Israel. Jesus had twelve disciples. The city described in Revelation 21 has a majestic and high wall with twelve gates. The twelve gates are twelve pearls. At each gate stands an angel. The wall is set on twelve foundations. I interpret the tree of life, bearing twelve kinds of fruit as meaning completion. It will not be possible to get any better. All the God-given longings and hopes we have in this life will blossom in full or be completely realized. "Wounds that heal" is a reference to the river flowing out of Eden in Genesis 2:10, as well as in Revelation 22:1–2. Part of it says, " . . . and the leaves of the tree are for the healing of the nations." The profound brokenness of this world has been clearly evidenced everywhere throughout history. Yet there will one day be absolute healing and restoration. Everything will be made right.

20. Chesterton, *Orthodoxy*, 97.

Revelation 21:26 says, "The glory and honor of the nations will be brought into it." Consider what you believe to be the most glorious and honorable aspects of any nation you have visited? Landscapes, majestic mountain ranges, architecture, art, foods, drinks, rivers, lakes, seashores, music, art, and on and on and on . . . all being brought into the new heavens and new earth! We will have renewed, perfectly healthy bodies that will never get sick, grow old, or die. The most intimate and memorable interactions we have experienced with family and friends here are but a foretaste of what will always be. Revelation 21:23–25 says, "The city does not need the sun or the moon to shine on it, for the glory of God gives it light, and the Lamb is its lamp. The nations will walk by its light, . . . for there will be no night there."

My favorite survival and rescue story is about Sir Ernest Shackleton's expedition in 1914 to Antarctica with a crew of twenty-nine men aboard the *Endurance*. His goal was to cross the entire continent of fifteen-hundred miles. In mid-December of that year, as the *Endurance* approached Antarctica, an unusual season of packed ice forced her to slowly push through. In January 1915, she got lodged in the ice. The crew and ship had to drift with the ice pack and wait for it to break. It finally began to do so in August 1915. By late October, however, the immense pressure of the breaking ice took a dreadful toll on the ship, and frigid ocean water began to seep in. In late October, the *Endurance* started breaking apart. The men were forced to abandon ship—which stranded them on an uncontrollable floating island of ice. After five months of floating, they spotted land. It was late March 1916. At this point they were being swept out of the Weddell Sea into the open ocean, and the island of ice upon which they had been floating had disintegrated to a size only large enough for their camp. In early April, they abandoned the floe and divided up between three lifeboats they had dragged with them. After a few days of turmoil in the sea, remaining wet, cold, often seasick, and desperately thirsty, they spotted land. It was an uninhabited place called Elephant Island. But how would they ever return home?

Shackleton knew the only way home would be to cross over seven hundred dangerous miles of ocean to the tiny island of South Georgia. In late April, a week after arriving on Elephant Island, Shackleton chose five other men, and together they boarded the twenty-two-foot-long *James Caird*. Of all the struggles they had endured, this would be the hardest. Turbulent storms, caked ice, the freezing cold, sleep deprivation, heavy seas, and high waves constantly threatened their survival. If they died, the remaining men would probably never be found. On top of this, they had to remain steadfastly focused on staying the narrow course to South Georgia Island. If off by any stretch, they would be lost in an endless ocean. Meanwhile, back on the island, the others restlessly waited. They built a tiny hut structure roofed by the two remaining boats. They longed to be rescued and return home.

Worsely, the navigator aboard the *Caird*, managed to somehow keep their small boat on track. After more than two weeks struggling to survive, they found their destination. But weather conditions forbid them from landing. After two more days of fighting weather conditions and exploring the area for a spot to land, the men found a small cove. The whaling station they needed to reach lay on the other side of the island. They would have to walk over and through the interior part of the island comprised of mountains and glaciers. After trekking thirty-six hours, they located the whaling station. Shackleton was anxious to rescue his men and bring them home. After three failed attempts, Shackleton finally broke through the pack ice on a fourth ship in late August 1916. It had been 126 days after they had set sail in the *James Caird*. The stranded men had begun to lose hope, yet every single one of them remained alive.[21]

In our ongoing struggles, we long for rescue. We long for the home where love will never leave. We long for that place where all that is loving, beautiful, and good runs wild; where our deepest hopes and longings are fulfilled, and wounds completely heal. Our hope rests completely in a Savior and King who endured the cross, died, and was buried, but rose again from the tomb. And he who is seated on the throne will come again. John, in Revelation 21:1–5 describes it:

> "Then I saw 'a new heaven and a new earth,' . . . I saw the Holy City, the new Jerusalem, coming down out of heaven from God, prepared as a bride beautifully dressed for her husband. And I heard a loud voice from the throne saying, 'Look! God's dwelling place is now among the people, and he will dwell with them. They will be his people, and God himself will be with them and be their God. He will wipe every tear from their eyes. There will be no more death or mourning or crying or pain.' . . . He who was seated on the throne said, 'I am making everything new!'"

"In the beginning of the book of Genesis we learn the reason why all people feel like exiles, like we aren't really home. We are told there that we were created to live in the garden of God. That was the world we were built for, a place in which there was no parting from love, no decay or disease.

---

21. If you are curious to find out more, here are some resources I've read or watched: *Endurance: Shackleton's Incredible Voyage* by Alfred Lansing. NewYork, NY: Basic Books, 2014. A documentary entitled, *The Endurance: Shackleton's Legendary Antarctic Expedition* directed by George Butler. Discovery Channel Pictures, 2000. A mini-series entitled, *Shackleton—The Greatest Survival Story of All Time,* directed by Charles Sturridge, featuring Kenneth Branagh. Released in 2002. A&E Networks.

. . . We have been wandering as spiritual exiles ever since. That is, we have been living in a world that no longer fits our deepest longings."[22] However, one day, . . . "We will not float through the air, but rather will eat, embrace, sing, laugh, and dance in the kingdom of God, in degrees of power, glory, and joy that we can't at present imagine. Jesus will make the world our perfect home again."[23] This is a great segue into the last chapter. God has not called us to sit and wait around for that future hope. Rather, that future hope summons us to participate with God in his mission to redeem and restore that home here and now, with and for ourselves and our neighbors. Jesus indeed taught us to pray in Matthew 6:10, "Your kingdom come, your will be done, *on earth* as it is in heaven."

22. Keller, *The Prodigal God*, 95-96.
23. Keller, *The Prodigal God*, 104.

CHAPTER 14

Beauty Arising and Growing
from the Ashes

Babylon

"From the ashes a fire shall be woken, A light from the shadows shall spring."[1]—J.R.R. Tolkien

A t the beginning of chapter 12, I brought attention to the atrocities regarding African Americans. We could say the United States was to exiled African slaves what Egypt was to the early Israelites, or later, what Babylon was to Judah (I will elaborate more on Babylon as we continue.) Allow me also to bring attention to the devastation in the US South, and in particular, the state of Alabama during and after the Civil War. Historian, professor, and author Wayne Flynt said that between the Civil War and the Great Depression that "no other cycle in American history resulted in so sustained and extensive downward mobility for so numerous a population."[2] One gentleman, for instance, owned several acres of land by 1861. But the war took the life of his son, a Confederate soldier, his wife soon after the conflict was over, and soon his fortunes. Many men going off to war left behind women and children to tend to their farms and fend for themselves. Even when enough crops were produced to feed Alabama's population, poor transportation thwarted distribution to those who needed it most.

A letter to a government official in 1864 said, "I find hundreds of them entirely destitute of everything upon which to live, not even bread."[3] In 1865, another letter from a prominent individual to the governor stated, "I pledge you my word, I've never heard such a cry for bread in my life.

1. Tolkien, *The Fellowship of the Ring*, 241.
2. Flynt, *Poor but Proud*, 36.
3. Flynt, *Poor but Proud*, 43.

And it is impossible to get relief up here. The provisions are not here and if they were there is no money here to buy with. . . . If anything can be done, for God's sake do it quickly."[4]

Layered upon daily hardships were delivered reports of loved ones killed in battle. Some families fled their homes as even the Confederate cavalry and home guards pillaged and looted their properties. After an army of federals encamped on her land, one widow of a large plantation wrote that there was "not a living thing on the place except a few chickens. God help us, for we have almost nothing. Of our abundant crop of corn, not an ear remains except that which is scattered on the ground."[5] In many cases, they stole both corn and cattle.

Often, the greater battle was not against the Union Army, but against neighbors. Bread riots broke out in Mobile in April and September of 1863. Thousands deserted the Confederate army. "Many poor whites express their resentment in guerilla warfare against affluent Confederate sympathizers. As a consequence, murder, random violence, robbery, and looting plunged some counties into anarchy."[6] War, drought, anarchy, starvation, robbery, pleas for help, and a thousand other small, daily sufferings became the norm for thousands of Alabamians and southern-state residents during and after the Civil War. All was "gloom and wretchedness and woe."[7]

Babylon—a place of gloom and wretchedness and woe

Out of the genealogy in Matthew 1, only one *place* is mentioned—and, no, it is not Bethlehem, the birthplace of Jesus, or even Jerusalem. The only named place is Babylon, in verses 11–12 (". . . and Josiah the father of Jeconiah and his brothers at the time of the exile to Babylon. After the exile to Babylon: Jeconiah was the father of Shealtiel, . . ."), and again in verse 17 ("Thus there were fourteen generations in all from Abraham to David, fourteen from David to the exile to Babylon, and fourteen from the exile to the Messiah."). It seems quite ironic that Babylon is the only place mentioned in the genealogical account because "throughout the Old Testament and New Testament, Babylon stands theologically for the community that is anti-God."[8] In Genesis 11, in arrogance and selfish ambition, the people

---

4. Flynt, *Poor but Proud*, 47.

5. Flynt, *Poor but Proud*, 43.

6. Flynt, *Poor but Proud*, 45.

7. Flynt, *Poor but Proud*, 47.

8. Bromily, *The International Standard Bible Encyclopedia,* 1:385.

of the world after the Flood sought to make a name for themselves in building the tower of Babel. In 2 Kings 20:17–18, Hezekiah was foretold by the prophet Isaiah, "The time will surely come when everything in your palace, and all that your predecessors have stored up until this day, will be carried off to Babylon. Nothing will be left, says the Lord and some of your descendants, your own flesh and blood who will be born to you, will be taken away, and they will become eunuchs in the palace of the king of Babylon." Second Kings 24:10–16 documents the fulfillment of that prophecy. While the city of Jerusalem was being besieged, King Nebuchadnezzar himself was there, and Jehoiachin, king of Judah, surrendered himself, his mother, servants, and palace officials to him. He captured all of them—the king's wives, the mighty men of valor, and thousands of others. No one remained except the poorest people of the land. Second Kings 25:9–11 describes the further destruction of Jerusalem. "Jerusalem and much of the Judean countryside were plundered and destroyed. The temple and palace were razed, more of the populace deported, and the upper classes punished. All of the tangible institutions and powerful people were gone or crippled. The state of Judah, its long history so closely associated with Yahweh and His servant David, was no longer."[9] The journey ahead of them to Babylon by foot would stretch hundreds of miles.

As God's people walked toward captivity, they could not have envisioned the scene painted in Revelation 18:2–3: "Fallen! Fallen is Babylon the Great! She has become a dwelling for demons and a haunt for every impure spirit, a haunt for every unclean bird, a haunt for every unclean and detestable animal. For all the nations have drunk the maddening wine of her adulteries. The kings of the earth committed adultery with her, and the merchants of the earth grew rich from her excessive luxuries." Babylon—a place of such corruption and evil—is where the people of God felt most ruined, wretched, and woeful. It was the setting of Judah's darkest days.

The book of Lamentations provides a sense of the raw emotion and mental state of the Jews afflicted in Babylonian captivity. How would we feel if we, our families, our friends, and our communities lost our homes, routines, traditions, places of worship, government, culture, security, property, opportunity, and freedoms? How would we feel if we were exiled to a foreign country? God's people had no protections. Lamentation 1:16 says, "This is why I weep and my eyes overflow with tears. No one is near to comfort me, no one to restore my spirit. My children are destitute because the enemy has prevailed." The latter part of verse 22 says, "My groans are many and my heart is faint." In Lamentations 3:1–3, we hear one man's

9. Bromily, *The International Standard Bible Encyclopedia*, 1:614.

heartache—"I am the man who has seen affliction by the rod of the Lord's wrath. He has driven me away and made me walk in darkness rather than light; indeed, he has turned his hand against me again and again, all day long." In verses 7 to 9, he continues: "He has walled me in so I cannot escape; he has weighed me down with chains. Even when I call out or cry for help, he shuts out my prayer. He has barred my way with blocks of stone." Toward the end of his lament (vv. 16–18), the man's despair rises to fever pitch: "He ground my face into the gravel. He pounded me into the mud. I gave up on life altogether. I've forgotten what the good life is like. I said to myself, 'This is it. I'm finished. GOD is a lost cause'" (MSG).

Babylon—not the end of the story

But . . . I hope by now— in the last chapter of this book—that we would be all chips in that Babylon is *not* the end of the story. The man with his face in the gravel transitions his thought process from a deep struggle with despair to inspired hope and faith—"Yet this I call to mind and therefore I have hope: because of the Lord's great love we are not consumed, for his compassions never fail. They are new every morning; great is your faithfulness. I say to myself, 'The Lord is my portion; therefore I will wait for him.' The Lord is good to those whose hope is in him, to the one who seeks him; it is good to wait quietly for the salvation of the Lord" (Lam 3:21–26). "Disappointment, even despair, metastasized throughout Israel as history, ever crueler, destroyed all hopes but one: the prophets' promise of a King of Kings . . . the Jews clung to that promise fiercely."[10] I'm reminded of Bilbo Bagins bursting out with a poem which included these words: "*From the ashes a fire shall be woken, A light from the shadows shall spring; Renewed shall be blade that was broken: The crownless again shall be king.*"[11]

The people of Judah did not want or choose to be in Babylon, but for a time, that's where they were. What is your current place? Let's go back to a thought from the introduction. Henri Nouwen exhorted his readers "to be present fully to the moment, in the conviction that something is happening where you are."[12] Your right-now moment is filled with possibility because God is always present with us and at work. Guard yourself, then, against the temptation to believe this moment and place right now are void of any meaning or significance even though it may be painful, sad, stressful, boring, or confusing. We should be willing "to stay where we are and live the

---

10. Yancey, *Disappointment with God*, 114.

11. Tolkien, *The Fellowship of the Ring*, 241.

12. Durback, *Seeds of Hope*, 158.

situation out to the fullest in the belief that something hidden there will manifest itself to us."[13]

Harvesting treasure from our struggles

Enduring through a struggle makes it especially difficult to maintain such a hope filled perspective. Disheartened, we are tempted to shut down. Yet consider this provoking thought from Richard Rohr. "It has been acceptable for some time in America to remain wound identified . . . instead of using the wound to redeem the world, as we see in Jesus and many people who turn their wounds into sacred wounds that liberate both themselves and others."[14] Reflecting on the parable of the talents (Matt 25), Frederick Buechner said God "expects that out of whatever the world in its madness does to us, we will somehow reap a harvest. He does not sow these things that happen, but he expects us to deal with these things in creative and redemptive and life-opening sorts of ways. . . . He does not sow the pain, he does not make pain happen, but he looks to us to harvest treasure from the pain. Like the girl in the fairytale, he looks for us to spin gold out of the straw of what happens to us."[15]

In the movie, *The Shawshank Redemption*, Andy Dufresne, a professional banker, is falsely accused of murdering his wife and her lover, and for that reason is sentenced to two life terms in prison. Inside this Babylon of gloom, wretchedness, and woe, the maximum-security prison where he is sentenced, guilty men are subjected to deplorable food, tiny concrete cells, abusive guards, a corrupt warden, unpaid labor, and gang violence. The place festers with evil, fear, and despair. Morgan Freeman's character, "Red," narrates the story, and becomes Andy's most trusted friend.

> "The first night's the toughest, no doubt about it," Red says. "They march you in naked as the day you were born, skin burning and half blind from that delousing shit they throw on you, and when they put you in that cell . . . and those bars slam home . . . that's when you know it's for real. A whole life blown away in the blink of an eye. Nothing left but all the time in the world to think about it . . . These walls are funny. First you hate 'em, then you get used to 'em. Enough time passes, you get so you depend on them. That's institutionalized."

13. Durback, *Seeds of Hope*, 158.
14. Rohr, *Falling Upward*, 34.
15. Buechner, *A Crazy, Holy Grace*, 23–24.

This is the atrocious world that Andy, an innocent man, was forced to enter and endure for years.

In time, Andy's hopefulness, skills, and kind-heartedness make an impact within those prison walls. His voice gains influence among not only the prisoners, but the guards as well. He uses his financial knowledge to help the prison guards and even the warden with their tax returns and financial planning. Through his perseverance, the prison receives enough funds and book donations to create a library. He helps several of his fellow prisoners obtain at least a high-school-level education. "Another way of dealing with your pain is to be a good steward of it,"[16] Buechner wrote. Andy was doing just that. He refused to allow unjust circumstances to define him.

Have we allowed hard circumstances to define us? Have we allowed our struggles to bury our light and capacity to love others? "To live a buried life is to say you have not really lived your life at all. . . . If you bury your life—if you don't face, among other things, your pain—your life shrinks. It is in a way diminished."[17] Buechner's own father committed suicide when he was young. He said his mother's life diminished because she had buried much of the sadness of her life. "She never grew in the way she might have. She never became the human being she richly had it in her to become. She never became the compassionate, outward-reaching person who had real friends. Her life shrunk . . . rarely leaving her apartment. First her apartment, then her bedroom, then her chair in her bedroom, and finally her bed—it was just this sort of gradual shrinking . . . That's what happens when you do not live your life, when you do not harvest your pain."[18]

As remarkably difficult as his prison life was, Andy did not shrink and bury his life in the injustice of his imprisonment. Instead, he stewards his pain. He doesn't remain "wound identified." He becomes an instrument of redemption. His wounds turn sacred as he works to liberate both himself and others. Beauty arises out of the ashes.

Andy intentionally breaks the rules one day. He locks himself in a communications room and plays a recording of opera singers on the loudspeakers for the inmates to hear throughout the prison. The moment is transcendent for Red:

> "I have no idea to this day what those two Italian ladies were singing about. Truth is, I don't want to know. Some things are best left unsaid. I'd like to think they were singing about something so beautiful, it can't be expressed in words, and makes

16. Buechner, *A Crazy, Holy Grace*, 21.

17. Buechner, *A Crazy, Holy-Grace*, 25

18. Buechner, *A Crazy, Holy Grace*, 26.

your heart ache because of it. I tell you, those voices soared higher and farther than anybody in a gray place dares to dream. It was like some beautiful bird flapped into our drab little cage and made those walls dissolve away, and for the briefest of moments, every last man in Shawshank felt free."

Andy was able to execute his planned escape from prison after almost twenty years. Upon doing so, he also exposed the outrageous injustices and corruption that had dominated the prison system for so long. In the end, justice prevailed. For two decades, Andy endured unimaginable trials within those prison walls, built lasting friendships, and maximized his knowledge and skills for the good of the place. His "lit" spiritual candle let the light of hope, beauty, love, and justice flicker in the darkness of his Babylonian captivity. "Sometimes it makes me sad, though . . . Andy being gone," Red said. "I have to remind myself that some birds aren't meant to be caged. Their feathers are just too bright. And when they fly away, the part of you that knows it was a sin to lock them up does rejoice. But still, the *place* you live in is that much more drab and empty that they're gone. I guess I just miss my friend."[19]

In the good news of God's redemptive story in Jesus, we are offered deliverance and freedom. "We are all invited—summoned, actually—to discover, through following Jesus, that this new world is indeed a *place* of justice, spirituality, relationship, and beauty, and that we are not only to enjoy it as such but to work at bringing it to birth on earth as in heaven."[20] N.T. Wright, in his book, *Surprised by Hope*, wrote:

> ". . . every act of love, gratitude, and kindness; every work of art or music inspired by the love of God and delight in the beauty of his creation; every minute spent teaching a severely handicapped child to read or to walk; every act of care and nurture, of comfort and support, for one's fellow human beings and for that matter one's fellow nonhuman creatures; and of course every prayer, all Spirit-led teaching, every deed that spreads the gospel, builds up the church, embraces and embodies holiness rather than corruption, and makes the name of Jesus honored in the world—all of this will find its way, through the resurrecting power of God, into the new creation that God will one day make.[21]

Wherever your place is, be not dismayed; God is there, and he is at work. Seeds lie as buried treasure within the sacred ground of your struggles

---

19. *The Shawshank Redemption*, directed by Frank Darabont (1994; Beverly Hills, CA: Castle Rock Entertainment, 2007), DVD.

20. Wright, *Simply Christian*, 92.

21. Wright, *Surprised by Hope*, 208.

as they did in the stories of the people we have reflected on from the genealogy of Jesus. A broken, disoriented, and scarred life is not a sign of failure—It's just normal. Matthew was an outcast. Abraham at seventy-five was
called to end his life as he had always known it, leaving behind relationships,
his home, and inheritance. Although given a promise, he and Sarah knew
not where they were going and struggled to believe in the face of uncertain
future outcomes. Jacob was blind to his own self-centered bondage and suffered through painful family division and drama throughout his entire life.
Judah severely wounded people close to him and remained as sick as his
secrets for a long time. Tamar was mistreated, mislead, and misrepresented
as a vulnerable minority female in a male dominated culture. Rahab was a
prostitute whose name poetically stood for an enemy of God. Ruth grieved
the death of her young husband, then sacrificially left her home to remain
beside her mother-in-law only to be destitute for a season. Jesse was nobody
significant living in no place important. David went from being a boy herd-
ing sheep to a king commanding armies, but then to a man who grievously
fell—having the affair, trying to cover it up, abusing his power, and commit-
ting murder. Solomon denied himself nothing his heart desired yet found
it all meaningless. Manasseh and Amon were wicked men. Hezekiah and
Josiah were good men. Babylon was a place of ruin, gloom, wretchedness,
and woe for the people of Judah. But woven through all these stories was an
unfolding story of divine redemption.

Beauty arising and growing out of the ashes

The seed of redemption planted initially in Abraham's story blossomed fully
in Jesus. "The Old Testament tells the story which Jesus completes."[22] Don't
miss *the* Bible story! "It is a unified and progressively unfolding drama of
God's action in history for the salvation of the whole world. The Bible is not
a mere jumble of history, poetry, morality lessons, comforting promises, and
guiding principles; instead, it is fundamentally coherent. Every part of the
Bible . . . must be understood in the context of one storyline."[23] Israel's story
had to go through Babylon to get to Jesus. Isaiah prophesied about the coming exile, but he also proclaimed that good news would be preached to the
poor, the brokenhearted would be healed, captives would be set free, prisoners pardoned, and mourners comforted (61:1–4). Messages of joy would
resound instead of news of doom. The old ruins would be rebuilt. A new
city would be raised out of the wreckage. In other words, *beauty would arise*

22. Wright, *Knowing Jesus Through the Old Testament*, 2.
23. Bartholomew and Goheen, *The Drama of Scripture*, 14.

and grow out of the ashes. It was not until *four hundred years after* the last biblical prophet that news started spreading about someone having arrived on the scene who might be the "sent one." The first words in the book of Matthew are "a new creation"—which, translated, mean, "book of genesis." Those words echo Genesis; indeed, the fulfillment of Scripture is signaled from the very start: "A new creation is now taking place."[24]

We expect to face struggles in life. But we never know what that will mean until they happen. I've attempted to invite you into parts of my own story and wish I could hear yours. Thank you for listening. It is our natural inclination to plead with God to remove or change our circumstances. But what God may be doing is changing *us.* Our lives can go the pathway of shrinking and remaining buried by our struggles. I was on that path for quite a while. Or, by God's redeeming grace soaking the soil of our struggles where seeds lie as buried treasure, beauty can arise and grow out of the ashes. A new creation can emerge out of the wreckage. Old ruins *can* be rebuilt.

Rather than shrinking and remaining buried, may you discover and experience the mercy of God cultivating your lowest moments into unknown treasure. May his mercy cause seeds of redemption to germinate and grow roots of deepened faith, hope, joy, and love. Recall from chapter 1 how such seeds grew out of the life of Valjean following his encounter with the bishop. Valjean would no longer be identified or live his life as a prisoner and a number, 24601. As you encounter Jesus and his redeeming love in and through your struggles, may the new life that emerges out of that dark soil of pain, sorrow, failure, or loss be an ever-growing source of love, liberation, and restoration for the beautiful and broken world and people around you—wherever you are planted.

---

24. France, *The Gospel of Matthew,* 28.

Bibliography

Alighieri, Dante. *Divine Comedy: The Inferno, The Purgatorio, and The Paradiso.* Translated by John Ciardi. New York, NY: New American Library, 2003.

Allender, Dan B., and Tremper Longman, III. *Bold Love.* Colorado Springs: NavPress, 1992.

Allender, Dan B. *The Healing Path: How the Hurts in Your Past Can Lead You to a More Abundant Life.* Colorado Springs: Waterbrook, 1999.

Alexander, Michelle. *The New Jim Crow: Mass Incarceration in the Age of Colorblindness.* New York: New Press, 2012.

Amorim, Vicente, dir. *Good.* 2008. Beverly Hills, CA: Good Films Collective, 2009. DVD.

Barclay, William. *The Gospel of Matthew, Volume 1.* Philadelphia: The Westminster Press, 1975.

Bartholomew, Craig G., and Michael W. Goheen. *The Drama of Scripture: Finding Our Place in the Biblical Story.* Grand Rapids: Baker Academic, 2014.

Bennett, Arthur, ed. *The Valley of Vision: A Collection of Puritan Prayers and Devotions.* Edinburgh: Banner of Truth Trust, 1975.

Blue, Ken. *Healing Spiritual Abuse: How to Break Free from Bad Church Experiences.* Downers Grove: InterVarsity, 1993.

Bnioff, David, and D. B. Weiss, creators. *Game of Thrones.* Season 1, episode 1, "Winter is Coming." Featuring Isaac Hempstead Wright, Lena Headey, and Nikolaj Coster-Waldau. Aired April 17, 2011, in broadcast syndication. HBO.

———. *Game of Thrones.* Season 8, episode 3, "The Long Night." Featuring Isaac Hempstead Wright, Alfie Allen, and Iwan Rheon. Aired April 28, 2019, in broadcast syndication. HBO.

———. *Game of Thrones.* Season 8, episode 6, "The Iron Throne." Featuring Isaac Hempstead Wright. Aired May 19, 2019, in broadcast syndication. HBO.

Bromiley, Geoffrey W., ed. *The International Standard Bible Encyclopedia.* Grand Rapids: Eerdmans, 1982.

Brown, Colin, ed. *The New International Dictionary of New Testament Theology.* Grand Rapids: Zondervan, 1986.

Buber, Martin. *I and Thou.* Translated by Walter Kaufmann. New York: Charles Scribner's Sons, 1970.

Buechner, Frederick. *A Crazy, Holy Grace.* Grand Rapids: Zondervan, 2017.

———. *The Magnificent Defeat.* New York: HarperCollins, 1966.

————. *Secrets in the Dark: Life in Sermons.* New York: HarperOne, 2006.

————. *Telling Secrets: A Memoir.* New York: HarperOne, 1991.

————. "What Believing Means" (an excerpt from the novel *The Return of Ansel Gibbs*). Frederick Buechner (May 3, 2016). https://www.frederickbuechner.com/blog/2016/5/3/what-believing-means?rq=christian%20commitment.

————. *Whistling in the Dark: An ABC Theologized.* New York: Harper & Row, 1988.

Carson, D. A. *How Long O Lord? Reflections on Suffering & Evil.* Grand Rapids: Baker, 1990.

————. *Matthew: Chapters 1–12.* The Expositor's Bible Commentary. Grand Rapids: Zondervan, 1995.

Carson, D. A., and Douglas J. Moo. *An Introduction to the New Testament.* Grand Rapids: Zondervan, 2005.

Cassidy, David. "The Gospel According to Mark: Scandalous Savior, *Splagxnizomai*—Mark 10:1:40–45." Christ Community Church (October 28, 2018). https://christcommunity.org/sermon/mark7/.

Chesterton, G. K. *Orthodoxy,* New York: Doubleday, 1959.

Clapp, Rodney. "Eugene Peterson: A Monk Out of Habit," *Christianity Today* (April 3, 1987), 25.

Cukor, George, dir. *Gaslight.* 1944. Hollywood, CA: MGM, 2004. DVD.

Darabont, Frank, dir. *The Shawshank Redemption.* 1994. Beverly Hills, CA: Castle Rock Entertainment, 2007. DVD.

Davids, Peter H. *The New International Greek Testament Commentary: The Epistle of James.* Grand Rapids: Eerdmans, 1982.

Defoe, Daniel. *Robinson Crusoe.* Garden City, New York: Doubleday, 1946.

Dempsey, Kristy, and illustrated by Sarah Green. *Papa Put a Man on the Moon.* New York: Dial, 2019.

Dostoevsky, Fyodor. *The Brothers Karamazov.* New York: Farrar, Straus and Giroux, 1990.

Dumas, Alexandre. *The Count of Monte Cristo.* New York, NY: The Modern Library, 2005.

Durback, Robert, ed. *Seeds of Hope: A Henri Nouwen Reader.* New York: Doubleday, 1997.

Edmundson, Mark. "One Nation Under Fear." *Hedgehog Review* 16 (Fall 2014). https://hedgehogreview.com/issues/thinking-about-the-poor/articles/one-nation-under-fear.

Ellul, Jacques. *Money and Power.* Grand Rapids: Eerdmans, 1984.

Flynt, Wayne. *Poor but Proud.* Tuscaloosa, AL: The University of Alabama Press, 1989.

France, R. T. *The Gospel of Matthew.* Grand Rapids: Eerdmans, 2007.

Frankl, Viktor E. *Man's Search for Ultimate Meaning.* New York: MJF, 2000.

Fraser, Sylvia. *My Father's House: A Memoir of Incest and Healing.* New York: Ticknor & Fields, 1988.

Friedman, Edwin H. *A Failure of Nerve: Leadership in the Age of the Quick Fix,* edited by Margaret M. Treadwell and Edward W. Beal. New York: Church Publishing, 2017.

Gay, Craig. *Cash Values: Money and the Erosion of Meaning in Today's Society.* Grand Rapids: Eerdmans, 2003.

Gilliard, Dominique DuBois. *Rethinking Incarceration: Advocating for Justice That Restores.* Downers Grove: InterVarsity, 2018.

Graber, Jennifer. *The Furnace of Affliction: Prisons and Religion in Antebellum America.* Chapel Hill, NC: University of North Carolina Press, 2014.

Guiness, Os. *The Call: Finding and Fulfilling the Central Purpose of Your Life*. Nashville: Thomas Nelson, 2003.

Hamilton, Victor P. *Handbook on the Pentateuch*. Grand Rapids: Baker, 1982.

Hendriksen, William. *Matthew, New Testament Commentary*. Grand Rapids: Baker, 1973.

Hester, H.I. *The Heart of Hebrew History*, Liberty, MO: Quality, 1962.

Holt, Rackham. *George Washington Carver*. Garden City, NY: Doubleday, 1963.

Houston, James M. *Joyful Exiles: Life in Christ on the Dangerous Edge of Things*. Downers Grove: InterVarsity, 2006.

Hugo, Victor. *Les Misérables*. Translated by Charles E. Wilbour. New York: Everyman's Library, 1909.

Hunter, James Davison. *To Change the World: The Irony, Tragedy & Possibility of Christianity in the Late Modern World*. Oxford: Oxford University Press, 2010.

Jackson, Peter, dir. *The Lord of the Rings: The Two Towers*. 2002. Los Angeles: New Line Cinemas, 2003. DVD.

James, Carolyn Custis. *Lost Women of the Bible*. Grand Rapids: Zondervan, 2005.

———. "The Perfect Storm." Carolyn Custis James (June 17, 2013). https://carolyncustisjames.com/2013/06/17/the-perfect-storm/.

Joffe, Roland, dir. *The Mission*. 1986. Burbank, CA: Warner Bros., 2003. DVD.

Kavanaugh, John. "Godforsakenness: 'Finding one's heart's desire.'" *America: The Jesuit Review* 197 (October 1, 2007). https://www.americamagazine.org/issue/627/columns/godforsakenness.

Keil, C. F., and F. Delitzsch. *Commentary on the Old Testament*: Peabody, MA: Hendrickson, 2006.

Keller, Phillip. *A Shepherd Looks at Psalm 23*. Grand Rapids: Zondervan, 1970.

Keller, Timothy. "By the Blood of Jesus Christ." Gospel in Life (March 15, 2009). https://gospelinlife.com/downloads/by-the-blood-of-jesus-christ-5995/.

———. *Counterfeit Gods*. New York: Penguin, 2009.

———. *The Prodigal God: Recovering the Heart of the Christian Faith*. New York: Dutton, 2008.

Keyes, Dick. *Seeing Through Cynicism: A Reconsideration of the Power of Suspicion*. Downers Grove: InterVarsity, 2006.

Kidd, Sue Monk. *When the Heart Waits*. New York: HarperOne, 1990.

Kidner, Derek. *Psalms 1–72*, Tyndale Old Testament Commentaries. Downers Grove: InterVarsity, 1973.

Kittel, Gerhard and Gerhard Friedrich, eds. *Theological Dictionary of the New Testament*. 10 vols. Translated by Geoffrey W. Bromiley. Grand Rapids: Eerdmans, 1964–76.

Langberg, Diane. *Suffering and the Heart of God: How Trauma Destroys and Christ Restores*. Greensboro, NC: New Growth, 2015.

Lee, Harper. *To Kill A Mockingbird*. New York: Grand Central, 1960.

Lewis, C. S. *The Four Loves*. New York: Harcourt, 1960.

———. *A Grief Observed*. New York: HarperCollins, 1961.

———. *Mere Christianity*. New York: HarperCollins, 1952.

———. *The Problem of Pain*. New York: HarperCollins, 1940.

———. *The Weight of Glory*. New York: HarperCollins, 1949.

Macaulay, Ranald, and Jerram Barrs. *Being Human: The Nature of Spiritual Experience*. Downers Grove, IL: InterVarsity, 1978.

MacDonald, George. *Life Essential: The Hope of the Gospel*. Wheaton, Il: Harold Shaw, 1978.

Mandino, Og. *A Better Way to Live*. New York: Bantam, 1991.

Manning, Brennan. *The Ragamuffin Gospel: Embracing the Unconditional Love of God.* Sisters, OR: Multnomah, 1990.

———. *Ruthless Trust: The Ragamuffin Path to God.* New York: HarperCollins, 2000.

Marty, Martin. *A Cry of Absence.* San Francisco: Harper & Row, 1983.

McCarthy, Tom, dir. *Spotlight.* 2015. Los Angeles: Open Road Films, 2016. DVD.

McKay, Adam, dir. *The Big Short.* 2015. Hollywood: Paramount Pictures, 2016. DVD.

McKnight, Scott. *One Life: Jesus Calls. We Follow.* Grand Rapids: Zondervan, 2010.

McLaren, Brian D. *We Make the Road by Walking: A Year-long Quest for Spiritual Formation, Reorientation, and Activation.* New York: Jericho, 2014.

Melville, Herman. *Moby-Dick.* New York: Alfred A. Knopf, 1988.

Merica, Dan. "Facing Death, A Top Pastor Rethinks What It Means to Be Christian." CNN (February 18, 2012). http://religion.blogs.cnn.com/2012/02/18/tending-the-garden-one-person-at-a-time/.

Merton, Thomas. *Contemplation in a World of Action.* New York: Doubleday, 1973.

———. *Thoughts in Solitude.* New York: Farrar, Straus and Giroux, 1958.

Nolan, Albert. *Jesus before Christianity.* Maryknoll, NY: Orbis, 1976.

Nouwen, Henri. *In the Name of Jesus: Reflections on Christian Leadership.* New York: Crossroad, 1989.

———. *Mornings with Henri J.M. Nouwen: Readings and Reflections,* compiled by Evelyn Bence. Cincinnati: Servant, 2005.

———. *Return of the Prodigal.* New York: Doubleday, 1992.

———. *Turn My Mourning into Dancing: Finding Hope in Hard Times.* Nashville: W Publishing, 2011.

Null, Ashley. "Thomas Cranmer's Gospel of Divine Allurement." July 9, 2014. Mockingbird Conference in New York. Vimeo, 56:09. https://mbird.com/tag/ashley-null/.

Peck, M. Scott. *People of the Lie: The Hope for Healing Human Evil.* New York: Simon & Schuster, 1983.

Peterson, Eugene. *Christ Plays in Ten Thousand Places.* Grand Rapids: Eerdmans, 2005.

Plantinga Jr., Cornelius. *Not the Way It's Supposed to Be: A Breviary of Sin.* Grand Rapids: Eerdmans, 1995.

Prior, David. *The Message of 1 Corinthians,* The Bible Speaks Today. Downers Grove: InterVarsity, 1985.

Rader, Dotson. "The Mixed-up Life of Shia LeBeouf." *Parade* (June 14, 2009). http://www.parade.com/celebrity/2009/06/shia-labeouf-mixed-up-life.html.

Robinson, Marilynne. "Fear." *The New York Review of Books* (September 24, 2015). https://www.nybooks.com/articles/2015/09/24/marilynne-robinson-fear/.

Rowling, J. K. "The Fringe Benefits of Failure, and the Importance of Imagination." *Harvard Gazette* (June 5, 2008). https://news.harvard.edu/gazette/story/2008/06/text-of-j-k-rowling-speech/.

Rohr, Richard. *Falling Upward: A Spirituality for the Two Halves of Life.* San Francisco: Jossey-Bass, 2011.

———. "A Santa Claus God." Center for Action and Contemplation. (January 27, 2016). https://cac.org/a-santa-claus-god-2016-01-27/.

Sarkis, Stephanie A. "11 Warning Signs of Gaslighting." *Psychology Today* (January 22, 2017). https://www.psychologytoday.com/us/blog/here-there-and-everywhere/201701/11-warning-signs-gaslighting.

Schaeffer, Frances A. *No Little People.* Wheaton, IL: Crossway, 2003.

Sittser, Jerry. *A Grace Disguised.* Grand Rapids: Zondervan, 1995.

Staub, Dick. "The Dick Staub Interview: Brennan Manning on Ruthless Trust." *Christianity Today* (December 2002). http://www.christianitytoday.com/ct/2002/decemberweb-only/12-9-21.0.html?start=2.

Stott, John. *The Message of the Sermon on the Mount.* Downers Grove: InterVarsity, 1978.

Stevenson, Bryan. *Just Mercy: A Story of Justice and Redemption.* New York: Spiegel & Grau, 2014.

———. "As Study Finds 4,000 Lynchings in Jim Crow South, Will U.S. Address Legacy of Racial Terrorism?", *Democracy Now* (February 11, 2015). https://www.democracynow.org/2015/2/11/as_study_finds_4_000_lynchings.

Taylor, Barbara Brown. *Learning to Walk in the Dark.* New York: HarperCollins, 2014.

De Tocqueville, Alexis. *Democracy in America.* Translated by George Lawrence. New York: Doubleday, 1969.

Tolkien, J. R. R. *The Fellowship of the Ring: Being the First Part of The Lord of the Rings.* New York: Houghton Mifflin, 1954.

———. *The Hobbit.* 75th anniversary ed. New York: Houghton Mifflin Harcourt, 2012.

———. *The Return of the King: Being the Third Part of The Lord of the Rings.* New York: Houghton Mifflin, 1955.

———. *The Two Towers: Being the Second Part of The Lord of the Rings.* New York: Houghton Mifflin, 1954.

Wallace, Daniel B. *Greek Grammar: Beyond the Basics, An Exegetical Syntax of the New Testament.* Grand Rapids: Zondervan, 1996.

Waltke, Bruce K. *Genesis.* Grand Rapids: Zondervan, 2001.

White, William L. *The Incestuous Workplace: Stress and Distress in the Organizational Family.* Center City, MN: Hazelden, 1997.

Wilkinson, Gary, dir. *John Newton.* 2011. Worcester, PA: Gateway Films/Vision Video. Amazon Prime.

Willard, Dallas. *The Divine Conspiracy: Rediscovering Our Hidden Life in God.* New York: HarperCollins, 1997.

Williams, Michael. *Far as the Curse Is Found: The Covenant Story of Redemption.* Phillipsburg, NJ: P&R, 2005.

Wolters, Albert M. *Creation Regained: Biblical Basics or a Reformational Worldview.* Grand Rapids: Eerdmans, 1985.

Wright, Christopher J. H. *Knowing Jesus Through the Old Testament.* Downers Grove: InterVarsity, 1992.

Wright, N. T. *Following Jesus: Biblical Reflections on Discipleship.* Grand Rapids: Eerdmans, 1994.

———. *Simply Christian: Why Christianity Makes Sense.* New York: HarperOne, 2006.

———. *Surprised by Hope: Rethinking Heaven, the Resurrection, and the Mission of the Church.* New York: HarperCollins, 2008.

Yancey, Philip. *Disappointment with God.* Grand Rapids: Zondervan, 1988.

Zahl, David. "What the Heart Loves, the Will Chooses, and the Mind Justifies: Ashley Null on Thomas Cranmer." *Mockingbird* (January 5, 2011). https://mbird.com/2011/01/ashley-null-via-thomas-cranmer-on/.

Zemeckis, Robert, dir. *Cast Away.* 2000. Los Angeles: ImageMovers, 2001. DVD.

9 781725 294967